# BACK FROM BETRAYAL

*Saving a Marriage, a Family, a Life*

# BACK FROM BETRAYAL

*Saving a Marriage, a Family, a Life*

by SUZY FARBMAN

Foreword by MARIANNE WILLIAMSON
Afterword by BURTON FARBMAN

CROFTON CREEK PRESS
SOUTH BOARDMAN, MICHIGAN

First Edition
10 9 8 7 6 5 4 3 2 1

Published by Crofton Creek Press
2303 Gregg Road SW
South Boardman, Michigan 49680
E-mail: publisher@croftoncreek.com
Web site: www.croftoncreek.com

Book and cover design by Angela Saxon, Saxon Design Inc.
Traverse City, Michigan

Cover art, *Looking Ahead IV,* from an original painting by
Angela Mathias Saxon. Used by permission of the artist.

*The River,* by Victoria Shaw and Garth Brooks. ©1991 BMG Songs Inc., Major
Bob Music Co., Inc. and Mid-Summer Music Inc. All rights reserved. Used by
permission. Warner Bros. Publications U.S. Inc., Miami, FL 33014

*When I Fall in Love,* by Edward Heyman and Victor Young. ©1952 (Renewed)
Chappell & Co. and Intersong-USA, Inc. All rights reserved. Used by
permission. Warner Bros. Publications U.S. Inc., Miami, FL 33014

Library of Congress Cataloging-in-Publication Data

Farbman, Suzy, 1944–
  Back from betrayal : saving a marriage, a family, a life / by Suzy Farbman
; foreword by Marianne Williamson ; afterword by Burton Farbman.-- 1st ed.
    p. cm.
  Includes bibliographical references.
  ISBN 0-9700917-2-9 (alk. paper)
  1. Adultery. 2. Husbands--Sexual behavior. 3. Marriage. 4.
Reconciliation. I. Title.
  HQ806.F37 2004
  306.73'6--dc22
                        2004002850

*To Burton, for his courage and heart and for
recognizing that this story was bigger than the two of us.*

*To our sons, David and Andy, for their loving and
even-handed support and for putting up with
any difficulties this book might cause them.*

*To my mother, Barbara, for building my confidence
and sparking my love of words.*

*And to my sister, Anne, for always being there,
even long-distance.*

*How poor are they that have not patience!*
*What wound did ever heal but by degrees?*

*OTHELLO*, WILLIAM SHAKESPEARE

# CONTENTS

## Author's Note

I have changed several names and details to protect certain people. Jim Myerson, Jody Sommers, and Sally Preston are invented names. Other altered names include Lori and Ronnie Wagner, Alan and Sheila Felstein, Jeanie Jewell, and Shirley Kramer. I have also changed the names of many individuals with whom I participated in psychotherapeutic programs. Because the experiences I relate in *Back from Betrayal* are true, I regret that they may bring pain to some people. I did not write my story to harm anyone or to bring malice by means of this book. My writing was inspired by a profound sense of calling, which, I believe, comes from a source greater than myself. My intention is to heal what was broken in me and in my marriage and, I hope, to inspire the same possibility in others.

# ACKNOWLEDGMENTS

Many people helped me develop the skills and the courage to tell this story. Marianne Williamson, you are an inspiration and a treasure. Thank you for believing in me. My deepest gratitude to my editor and publisher, Doug Truax, for smart and patient guidance, and to his gracious assistants Grace and Tess. Thanks also to friend and mentor Bill Haney for cheering me on. For teaching me the craft of creative nonfiction, I'm grateful to Mike Steinberg and Joyce Maynard, Elizabeth Cox and Eric Jerome Dickey, and John D. Lamb and the Walloon Writers Conference. For keeping me going when doubts got me down, I'm grateful to Mary Kay Crain, Margie Miller, Ginny Beauregard, and my sister, Anne Smith, who saw a swan in some ugly-duckling early drafts.

Thanks to Denise Tietze for backing me up in countless ways, and to Rodney, Christina, Thelma, Debra and other friends at Farbman Group. Thanks to Maureen Stanton and Kate Petrella for insightful editing. To Amy, Anita, Barbara, Beth, Bobbye, Brenda, Cara, Carol, Donna, Francene, Henrietta, Jeannie, Jennifer, Julie, Kathy, Lila, Linda, Lynne, Margo, Marjie, Marilyn, Mary Lou, Mickey, Missy, Nancy, Peggy, Rita, Sally, Sandy, Shelley, Sue, Terry, Zina and Rick—thanks for so much support. Thank you, Angela Saxon, for my amazing cover, and thanks to publicist Grace McQuade for spreading the word. Thank you Debbie Ford, Sonya Friedman, Ted Klontz, Jim Maas, Terri Orbuch, and Jim Rowe for your confidence in me.

Most of all, thanks to my remarkable husband, Burton, for so much love and support.

# FOREWORD

## By Marianne Williamson

EVERYONE HAS A STORY, but not everyone understands theirs. And in the absence of understanding, we stumble and fall on the rocks of our own unconscious behavior. "An unexamined life is not worth living," said Socrates. One might respond to him across the ages, "Yeah, and it hurts, too."

Suzy and Burt Farbman lived in many ways the American dream: a life of fabulous happenings and external bounty. Yet their dream, like so many of ours, turned sour. Not from one big hit here or another there. It turned sour the way any situation does when the emotional, psychological, and spiritual attention we pay to it doesn't match our material efforts.

Suzy and Burt descended into an American nightmare—where all is good on the outside but crumbling on the inside. And then they awoke. They ultimately took on their inner world with the same commitment with which they once addressed the outer. And in so doing, they brought the two worlds together. They saved their marriage, and in an emotional sense they saved their own lives.

We learn from hearing stories, the way we learn from nothing else. The Farbmans' story—of a marriage gone bad, then ultimately redeemed—is a story of human foible and redemption, made all the more meaningful because from a human perspective this marriage didn't have a chance. Not because of a lack of love—but because of a lack of consciousness, a lack of authenticity, and a lack of forgiveness. In order for a marriage so devastated to be reborn, two people needed to change. They needed to grow. The needed to transform. And they did.

Reading *Back from Betrayal* is like watching Humpty Dumpty fall off the wall and then be painstakingly put back together again. You're amazed it can happen; yet you see it with your own eyes. And having seen it happen, you believe it can happen for you.

This is a story of a modern miracle. It is the story of a power that healed two people and through this book will surely heal many. For the shattered loves that still hold promise, may this book be medicine. May it call us home to one another, and in doing so, to ourselves.

# DON'T WORRY ABOUT IT

———— ∞∞∞ ————

IF YOU HAVEN'T LIVED IT,
IT WON'T COME OUT OF YOUR HORN.
*Charlie Parker*

WHEN BURTON AND I FIRST GOT MARRIED, I didn't understand the "death do us part" part. I didn't foresee all the head colds and the whiskers in the sink and the slammed doors that added up to a marriage. I didn't calculate the checks we hoped wouldn't bounce or the times I wished my husband would read a book when he just wanted me to watch TV with him. But over the years, the "death do us part" sank in, and I began to believe we were partners for life. We survived the germs and the hurt feelings, and we paid the bills and stayed together through several friends' divorces. We raised two loving and talented sons, built a real estate company, bought nicer homes, went on dates by ourselves. We hugged and laughed a lot. Some friends turned to us for advice, called us the perfect couple. I knocked on my head when anyone talked that way.

ONE BLUE SKY SUMMER DAY twenty-nine years into our marriage, Burton and I took a break from the office to visit our construction site. We could finally afford to build the house I had dreamed about. We had lived in Huntington Woods for twenty-six years and raised our sons there. Our house had hosted Thanksgiving dinners, my mother's sixtieth birthday, my mother-in-law's seventieth, my grandmother's Shiva. The tiny backyard had graduated from a swing set on patchy grass to a stylish deck and bluestone pavers. The large front yard no longer filled in as the local football field. It was a good house. A solid house. But not the house of my dreams.

Having been a design editor writing about other people's beautiful homes for twenty-five years, I was happy to create one of my own. I had worked with an architect and a designer, spent almost twelve months on the plans. Now those plans had turned into concrete and wood and every visit brought new excitement. The house, with a three-car attached garage, was rising at the top of a steep ravine in Franklin, north of Detroit. Its plywood exterior would receive rough cedar siding. Inside, we would have a first floor master suite, a Jacuzzi tub, and two wood-burning fireplaces.

With large rolling yards and acres of hardwood trees, our future neighborhood felt farther out in the country than a ten-minute drive from our office. An old-fashioned cider mill came alive every fall. There was a gift shop in an old barn, a small post office where the clerk knew your name, and a gas station at which neighbors maintained house charge accounts. A sign said Franklin Village: The Town That Time Forgot.

As we drove that afternoon, impatiens and petunias beamed pink and purple welcome to low-rise office buildings and strip centers along Northwestern Highway. We passed the bakery where I stopped to buy apple pie for my invalid mother, the party store that smelled of cigarettes but where I could buy skim milk at the last minute, the photo store that developed my scouting slides.

We rode in Burton's Cadillac STS. Burton loved cars and owned only those that were locally made. Our company leased office space to General Motors; we drove GM cars. Burton bought a new Cadillac almost every year. Most were black. This one was gunmetal gray.

I chattered about our new house. About how I had designed a wall in the foyer wide enough to show off the antique red lacquered bombé chest I had inherited from my grandmother. About how pleased Burton would be to have an office with cabinets to store the mounds of paper that now collected in our kitchen. "Just give me someplace comfortable to sit," he said.

Burton's mobile phone rang. Usually he answered on the hands-free microphone. This time he lifted the black receiver from its plastic cradle.

"Hello."

One of the selling points of a Cadillac is its quiet V-8 engine. The engine emits a soft purr, a purr that would not muffle, for instance, the sound of a loud voice through a telephone receiver. Sitting beside my husband in our quiet luxury car, I heard such a voice. It rang out "Hiiiiiiiiii," extending a simple two-letter word by at least seventeen extra vowels and sliding up and down the better part of an octave. It was a woman's voice.

The blood in my veins turned to sleet.

Burton answered in a businesslike manner. "No." "Yes." "Talk to you later."

I strained every aural fiber and nerve ending to pick up more from the other end, but couldn't hear another word. When Burton hung up, I turned to look at him. His face was suntanned. His color hadn't changed, but then it never did. He stared at the road.

In a casual tone of voice, a tone I'd use to ask what he'd like for dinner: "Who was that?"

Still looking at the road: "Jerry. He was calling on business."

The sleet in my veins turned to ice. For the first time in almost thirty years of marriage, I knew my husband was lying.

As the middle child between two sisters, Burton had always been comfortable around women. He would talk about our West

Highland Terrier Maggie or someone's kid's role in *Brigadoon* as readily as about the latest Red Wings game or the price of IBM stock. When I spotted him conversing with an attractive woman at a party, I'd tell myself to relax. I was attractive, too. I was glad my husband had depth.

I hoped Burton's sound character would ensure his fidelity. If not his complete fidelity, at least the appearance of it. Appearances mattered more to me then. I knew Burton enjoyed *Playboy* magazine and had slept with dozens of women before we met. As much as he loved me, in some private cranny of my mind I figured he might be tempted to stray on occasion. It was a simple equation: he was a guy; guys liked sex; three decades added up to a long time with one woman. Without planning or looking for it, Burton might succumb to a one-night stand on a business trip. But if he did, as long as it lasted only one night, as long as I didn't find out, it wouldn't have to change his love for me. He valued his family. He wouldn't jeopardize our relationship.

I should have suspected I was pushing my luck when I took my new job, but I didn't want to think about it. With our children grown and out of the house, just as Burton started talking about taking more time off, I had become a regional editor for *Better Homes and Gardens* and some sister publications. For the past three years, I had sought out, visited, and produced articles on great Michigan homes. I loved meeting passionate homeowners, getting to know editors, winning national recognition for local design talent, finding my features on newsstands in Aspen or Santa Barbara. It felt good to know I could make enough money to support myself if I had to. I had backed Burton's efforts to build his career. Now he could back mine. It was only fair.

BURTON TURNED THE STEERING WHEEL, cruising onto Inkster Road. "I heard a woman's voice," I said. I imitated the tone: "Hiiiiiiii."

Burton drummed his fingers on the steering wheel. "If you say so."

"Who was she?" Some hostile force twisted my stomach.

"Don't worry about it."

"A strange woman carries on like she's your long lost best friend. You tell me it's a man on a business call. And I shouldn't worry?" My voice rose to such a high pitch, I almost didn't recognize it as mine.

Burton's eyes did not veer from the road. "There is an explanation."

"What would that be?"

"I can't go into it."

"Why not?" My heart pummeled my ribs.

"I just can't."

I stared out the car window, not seeing a tree or a branch or a leaf.

"You don't want to know," he said.

I mentally replayed the voice. The connection between my ear and my brain had severed. If I knew the caller, I couldn't identify her.

We drove on in silence. We parked the car on the dirt in front of our future dream house in silence. We walked through the side door in silence. Two carpenters measured something in the kitchen. "How's it going?" I asked in what I hoped passed for a normal tone. If they had told me we had foundation problems and the house was about to slide into the ravine, I would have said, "That's nice."

Burton and I wandered around in silence. We checked out the living room. New wood trusses defined the shape of the fourteen-foot-high tray ceiling. The original trusses had come in short a few weeks before, requiring an emergency meeting with the builder, the truss company salesman, the architect, and me. At the time, the problem seemed so urgent.

We walked out to the framed-in porch that cantilevered over the ravine. The river that snaked through the woods below was almost totally hidden by leaves. Burton and I first saw this property one and one-half years before, in January. Trees stood tall, slim and naked, like thousands of Giacometti sculptures. I had envisioned the porch we could build here, enfolded by treetops, a dramatic setting for entertaining. I wasn't thinking about cocktails now. Like a burglar alarm blaring in the middle of the night, Burton's cell phone had sounded a warning. Could that call mean we might never live here together?

"Alright," Burton said. "The woman on the phone is having an affair with a buddy of mine. His wife doesn't know. I'm a go-between." His eyes remained focused on the woods.

"You're too smart to put yourself in such a position."

"I was stupid to get involved. But that's the fact," he insisted. "Look at that squirrel."

End of conversation.

As I sat in bed that night, my muscles twitched, my feet flicked back and forth. I traipsed downstairs to our library, pulled crystal glasses out of the built-in bar, stuck them into segmented cardboard boxes. From upstairs came the muffled sound of TV channels switching.

THE NEXT DAY I SAT IN MY OFFICE, down the hall from Burton's, attempting to concentrate on a photo order. I tried to focus on what props I would need to liven up a dining room shot. My telephone rang.

"I want to talk to you," Burton said.

As I walked down the hall, my knees trembled. I felt as though I were on the way to the doctor to learn the results of a biopsy.

"Close the door," Burton said. There was a grim set to his jaw.

Burton sat behind his ebony-stained oak desk, an oval wood slab topping two round pedestals. I had selected this piece for him when we moved to this space, thinking it reflected his management style, relaxed yet authoritative. Pens protruded from a black leather canister. A black leather box contained correspondence. Windows wrapped around two walls of his office. Beneath one of them, several framed photos topped a black wood credenza. Burton stood beside Michigan Senator Carl Levin. Beside Detroit Mayor Dennis Archer.

On a golf course with Wayne County Executive Ed McNamara. There were framed family photos as well and sweet birthday notes from our boys.

I sat in a chair in front of Burton's desk, the same chair where his secretary, Denise, sat to take dictation. A muscle twitched in my left knee.

"I know you've been worried about that phone call," Burton said. "I'm going to tell you who it was."

I gripped the arms of the chair.

"Last week I drove out to South Lyon. I wanted to check into boarding one of my horses so I'd have someplace nearby to ride. I ran into Jody Sommers. She lives in a farmhouse in the area. She showed me around, and I spent the afternoon with her. We had lunch together; that was all. I figured you wouldn't like it, so I didn't tell you. But there's nothing to worry about. I'm not even attracted to her."

He was right about one thing: I didn't like it.

"Why did she call you?"

"She's thinking about going into the real estate business. She wanted my opinion."

Burton's explanation felt like the truth. Jody Sommers was a beautiful woman we had both known casually for several years. She had been married at least three times. She had wavy auburn hair and eyes the color of translucent green seaweed. I remembered Burton's once commenting on them. Several years ago, Jody had moved out to South Lyon, a rural area where many residents kept horses, about an hour's drive from our office in Southfield.

"I'm glad you told me the truth," I said, although the truth did not relieve the pressure in my gut. "You're right. I don't like it. Jody's an attractive woman. She's looking for a husband. You'd be her fantasy—a cowboy entrepreneur. If I were you, I wouldn't want to tempt fate."

"Neither would I," he said. "Forget about it."

I stood up and walked out of his office. But I didn't forget about it.

*Chapter One*

# A KISS TO BUILD A DREAM ON

———— ⚬⚬⚬ ————

WE DO NOT SEE THINGS AS THEY ARE.
WE SEE THEM AS WE ARE.

*Talmud*

BY THE TIME BURTON AND I MET IN 1966, I was twenty, he almost twenty-two, and I was ready for some excitement. My sex life hadn't improved much since the seventh grade, when Jon Flowers abandoned me on the hayride to make out in the back of the flatbed trailer with Joanie Garabrand, a more willing participant. I had gone from being a sexually stunted adolescent in a private girls school to a sexually stunted coed at the University of Michigan. I was afraid of my urges, afraid of getting pregnant, afraid of sacrificing my virginity to someone who didn't deserve it.

There was also the matter of Jim Myerson, my long-distance boyfriend. Although we had agreed to see others during college, I was saving myself for him, for our eventual marriage, which was what most nice girls did—or pretended to do—in the first half of the 1960s. My feelings for Jim inhibited my relationships with U of M

9

guys. I couldn't acquire the knack for juggling two boys at once. Even though I made it a rule not to kiss on the lips until the third date, I still felt uncomfortable kissing one boy one week and my real boyfriend the next. And if a patient young Michigan man stuck with me long enough to wriggle his hand inside my bra—not that much awaited him—I'd manage to end the relationship before his hand ventured further.

Jim was my high school sweetheart. We had begun dating in spring of 1961, when I was a junior at Kingswood and he a senior at Cranbrook, our brother school. Jim graduated and went on to attend Duke University, in North Carolina. We'd get together on vacations and on occasional weekend campus visits. In his senior year of college, Jim became president of his fraternity, Zeta Beta Tau, the cool Jewish house. His position rendered me the Sweetheart of ZBT during Homecoming. I loved the distinction, especially since I hadn't scraped up dates with any ZBTs at the U of M. Jim was a catch. Sweet, cute, well educated. My mother adored him. He sent her cards on her birthday. I adored him, too. But something was missing.

The year Jim entered law school, I admitted to myself what that missing something was: My boyfriend didn't turn me on. And so I did the honorable thing, the brave thing—flew down to North Carolina to break up with Jim face-to-face. Jim met me at the airport with roses in his arms and love in his eyes and delivered a heartfelt proposal. I hated to hurt anyone's feelings, especially someone who had just expressed his undying love for me. Instead of saying no and coming home a free woman, I said yes. Over the next few weeks, I tried to talk myself into feeling happy about my engagement. Hard as I tried, I felt miserable. I resolved, once again, to break up with Jim. This time I didn't take any chances. I did it in a cold, cowardly way, the only way I could—through a long-distance phone call.

Ricocheting between guilt and relief, I spent a lonely Christmas vacation with my family in Florida and returned to Ann Arbor longing to meet someone new. My roommate, Vicki, suggested Burton Farbman, her boyfriend Michael's best friend. Burton was cute, nice, and more mature than most guys his age, she said. He worked full-time, having dropped out of college. My former fiancé had the academic credentials I thought I wanted. Burton's dubious scholastic record could signal an independent streak. "He's really sexy," Vicki added. That was all I needed to hear.

My blind date's gold Plymouth Barracuda looked like a baby humpback whale, but Burton said he appreciated its affordable price and its high-performance transmission, and I appreciated his frugality. I also appreciated how smoothly he shifted in and out of gears, moving the lever with his big hand while pressing on the clutch with a muscled leg. He inhaled Camel cigarettes as we drove the 'Cuda downtown on the John Lodge Expressway.

While most college guys tried to impress you with their T-bird or Corvette or the number of beers they could guzzle, Burton seemed more stable. His father, a family physician, had died when Burton was eleven. His mother had then obtained her master's degree and gone to work teaching high-school math. When his father grew ill, Burton, age nine, had become a newsboy. He had saved all his earnings to take his mother to lunch on Mother's Day. "I didn't have enough for the tip," he said. "I had to borrow the money from my mom."

Boarded-up buildings flashed by as Burton told me he had struggled through elementary school and been expelled from Mumford High School for cutting classes. "As hard as I tried, I didn't get what the teachers were talking about. So most days I gave up and spent my time down the street at Fredsons Deli. I got an A in Mustard." Many years later, Burton and I would both learn he suffered from Attention Deficit Disorder. That discovery helped explain a lot of behavior, both good and bad, that I didn't understand when it happened.

Expelled from Mumford, Burton had enrolled at Valley Forge Military Academy in Pennsylvania. Another dismal academic experience. "Aside from hating my classes, I hated the dorm food," he said. "And I couldn't afford the hoagies sold at the PX." He solved the problem. Temporarily. He smuggled in a telephone and called in students' orders to a local pizza parlor. He snuck out of the dorm, met the deliveryman by the fence, paid for the contraband, carried it back, distributed, and collected. On the night of his biggest order, as he hauled back an armload of pizzas, the beam of a flashlight hit him in the eyes. "A student sentinel confiscated everything," he said. "The faculty had a party on me."

Burton Farbman had the guts to take on the military establishment, and he'd lived to laugh about it. As a conventional middle-class girl who went to the right schools and studied hard and seldom drank or used the "f" word, I was impressed by Burton's spunk.

By 1966, downtown Detroit no longer bustled with people heading in and out of shops and doctors' offices the way it did when Burton and I were kids. But there were still some good restaurants and entertainment spots. *Dr. Zhivago* was playing at the United Artists Theater. We walked up the stairs and found seats in the mezzanine. I remember being dazzled by Omar Sharif's poem to Julie Christie, written at a frozen country estate, and by snowy Russian vistas on the wide screen. I remember weeping to the melancholy lyrics of "Lara's Theme." I remember the warmth of Burton Farbman's solid shoulder next to mine.

LATER, BURTON PROPOSED ICE SKATING. We headed to Franklin Hills Country Club, to which my family had belonged since I was a child. My father's late uncle Albert Kahn, an architect, had designed the clubhouse. He had also designed the General Motors World Headquarters, Ford factories, and hundreds of other buildings in Michigan and around the globe—a fact I hoped gave me some artistic provenance, and a fact I'm sure I mentioned as Burton's tires bounced through the snow behind the clubhouse.

Half a moon cast a glow on the frozen, partly shoveled pond and the cabin beside it. Burton pushed open the cabin door and started a fire in the large fieldstone fireplace. We sat side by side on a bench to pull on ice skates. Burton knelt down and tightened my laces.

Our blades sliced across lightly rippled ice. My ankles wobbled and I grabbed Burton's arm as we looped around and around, laughing at our awkward circles. After, we warmed our hands by the fire and sipped hot chocolate from the plastic cup of our thermos. Sharing a drink with Burton Farbman, alone in that secluded cabin, sent a quiver to the bottom of my spine. Without thinking, I found my feet stepping forward, my face tilting up, my lips pressing into Burton's warm mouth. I found my fingers running through soft bristle on a thick neck, my tongue tasting chocolate and tobacco. I found my controlled, strait-laced self giving in to a serious kiss, a prolonged kiss, a kiss that took my breath away. No matter how much time has passed, remembering that kiss still stirs a tingle in my chest.

A couple of years later, as a married couple, we joined Franklin Hills Country Club. Soon after, the cabin in which we shared our first kiss was condemned and torn down. At forty, Burton became president of the club. For his first official act, he commissioned the cabin's rebuilding. Years later, that little log structure still stands, although most golfers don't recognize its romantic significance. They see it merely as a rustic marker to a dreaded water obstacle on the eighteenth hole.

But I'm getting ahead of myself.

*Chapter Two*

# HIGH HOPES

---

OUR POWERS OF OBSERVATION ARE ESPECIALLY ACUTE WHEN
WE ARE LOOKING FOR A MATE, BECAUSE WE ARE SEARCHING FOR
SOMEONE TO SATISFY OUR FUNDAMENTAL UNCONSCIOUS DRIVES.

*Getting the Love You Want*, Harville Hendrix, Ph.D.

A FIRST KISS WAS ONE THING. Marriage was another. When I started dating Burton, marrying him was not an option. Without a college degree, he wasn't marriage material. Besides, I wanted to pursue a career. Marriage could come later.

But the better I knew Burton, the more I liked him. We held long conversations each night when he called my apartment in Ann Arbor from his office in Detroit, where he often worked late. He worked for a mortgage company, having started in collections. He hated calling delinquent mortgage holders, pressuring them to pay up, especially at Christmas time. "It killed me to bully some poor father into paying his mortgage instead of buying a bike for his kid," he said. Recently promoted to head the department, he felt relieved not to personally make those calls any longer.

I loved hearing tales of Burton's wild youth. Nearing eighteen, he had worked in California researching mortgage titles. For fun, he had hung out with cowboys, joined an amateur rodeo circuit, and ridden Brahma bulls. I thrilled to picture my boyfriend atop a bucking wild animal, loins gripping, sweat dripping. While college guys memorized the dates of battles or ran around in togas at frat parties, Burton had defied death on the back of a raging beast.

One night when Burton phoned, I heard his lighter click open, heard him inhale and exhale. For several years he had smoked three packs a day.

"You should give that up," I said.

"Why?"

"Aside from being unhealthy, it gives you bad breath."

"Then I'll never smoke again."

And he didn't. Nor did he whine about withdrawal symptoms as I had for weeks, when I quit at nineteen, having smoked one pack a day for three years. The stoic way Burton gave up cigarettes made me see him as a man of character, someone I could trust to keep his word.

I GRADUATED, MOVED TO CHICAGO, found an apartment at the Carl Sandburg apartment complex, and became a fashion copywriter for Carson Pirie Scott, a department store chain. I loved the city and the job and the discount that came with it. By coincidence, Burton was transferred to Chicago to head up his company's branch office. We continued to date. We savored cannelloni at the Italian Village, a downtown spot festooned with tiny lights. We spent weekends in Waukegan, Illinois, and Appleton, Wisconsin, where we fished, built fires in park grills, and fried the speckled bass we caught.

Burton was transferred back to Michigan. A few nights later, I was about to step into the shower when I heard a knock. I pulled on a robe and opened the front door. Burton stood in the hall. "I had to see you," he said.

He dropped me at his motel room and drove off while I show-ered. Minutes later, I came out of the bathroom, wrapped in a towel. Burton had returned, drawn the curtains, and turned off the lights. On a side table, he had arranged two lit candles, two hot dogs on paper plates, and two motel glasses filled with champagne.

"Sit down," he said, pointing to the bed.

Across a pillow, he had draped a navy sweatshirt with "Michigan" printed in yellow on the front. I slipped it over my head.

"I hoped to create a romantic setting with a gourmet meal," Burton said. "I drove around looking for something to impress you. Hot dogs were the fastest thing I could find. Imagine they're filet mignon."

I laughed. Hot dogs seemed more appropriate to the setting, to the flimsy brown bedspread and the matted, stained beige carpet that made me want to put my shoes back on.

Burton bent down on one knee and took my hands in his.

"I want you home with me," he said. "I don't have the college degrees or the family money you might have wanted. But no one will make you happier or take better care of you or love you as much as I will. Will you marry me?"

There must be women who answer such a question with complete certainty. I wasn't one of them. The ambivalence I felt that day had shadowed me through our courtship and would follow me through much of our marriage. Sitting in a seedy motel, I knew that I loved Burton Farbman, but I didn't feel ready. Contrary thoughts vied for my attention. He's smart. But he can't quote Shakespeare. He works hard. But I want to stay in Chicago. He takes care of me. But I need to know more men. He gets my car unstuck. And if I ever decide to be a mother, we'd make amazing children together.

In the span of a few seconds, I washed down the "buts" with a bite of cold hot dog and a gulp of flat champagne. "If I were stuck on a deserted island, there's no one I'd rather be with."

"Then the answer is yes?"

Before I could say so, Burton jumped up, threw his arms around me, and pressed me back on the bed.

"Yes," I said between kisses, hoping I'd given the right answer because I'd given the wrong one once before. Hoping because I was only twenty-two; hoping because how can anyone know for sure.

Burton propped himself up on an elbow. He looked at me with a determined glint in his eyes. "Someday," he said, "I'll buy you an island."

SIX MONTHS LATER, on April 8, 1967, we were married in the Cotswold Tudor–style, brick-and-stone clubhouse behind which we had shared our first kiss. A few hours before the ceremony, in a guest bedroom with my bridesmaids, I almost lost my nerve.

I sat on a chair that afternoon, turning my fingertips into shimmering pink pearls. I frowned at the broken nail on my baby finger. It would forever linger in our wedding album, in the shot of our newly ringed hands, a flaw all the more unfortunate since the photo would capture the only time Burton intended to wear the brushed gold band I had bought for him. "I hate to see a man wearing jewelry," he'd said.

My hands shook so that polish strayed onto my cuticle. I rubbed it off, fled to the bathroom, slammed the door, and plunged into the tub. Hot water rose to my shoulders, just short of my hair, which I'd had styled that morning. Mom pounded on the bathroom door. "Can I get you something?" "A Scotch," I muttered.

For years, I had watched my parents retreat to separate parts of the house—Dad to the television in the downstairs den, Mom to her books in their bedroom above. I had listened to the arguments, and the silence that swelled in between. When Mom and Dad separated, I was a sophomore in college, on my own and living miles away, but my forehead started to throb the day Mom called to tell me. It throbbed for weeks. A few months later, Mom and Dad got back together. They were still together, though living in their separate spaces, as far as I could tell.

As heat dissipated from the water, I knew that ready or not, I would dry myself off, step into my gown, and glide down the aisle into the same trap as my mother. A month short of twenty-three, I was going to sign away my freedom, to kiss my youth goodbye before I had even enjoyed it. Dad had already complained about the flower bill. But flowers weren't the problem. My married friend, Trudi, had promised, "When it's right, you'll know." The problem was, I didn't.

The soak and the Scotch and some soothing words from Rabbi Hertz pulled me through my last-minute panic attack. Dad walked me down the aisle. Burton and I said our vows in front of the fireplace at one end of the clubhouse. We danced to "Lara's Theme."

IN ACAPULCO, I BECAME A TRUE WIFE. Proof seeped into the sheet in the form of a lovely red stain, smaller than a rose petal. I had been the good girl I was supposed to be. Aside from growing up in an era that discouraged premarital sex, I'd had an extra incentive for remaining a virgin. With the maiden name of Fuchs, I, like Smuckers, had to be good. Now I was free of a name that had made me cringe on the first day of class when a new teacher read it out loud. I was also free of the burden of sexual restraint. The next day I wore a two-piece bathing suit and a grin.

The swimsuit disappeared when my arms and legs broke out with sun poisoning. The grin did, too, when I ate something I shouldn't have. Burton's smile disappeared as well in rough waves on a deep-sea fishing trip. But there were lots of fun times. Frozen margaritas. Chess on the terrace of our casita. Jumping in the surf. Watching Burton join Mexican children in a street game of tossing pesos. Our honeymoon proved an early lesson in the better and worse times we had vowed to share.

Returning from Acapulco, Burton gave our cab driver all the dollar bills he had left. When we arrived at our two-bedroom, $129-a-month townhouse in Detroit's Palmer Park, my husband had one dime and three pennies left in his pocket.

Burton and I like to say we began our married life with thirteen cents. The truth is we also had a few hundred dollars in the bank, some bar mitzvah savings bonds Burton had received, and several shares of stock my grandfather had given me. Inheriting my father's conservative spending habits, I viewed our meager funds as a challenge. I looked forward to working with my husband and building what we could together.

A few months earlier, Burton had picked me up at Detroit's St. Regis Hotel, where my mother's friends had thrown a shower in my honor. He'd opened the hatchback of his Barracuda and loaded the car with boxes of dishes, glassware, and appliances. As we turned off Grand Boulevard, he said, "I didn't want to spoil the shower, so I waited to tell you."

My stomach flopped. I hate it when people warn me about bad news.

"Tell me what?"

"The delinquency rate in my department kept rising. Yesterday, I got fired."

I'm a Taurus—stubborn, loyal in crisis. "This is an opportunity," I'd said.

Together, we had agreed that Burton should enter real estate. The field had afforded my late grandparents a stately Georgian home on Boston Boulevard, world travels, a chauffeur, and a cook. One day it would afford us a stately home as well, but it would be many years later.

Back from our honeymoon, Burton left the small residential company he had joined earlier for a larger commercial and industrial real estate firm, Schostak Brothers. It took him six months to close his first deal. When he leased a small office building to the Silber party supply company, we were as excited as if he'd sold the Empire State Building. His first commission was $250; he took home $125. We blew much of it on broiled lobsters at Joe Muer's, one of our favorite Detroit restaurants.

I had become the Detroit correspondent for New York–based Fairchild Publications, writing mostly for *Women's Wear Daily* (WWD) and *Home Furnishings Daily*. I felt proud that my $110-a-week paycheck kept us going for several months. I fell in love with journalism, with the way it dropped me right into the center of the action.

During the summer of 1967, a race riot broke out in Detroit's inner city, and I wanted to cover it. Burton insisted on driving me. Plumes of smoke signaled the way. When we reached Grand River Avenue, we saw burning buildings, smashed store windows, and mobs of dark-skinned youth surging through the streets. Young men ran in and out of shops, arms piled with radios and TVs and clothing. Others rocked cars, trying to flip them over. The Michigan National Guard was called out the next day.

As disturbing as they were, the Detroit riots earned me my first front-page story in WWD. They also gave me a chance to help my struggling husband. Researching the impact of the unrest on the home furnishings business, I came across a carpet supplier whose warehouse had burned down. Burton found him new space. We celebrated with another lobster dinner.

Burton worked from seven in the morning to seven at night, and frequently attended zoning meetings in the evenings. He logged thousands of miles seeking listings and showing space. He contended with obstinate lawyers and clients demanding commission reductions or trying to circumvent him. We owned one car, his Barracuda. I rode the bus back and forth to work downtown. As Burton's business improved, we treated ourselves to a housekeeper once a week. Burton installed a window air-conditioner in our bedroom. On hot summer nights, we raced upstairs to cool off and eat egg foo yung in bed.

At night, Burton watched TV while I read. As rifles banged and horses whinnied, I reclined beside my husband feeling my muscles tense. As I saw it, when Burton could have been enriching his mind, he chose to waste his free time. Books or magazine articles I handed him lay beside him on the blanket. One night at around 2 A.M., I broke into tears. Burton stomped downstairs, flung himself on the olive green sofa, a hand-me-down from his mother, and covered up with the olive and gold afghan his mom had crocheted for us. An hour later, still sniffling, I heard his footsteps trudge back up to our bedroom. "That damn blanket's too small," he said. "If something bothers you, tell me earlier." I cried some more; he held me; we made up. He stomped downstairs before dawn many times that year.

When we returned to Joe Muer's to celebrate our first anniversary, we drank champagne with our lobster.

I SKETCH OUR HISTORY to give you some background as to who we were and who we became. And to let you know our marriage was no more or less likely to be hit by infidelity than most, though neither of us had grown up in a happy home. We were both inconsistent— sometimes loving, sometimes reserved. We were neither perfect nor imperfect together, although there were years when some friends called us the perfect couple, when I did what I could to foster that image, when I almost believed it myself. We overcame our measure of problems and enjoyed our share of blessings. We developed our own strategies for avoiding each other's sore spots, as most couples do. Looking back, I see how we both contributed to a culture in which infidelity could occur. At the time, I didn't see so clearly.

*Chapter Three*

# ONWARD AND UPWARD

MOST OF US LEARNED TO HIDE OUR TRUE SELVES IN ORDER TO
SURVIVE GROWING UP. IT IS NOT SURPRISING THAT WE TAKE THIS
PRACTICE INTO OUR LATER RELATIONSHIPS. IT COSTS, BECAUSE
A CLOSE RELATIONSHIP THRIVES ON TRANSPARENCY.

*Conscious Loving*, Gay Hendricks, Ph.D.
and Kathlyn Hendricks, Ph.D.

SPURRED BY THE 1967 RIOT, affluent residents fled the city.
Unable to afford the suburbs, we moved from our townhouse across
from litter-strewn Palmer Park into a spacious rented flat in
Green Acres, a safer Detroit neighborhood.

Through my job, I met Detroit leaders. When Semon (Bunky)
Knudsen became president of Ford Motor Company, I visited his
Bloomfield Hills estate and interviewed his wife, Florence, for a
feature in WWD. I became pals with GM president Ed Cole's
effervescent wife, Dollie, who helped Burton and me obtain executive cars at bargain prices. My feature on Henry Ford II's glamorous

wife Cristina earned me a center spread in WWD and a handwritten note from publisher John Fairchild. Burton escorted me to charity balls, which we attended at no cost. As a teenager at a private girls school, I had tried to win over classmates whose fathers or uncles were titans of the auto industry. I ached over each slumber party to which I wasn't invited. Now I no longer worried about invitations. I was hobnobbing with the titans.

I accepted an offer from the *Detroit News* to start a gossip column and write feature stories. Soon after, Fairchild flew me to New York to meet with editor June Weir and her boss, Jim Brady. They countered the *Detroit News* by offering me a spot on *W*, their planned start-up publication. Had I been single, I'd have begun apartment hunting that day. But my husband was in Detroit, moving ahead in his career. He had become assistant manager of Schostak's brokerage department. Although thrilled by the New York offer, I did what most young married women of my generation would have done. I declined.

In 1970, my photo was splashed on top of the Sunday *Detroit News* women's section, along with the headline: InSight by Suzy Farbman. My first column revealed that high-profile GM exec John DeLorean had undergone facial plastic surgery. The item stirred outrage and glee and propelled me into the public spotlight.

That same year, I attended and reported on the first meeting of the Michigan chapter of the National Organization for Women (NOW), started by two of my friends, journalist Marj Levin and painter Patricia Burnett. I still remember the energy of the two-hundred-plus women gathered at Detroit's Scarab Club for that first NOW meeting. I came away with a new feeling of pride in being a woman and the sense that I had been right to pursue a profession. Soon after, I interviewed Gloria Steinem, co-founder of *Ms.* magazine. I was astonished at how confident she seemed about remaining single and childless.

I CALL THOSE OF US WHO CAME OF AGE in the 1960s Generation

S—a generation of straddlers. We early Baby Boomers straddled a cultural divide. Some of us protested the Vietnam War and advocated free love, hung beads around our necks and became flower children. Others did what our parents expected: married, moved to the suburbs, and planted flower gardens. I admired Peter, Paul and Mary and sang along to "Blowin' in the Wind," but cared more about pruning my rosebushes than marching for peace.

Burton wanted to begin a family. Once again, I was ambivalent. My mother had left college to marry my father. While he navigated bomber airplanes over Germany during World War II, she gave birth to me. Three years later, my sister, Anne, was born. As we grew up, Mom told us, "Don't be like me. Find a profession to fall back on." I was glad I had followed her advice. But now friends had started having babies. Burton and I had expected, and had been expected, to do so. We were twenty-six and twenty-seven, the right age to become parents. I loved my career and knew raising children would hamper my ambitions. But I was no Gloria Steinem.

We had been married three and one-half years when David was born and I gave up my job. Having secretly wished to write something more meaningful than gossip, I decided to author a novel. While trying to squeeze writing into nap times, I found that days of bottles and burps and nights of lost sleep dragged me down. I felt guilty for not enjoying motherhood the way women were supposed to. My literary efforts floundered.

After five months of listening to my complaints, Burton said, "I can't stand seeing you so unhappy. You need to go back to work." I raced to the phone, called the editor of the *Detroit News* Sunday Magazine and was hired as the fashion and design editor. Working part-time, I began to enjoy motherhood. I shivered along with other moms slipping into the tepid pool with their babies for swim class at the Y. I tugged on David's arms and legs at mother/toddler gym at the Jewish Community Center. Burton, David, and I tried out swings and slides at every public park we came across.

Three years later, Burton paced the floor beside me while I

groaned and pushed through eight more hours of severe labor. As I lay in the recovery room after Andy was born, Burton kissed my forehead and whispered in my ear, "I'll never do this to you again." We were jubilant. We had two sons to carry on the Farbman name. Freedom was a long way off, but the seed had been planted. Someday I could nurture more than children. I could grow my career again.

WHILE I WAS PREGNANT with David, we had moved into a three-bedroom house in Huntington Woods. Three years later, Burton had closed enough real estate deals that we purchased a larger home nearby. With four bedrooms, a sunken living room, and a screened-in porch, our new home was bigger than anything I'd ever lived in.

Huntington Woods was a friendly town. Sidewalks. Tall trees. Good schools. Little League teams. Ice cream socials. Fourth of July parade. As time passed, friends moved to fancier suburbs such as Birmingham or Bloomfield Hills. We stayed. Our neighbors cared about our children. No one tried to keep up with any Joneses, or any Fords or Fishers either. Our lives revolved around our growing sons. I carpooled to elementary and middle school, Sunday school, sports activities. In summer, we rented homes in Charlevoix, a northern Michigan resort town.

Driving north, our sons fought so that I separated them in the car. I sat in back with Andy on odd calendar dates, with David on even. The child in back inevitably developed a cramp, requiring him to stretch his ailing leg across the armrest into the cheek of the child in front. The child with the damp, smelly sock pressed against his face gagged, grabbed the offending foot and twisted. Blows ensued.

To distract our sons, Burton invented Squeaky the Squirrel, a character played by his left index finger. Squeaky bobbed and skittered along the steering wheel, sometimes joined by Lucy the Lizard, Burton's right index finger. Plots involved two little boys, David and Andy, who were lost in the woods. Squeaky investigated fallen logs, dug through leaves, and fended off wolves to rescue the boys. By the time our sons outgrew Squeaky, we could afford a van with a television monitor and a supply of videos.

Kids' sports, a national passion for American moms and dads, provided more fun times. Fortunately, both boys inherited their father's athletic ability. Burton and I cheered them on at hockey, baseball, basketball, and football games.

I remember one afternoon on the diamond behind Burton Elementary School. Andy, about nine, had pitched a flawless game. The score was 8–0 at the end of the fourth inning. Spectators yelled; players bumped shoulders; victory seemed certain. With two innings left, the coach replaced Andy. Hoping to watch our son pitch a shutout, I kicked the chainlink fence. "Other kids deserve a chance, too," Burton said. He had coached Andy's team the year before.

The new pitcher threw singles and doubles and walked several players. By the end of the fifth inning, the score stood at 8–7. Andy's team failed to score in the first half of the last inning, then took their places on the field. Two batters walked; the next hit a single to left field. Bases loaded. Tying run on third.

The coach clapped Andy on the shoulder. "Farbman, you're in."

Knocking his fist against his glove, Andy strode to the mound. Our son had been toughened by battles with his brother, but this pressure seemed more than any nine-year-old could bear. I gripped Burton's arm, afraid to blink or to breathe. Together we watched our little boy strike out the next three batters.

Andy's victory that day was the kind of memory that strengthened the muscles of a marriage. Like most memories, it was remembered best when shared. Years later, memories like that golden day on a dusty baseball diamond would keep me going, propel me through bitter heartache, and help me find the strength to stay in the game.

OVER TIME, THE FINANCIAL STRAIN of our early marriage eased. Burton became manager of Schostak's brokerage department. He stopped groaning over our monthly Visa bills. We joined Franklin Hills Country Club, where our kids learned to swim. We purchased four season tickets to the Fisher Theater. At twenty-nine, although I thought him too young for such a fancy car, Burton would buy his first Cadillac.

In our ninth year of marriage, Burton and his immediate boss, Lee Stein, started their own company. Farbman/Stein opened its headquarters in the Top of Troy, receiving a low rental rate in return for leasing out the new high-rise building. I moved into a small office where, in addition to working as a freelance journalist and copywriter, I handled public relations for our company.

Red, white, and blue Farbman/Stein signs began popping up around the city. After a couple of years in business, the company opened a branch in Southfield, closer to our home. Moving my office into the new building made it easier for me to drive our sons to school, sports activities, and checkups. Burton remained in Troy.

BY THE TIME WE HAD BEEN MARRIED for fifteen years, our sons were eleven and eight. They required less attention than they once had, and I appreciated them more and more. Although I still missed being a full-time reporter, I enjoyed implementing company projects and writing freelance articles. Our lives were busy and full. David and Andy tended to burst into our bedroom unannounced, so there was little chance for romance. Burton minded it more than I did. One afternoon when we were in our mid-thirties, he picked me up and drove me to a motel room that he had reserved and stocked with a bottle of wine.

At thirty-nine, Burton had put on a few pounds; his black hair had started to gray, making him look more distinguished than ever. At thirty-eight, I was grateful that my weight and my brown hair had stayed the same. I felt happy and in love. I thought Burton did, too.

WORKING IN OUR SOUTHFIELD OFFICE, I got to know a bookkeeper named Annie who loved doing crossword puzzles. On lunch breaks, I'd help her with them. One afternoon, I sat in my office writing an article for the *Detroit News*. Annie poked her head through the door.

"Got a minute?" she asked.

"Sure. Stumped for a word?"

Annie shook her head. I gestured toward a chair on the other side of my gray steel desk. She remained standing.

"I don't want to keep you," she said. She closed the door, put her hands on the edge of my desk, and leaned forward. She lowered her voice. "I'm sure you've heard the rumors. Everyone in the office is talking about Burt's having an affair with Sally Preston. I just wanted to tell you: I don't believe a word of it."

I felt as though I'd been thrown from a runaway horse. I tried to catch my breath.

"Thanks, Annie," I said in the steadiest voice I could manage. "I'm sure there's nothing to it. People like to talk."

Sally Preston was a curvy young blonde lawyer who worked for a firm that handled legal matters for our company. I knew Burton appreciated Sally's ability to analyze a lease. I hadn't thought his appreciation extended further than that.

Later that evening, in our 1950s pink-tiled bathroom, which needed renovating, Burton stood in his blue cotton pajamas, brushing his teeth.

"An employee stopped by my desk today," I said. "She told me everyone in the office says you're having an affair with Sally Preston. She said she didn't believe it."

Burton rinsed his toothbrush and tapped it against the sink. "There's no truth to the rumor, but it got so out of control that I had Sally taken off our account." He took a swig from a bottle of clear red mouthwash, swirled it around, and spat.

"If there's nothing to the rumor, I feel sorry for Sally," I said. "It doesn't seem fair to punish her for something she didn't do."

"I know, but I have a business to run."

"I hope you're telling me the truth. If I found out otherwise, I'd have to deal with it."

"I'm glad you're not making a big issue out of nothing."

I thought about the incident for a while. Burton hadn't shown much interest in making love lately, but it could have been because he was working so hard. He'd denied the affair. That was good enough for me. I had young boys who needed their daddy. So did I.

A few nights later, as I rubbed moisturizer into my cheeks, I managed to make light of the rumor. "For being such a good sport about the Sally thing, I figure the least you can do is buy me a new fur coat."

"It's yours," he said. "With or without the rumors."

Life went on. I didn't need the fur coat so I didn't buy it. But I remember feeling proud of myself for rising above the Sally scare.

WITHIN A FEW WEEKS, Burton slid into a depression. He dragged himself out of bed later in the mornings, stared into space with the newspaper in front of him. He stopped telling jokes. His mother, whom he adored, had died three months before. Business had deteriorated. He would soon turn forty. I tried to help him figure out what was wrong.

"Maybe you're having a delayed reaction to your mom's death," I suggested one night at Lafayette Coney Island downtown.

"Maybe," he responded with a shrug, taking another bite of his hot dog with onions and extra chili and mustard.

On a morning walk through our neighborhood, I came up with a different theory. "You're probably dragged down from so many business problems."

"This recession sucks." He kicked at a twig.

In the stands at David's baseball game, I said, "You might be suffering from executive burnout."

"Pay attention," he said. "David's on deck."

One night in bed as Burton watched a Western, I tried again. "You could be going through male menopause. I'm reading *Passages* to understand."

His eyes were lassoed to the TV screen. "Look at that horse."

Despite my best efforts, nothing had helped. I had known

Burton to slam down a telephone when someone tried to cheat him or to sulk for several days if he thought a guy flirted with me. Many nights when he heaved back and forth in bed, I awoke and stayed up with him, listening as he talked through business problems. Those moods had always passed.

OVER SEVERAL WEEKS, Burton grew more withdrawn. We traveled to Manhattan to attend a charity function. Together we walked from the Plaza to the Waldorf Astoria. Burton stared at the sidewalk.

"Maybe I should get away, escape to an island, take some time for myself," he muttered. "I need to figure out what's wrong with me."

I started to cry.

"I held back on my career to support you and raise our kids," I sobbed. "We're falling apart anyway."

At the hotel, we found an out-of-the-way sofa and sat down. I fumbled in my bag for tissue, wiped my bleeding mascara, and waited for my heartbeat to slow. Our marriage had seemed solid for so long.

"Could something be bothering you that you've never told me?"

Burton studied his short, square fingernails.

"There is one thing. It could upset you."

My brain sped through a grim list. Embezzlement. Murder. Drug addiction. All unlikely. Homosexuality? I couldn't imagine it, but if that were so, we had trouble.

"Go on."

"You always knew I dropped out of college. It bothered you, but you lived with it. The truth is: I didn't finish high school."

I should have been appalled that my husband of fifteen years had kept such a big fact from me. But instead I was relieved. He had revealed his dark secret.

"I was afraid you were going to tell me you were gay."

Burton's lips flickered in an almost-smile.

"I am definitely not gay."

"How did you get into the U of M Dearborn?"

"I talked them into letting me work toward high school and college degrees. I dropped out even before I got the one for high school."

"Why didn't you tell me this before?"

"You might not have married me."

"Well, I did, and I'm glad I did. Look at our kids. They come from both of our genes. Look at the company you've built. You should feel proud, not ashamed."

Later that night, Burton joined a friend in the Plaza Oak Room bar. Peter, a television producer, lived with his wife, Kathy, in Manhattan. We had met on an earlier trip to France. Burton returned to our room a couple of hours later and climbed between the soft sheets.

"How about a hug?" he said.

He held me tight, for a few extra seconds, not like recent hugs when he seemed to push off just as we connected.

"Peter told me what he's dealing with," he said. "He's addicted to gambling and alcohol. He's been through a string of bad love affairs. Kathy's Mercedes was repossessed. Peter's life is out of control. Listening to him, I realized I don't have it so bad."

After that weekend, Burton began getting up early and telling jokes again. Hearing about Peter's troubles had helped him realize how insignificant his own problems were, he said. I believed he felt better because he'd cleared his conscience with me about his academic history. In any case, we got back to leading our lives. Over the next few weeks I put Burton's depression out of my mind the way I'd forget about a spill that I'd eliminated with a good stain remover.

*Chapter Four*

# HAPPY TRAILS

A COUPLE OF YEARS BEFORE, in 1980, Burton had purchased a single engine Cessna 182 and learned to fly. On weekends, he piloted the family to small towns around Michigan. We landed at airports with terminals mostly consisting of a desk, a wall-hung aviation map, a bathroom, and a vending machine. We went for walks, hoping to stumble across a ma-and-pa diner with a good cheeseburger or mess of perch. Usually we ended up at a deserted road or a local garbage dump. In the summer of Burton's bad mood, we purchased a renovated, two-story Victorian home in Charlevoix, where we'd rented in the past. Our new northern Michigan vacation home provided a destination for Burton's plane and a boost for his spirits.

Three years after buying our house in Charlevoix, we purchased a farm with a barn, nine miles away. We named the farm Timber

Ridge. We leased, and later bought, six horses. As a child, Burton had hung around and ridden at a stable in Rondeau Park, Ontario. As a teen, I had come to love horses as well, spending a summer at the Quarter Circle H Dude Ranch in Colorado. Together we explored the farm, Burton astride T.R., a 16-hand quarter horse, I atop a small, part Arabian named Beauty. Burton clicked his tongue and stroked T.R.'s soft brown neck, guiding him through emerald green woods. The grin on his face stretched from east to west.

As MUCH AS WE LOVED NORTHERN MICHIGAN, we spent most of our time downstate in those days. The city of Detroit continued to deteriorate. By the mid-1970s, downtown Woodward Avenue had given way to liquidation sales, empty buildings, and discount shoe and wig stores as shoppers flocked to suburban malls. The J.L. Hudson Company, which occupied a full city block, would eventually shut down. Hudson's had been one of the country's great department stores, like Macy's in New York or Marshall Field's in Chicago. As a little girl, I had ridden in Hudson's brass-gated elevators and perched on Santa's lap amid a Christmas wonderland. Other fine stores also would close their doors: Himelhoch's downtown, where many years before, my family had stood, warm and comfortable, behind big plate-glass windows to watch the Hudson's Thanksgiving Day Parade pass by in the street below. And Saks Fifth Avenue, in the New Center area a few miles to the north, where my grandmother took me shopping.

Hoping to turn the city around, Mayor Coleman Young convinced Ford Motor Company chairman Henry Ford II to spearhead the development of a large office and hotel complex on the Detroit River. The Renaissance Center opened in 1976, the same year that a new city magazine debuted and I became its fashion editor. For the first issue of *Monthly Detroit* (later, *Detroit Monthly*) I wrote a feature on the Cartier and Yves St. Laurent boutiques that opened in the new four-tower RenCen. Both shops would close before long, a passing I did not write about.

Over the years, doing what we could to prop up our city, Burton and I served on several boards of directors. In 1987, our twentieth year of marriage, we chaired fundraisers for our art museum and our historical museum.

As a real estate man, Burton hated to see Detroit lose landmarks of its former glory as the automotive capital of the world. The wrecking ball had demolished the old French Renaissance–style City Hall downtown, the Crowley Milner and Ernst Kern department stores, the Baroque-ornamented Michigan Theater, and more. Burton was determined not to let the same fate destroy the classical Beaux-Arts, block-square, granite-and-sandstone Wayne County Courthouse. He joined a private multiracial partnership to redevelop the dilapidated turn-of-the-twentieth-century structure, which would be renamed the Wayne County Building.

Early that same year, Lee Stein suffered a fatal heart attack. Losing a partner and old friend proved hard on my husband. I tried to fill in as a sounding board. But understanding concepts like internal rate of return, warranty deeds, and mezzanine financing felt like slogging through deep snow without snowshoes.

Burton, then forty-four, threw his energies into the Wayne County Courthouse project. In twenty years of marriage, I had never seen him work so hard. Local banks refused to finance the renovation. Burton tracked down out-of-state funding. The project became the victim of political infighting. Burton lobbied reporters and politicians. Construction problems threatened the budget. Burton assembled engineers, architects, and contractors in one room, urging them to work together. "Someday," he told them, "we will bring our grandchildren to this building and show them what we did here."

On a clear, cold day in late fall 1987, the former courthouse was renamed the Wayne County Building and rededicated as the county headquarters. The podium for the ceremony rose at the top of a wide granite stairway in front of the building. Hundreds of onlookers gathered on the steps and sidewalk below. Burton shared the microphone with Wayne County Executive Edward

McNamara and Coleman Young, the powerful first African-American mayor of Detroit.

Standing a few steps below, I gazed up at the heroic copper-clad four-horse chariots, which symbolized Progress, on top of the building. I dropped my eyes to the portico pediment and its carving of General Anthony Wayne conferring with Indians, and then to my husband, in a charcoal gray wool overcoat, at the microphone. As I listened to him speak about the challenge of saving this masterpiece, my chest swelled with pride. I knew this project would not have succeeded without Burton's relentless efforts. And I knew what this renovation meant to a city in desperate need of hope.

IT'S OFTEN SAID IN THE MOTOR CITY that when the nation gets a cold, Detroit gets pneumonia. From the mid-1980s into the early 1990s, real estate holdings around the country suffered, especially in Detroit. Aside from his achievement with the Wayne County Building, Burton struggled to hang on to our investments during a severe economic downturn. Neighborhood shopping centers and office and light industrial buildings that we had developed lost tenants. Burton granted rent concessions. During this period, the company moved into one of our investments, an office building in Southfield, and changed its name to The Farbman Group. I oversaw the interior design of the new space and took an office in the executive wing.

The Farbman Group managed Riverfront Towers apartments on the Detroit River, the finest rental housing downtown, owned by financier Max Fisher and shopping center developer Al Taubman. In 1991, Burton oversaw the development of a third tower, bringing in the project on time and on budget, and bringing in needed funds to our company. To inaugurate the third tower, I organized a benefit for the Detroit Institute of Arts—a sellout party and auction of original Detroit-themed art, created and donated by local celebrities. Chrysler Chairman Lee Iacocca's sketch brought the highest price— $1,100. I bid on a silver belt buckle shaped like the back of a car, but lost to someone across the crowded room. I soon discovered that Burton, the competing bidder, had purchased the buckle for me.

IN THE MID-1980s, Burton joined the Young Presidents Organization. I was thrilled when he was accepted into this international group of businesspeople who had become presidents of significant companies by age forty. YPO would be good for business, provide Burton with a group of confidants, and offer us exciting travel possibilities. With YPO, we visited Sydney, Buenos Aires, and Hong Kong. Burton joined a forum of Detroit chapter members who met monthly, helped each other through business and personal challenges, and became close friends. Nearing fifty, Burton would chair the Detroit chapter of YPO.

LIKE THE LINES ON OUR FACES, with time Burton's and my differences grew more pronounced. I loved visiting art museums and galleries and attending lectures. Burton preferred flying, photography, and horseback riding. After several bad falls, I stopped riding with him. When we first married, we fished or played chess together. After a while, my love of reading prevailed. In my spare time, I chose a book over a boat or a chessboard.

Couples sometimes find traits that attracted them to each other in the first place cause problems later on. I admired Burton's spontaneity; he, my sense of organization. Burton made up his mind at the last minute; I planned ahead. Burton woke up on a Saturday morning and suggested we visit properties he hadn't seen for a while. I had five flats of geraniums in the backyard waiting to be planted. He wanted to take off early from work for a round of golf. Sorry, I said. I'm on deadline. He urged me to sit beside him on the sofa and watch John Wayne in *True Grit*. I was busy setting the table for a dinner party. He proposed flying to the Win Schuler's restaurant in Marshall for Swiss onion soup on a day I had a date with my friend Brenda. "Let me know when you can work me into your schedule," he grumbled.

I did, however, arrange many times together. Burton and I rode bikes or played golf, piled the kids in the car for a Detroit Tigers baseball game, headed up north for a weekend, caught every good movie that didn't have subtitles. Burton hated subtitles. We walked through our neighborhood many mornings, went on frequent dates, hosted dinners for friends and clients, enjoyed private parties, attended charity events.

In 1992, when we reached our twenty-fifth wedding anniversary, I considered it an achievement. We had survived the swinging 1970s, when open marriages were a trend and certain friends invited us to parties, passed around marijuana joints, and ended up in a hot tub and in each others' beds. We excused ourselves before the hot tub. We didn't frequent sex clubs like Plato's Retreat in Manhattan, though we knew people who did. We got through the 1980s, when the production of X-rated videotapes exploded and Dial-A-Porn services began, when the marriages of three close friends split up and our nation elected Ronald Reagan, its first divorced president.

Society had grown more promiscuous, but we had made it through twenty-five years together. And, as far as I knew, we had made it unscathed. Our marriage wasn't problem-free, but I didn't know one that was. We were a happy couple. We deserved to celebrate.

WE CELEBRATED OUR ANNIVERSARY with an outdoor party on a day in late June. Although rain had fallen for weeks, sun glinted off the white canvas tent. It brightened the smiling faces of the nearly two hundred guests who arrived at our farm in northern Michigan dressed in denim jeans and skirts, suede vests and turquoise jewelry. They had come to share our good fortune, to witness our anniversary as, in 1967, dozens of them had witnessed our wedding.

I had nailed enlarged family snapshots to the barn's newly painted red boards. The photos showed the four of us straddling each other on the slide of Clarence Burton Elementary School;

sitting on swings at a park; standing in the Temple Emanuel lobby at David and Andy's bar mitzvahs. A history of our happy lives— a chance to show off a little.

Though David was spending the summer in Hawaii, most everyone else we cared about was there: Our younger son, Andy. My mother, who still felt well. Burton's sisters, both divorced. My sister, Anne, from California. Old friends like Brenda, my fashion guru, and Michael, Burton's childhood buddy, who introduced us. Important real estate clients.

A band played western music. Instructors taught line dancing to some of our less-inhibited friends. Other guests helped themselves to drinks at the bar, set up in a horse-drawn carriage. We dined on barbequed ribs and chicken and warm tomato pudding, a northern Michigan specialty. Guests tied red bandanas around their necks. The borders were printed with a message. Over the microphone at dinner, I said, "People ask how Burton and I have stayed married for twenty-five years. You're wearing the answer." I explained that the message on the bandanas came from the story of a frog on a dairy farm who fell into a bucket of cream. Unable to escape, he flailed his legs in fear. Before long, he churned up a pat of butter and climbed on top, licking the flies that swarmed from all directions. "The moral of the story is printed on your bandanas," I said. "It is also the secret to making it through twenty-five years: Keep Paddling."

To celebrate Burton's upcoming fiftieth birthday, the caterer carried in a cake shaped like a cowboy boot. The shaft of the boot sagged so the cake looked more like a slipper than a boot. But guests sang "Happy Birthday" and Burton laughed and kissed me and blew out the candles.

At dusk, we climbed onto hay wagons and lumbered, wheels creaking, to the lake. As we neared the water, I whispered to Burton, "Remember what you promised when you proposed?"

"To buy you an island."

"I like our lake better. Consider the debt paid."

Beside the water, a bonfire blazed. Guests sat on logs surrounding the fire. Marshmallows skewered on the tips of long branches hovered near flames, turning brown. A friend strummed his guitar. Dozens of voices sang "The Gambler" and "Country Roads."

Tiny sparks floated up into a black velvet sky, hung with a slice of moon. We wrapped our arms around each others' shoulders and swayed, singing "Happy Trails (To You)." I absorbed the scene—the music, the smoke, the breeze, the faces of grownups getting to be kids around a campfire again. I wanted to seal this moment in my memory forever. I could see us here again on our fiftieth anniversary, at seventy-three and seventy-four, with grandchildren roasting marshmallows. I felt so lucky to have been blessed with gentle weather, to have thrown such a fine party, to be surrounded by family and friends, to have my loving husband by my side.

*Chapter Five*

# FALLING APART

———⊗⊗⊗———

DEAR ANN LANDERS: FRIENDS AND FAMILY MEMBERS HAD BEEN AWARE FOR
YEARS THAT MY HUSBAND WAS SEEING ANOTHER WOMAN. I FOUND OUT LAST
MONTH . . . I CANNOT BLAME THOSE AROUND ME FOR NOT SPEAKING UP, YET
SOMETHING AS SIMPLE AS AN ANONYMOUS NOTE WOULD HAVE OPENED MY EYES.
*Signed, The Last to Know in New York*

DEAR NEW YORK: . . . A CHEATING MATE ALWAYS LEAVES CLUES,
EITHER WITTINGLY OR UNWITTINGLY. I BELIEVE THE CLUES
WERE THERE, BUT DEEP DOWN, YOU DIDN'T WANT TO SEE THEM.

MAYBE THE TROUBLE BEGAN when my mother's foot surgery
failed, and I spent so much time trying to help.

Maybe it was when Burton lost interest in making love. At first
I blamed it on his stomach pains. But after his gall bladder was
removed, he still didn't turn to me at night to stroke my arm or
murmur that funny little "hmm" into my ear. If we had sex, I turned
to him.

Maybe it was when he no longer wanted to play golf with me.
When he stopped holding my hand at the movies. When he didn't
call me Gorgeous anymore.

Maybe it was the morning at the breakfast table when he slammed down the newspaper and said, "I can't keep taking this pressure."

Five years after our farm party, Burton was featured on the cover of *Commercial inc.* magazine along with four other prominent Detroiters. I framed the 1997 article and hung it on the wall of his corner office, next to the plaque with the ball from his hole-in-one. The article hangs there still, several years later. The headline reads "Five For The Future." The subjects, including Burton, say they plan to continue helping Detroit's business renaissance move forward. The truth was a different story. In private, for the past two years, Burton had complained he was tired of working, needed time off. I didn't want to hear him.

I had had enough time off. I had held back on my career, worked part-time as a freelance journalist, helped Burton build the company, raised our children. Once our sons were grown, just as Burton started to talk about retiring, I took a new job. I became a regional editor for a group of national design magazines. The work was demanding and creative, and I loved it. More time off did not fit my plan.

I came home from work one day to discover Burton brooding, staring at the TV. I came home another day and couldn't find him at all. At first I tried to ignore the signs of trouble. After a couple of years, I could not ignore them any longer. Or wish them away.

The signs seem stark and obvious now, but they didn't at the time. A marriage that has lasted more than thirty years doesn't dissolve in an instant. It happens slowly, like using a bar of soap. It vanishes little by little. Six years after we celebrated our twenty-fifth wedding anniversary, I realized we were down to a sliver.

IN THE TWO YEARS PRECEDING THE CALL I overheard on the way to our future house, Burton had complained he was bored. We should travel and play, he'd said. Our kids would marry soon and have babies. We'd want to be home for our grandchildren.

A wife who had been forced to work or who'd fulfilled her career ambitions might have been thrilled by such a proposal, might consider me an ingrate. I did, in fact, look forward to traveling extensively with Burton. In the future. One day Burton insisted, "This is our chance to see the world." I had just received a bonus for a cover shot. "I'm too young to retire," I said. "I'm having too much fun."

Unable to convince me to take off with him, Burton had found something to do closer to home. Soon after that cell phone call, Burton had trailered Gypsy, his favorite quarter horse, from northern Michigan to a stable in South Lyon. Many afternoons he drove there to trail ride or take horseback jumping lessons from an instructor.

ASIDE FROM MY MAGAZINE RESPONSIBILITIES and working on our new house, my mother's problems cut into my time. Twice divorced and alone in her early seventies, Mom had undergone orthopedic surgery to straighten her big toe, which had popped up and out into a hammer/monkey toe. During the surgery, her foot contracted and was casted in a contorted position. When we returned to the doctor to have the cast redone, her foot would not flatten out. After the second cast came off, my mother was left with a clubfoot. Before the surgery, she had walked slowly, unassisted. Now she hobbled on her ankle, supported by a metal walker, and required aides around the clock.

Several months later, also suffering from Parkinson's and arthritis, Mom tripped and broke her leg. The fall left her bedridden in a convalescent home, wearing a cast up to her thigh. I delivered pep talks to her aides, who had displayed a distressing tendency to quit. I visited Mom and worked crossword puzzles with her. Consulted with doctors. Researched senior citizen apartments. When Mom was released from the convalescent home, my sister and I moved her into the best apartment complex I could find.

Busy working and spending time with my mother, I tried not to worry about Burton, whose frequent visits to South Lyon put him within dangerous reach of Jody Sommers. I told myself to be glad my spouse wasn't sitting home pouting, to be grateful he had a hobby he enjoyed and a place in which to enjoy it.

Now and then I asked if he had seen Jody. "Hardly ever," he said. "Don't worry about it." I longed to believe him the way I longed to believe the powder-room mirror with the soft, flattering light.

NIGHTS WHEN I RETURNED from visiting my mother, I held my breath as I pulled into our driveway. I pressed the button for the garage door and glided in, hoping to find Burton's Cadillac parked in the next bay. More often than not, his car was missing. I tried to reach him on his mobile phone. A mechanical voice apologized that the party I was calling was out of range or had his cell phone turned off.

When Burton was around, I initiated our hello or good-bye kiss, or it didn't happen. His lips twisted to the side and felt hard as marbles. He seldom told me he loved me any longer. When I said it first, he mumbled the words back.

I began to feel like an abandoned old putter, tossed in a corner of the basement, replaced by a newer model. Once I had prided myself on being an amusing dinner guest, the type seated next to the host. Now I felt I had nothing to say. I scoured the newspapers and watched CNN to prepare for party conversation, but nothing stuck. I had lost my spark. I hated how miserable I felt. I hated having let myself sink so low. I hated confronting the degree to which I had measured and defined myself by my husband's love.

A saying I'd heard haunted me: Once two people know something, it's no longer a secret. However tortured I felt, I kept my fears to myself. Having written a gossip column, I knew how people loved to talk. Confiding in anyone could make our problems worse. If word of my doubts got around, people would whisper behind my back. Friends would feel sorry; enemies would gloat. And if I created more trouble by opening my own big mouth, I'd have only myself to blame.

Current events added to my anguish. Actor Hugh Grant was

caught in a car with a street hooker. Sportscaster Frank Gifford was discovered with some "tramp" in a tabloid-induced setup. Bill Clinton carried on with an intern young enough to be his daughter.

Drop-dead model Elizabeth Hurley wasn't glamorous enough to keep Hugh from straying. Vivacious TV host Kathie Lee failed to command Frank's loyalty. Savvy Hillary could not inspire the President of the United States to keep his fly zipped. I was no cover girl of the glossies, no sassy star of the tube, no brilliant First Lady. These high-powered women couldn't ensure the fidelity of their significant others. I didn't stand a chance.

Men strayed. A universal fact of history. The Chinese had their concubines. The Dutch, Philip the Good and his thirty-three mistresses. The French, Louis XV and Madame de Pompadour. The British, Prince Charles and Camilla. Here at home, we had blatant examples, too: FDR and Lucy Mercer; JFK and his stable. You didn't have to be a scholar to know these things.

OVER THE YEARS, WHEN BURTON WAS FEATURED in newspaper articles, he said, "Never believe your own press." He'd said it so often that for one of his birthdays, I gave him a black leather album filled with his clippings, his cautionary words gold-embossed on the cover.

When Burton started leaving the house earlier and earlier in the morning, I realized something about myself: I had come to believe my own press. I was the lucky wife whose husband provided two nice homes and traveled the world with her, the good mother whose handsome sons joined her on Sunday nights for Moo Shu Chicken at the Peking House, the talented journalist whose office wall was hung with her own framed cover shots. I led a life that sounded enviable in the holiday letter I sent out each year.

Every six months I pasted family photos into matching black pigskin albums. These books nested in our new library on shelves I had designed deep enough to hold them. Page after page showed us smiling at cookouts and birthday dinners. There were color photos of our young sons in their red and silver Michael Jackson fake-leather jackets, of David smiling beside his orthodontist on the day his braces came off, of Andy shouldering a backpack on top of a mountain. Photos of me only made the cut if I looked good in them. Looking good had become another occupation.

I kept a journal in which I jotted down details about Burton's business deals or articles I had written. I mentioned parties we attended, recounted anecdotes about our children. I wrote about how excited Burton was to graduate to a Cessna 421 airplane. Someday, I thought, our sons would come across these slender little books and be transported back to their childhoods, to their G.I. Joe and Lego collections, to the wavy slide in the park, to Berkley High School tennis tournaments and Cranbrook football games.

I wrote about David's initial fear of riding his new bike and how I enforced practice every day and how he finally mastered his two-wheeler on his six and one-half birthday: *He was so proud we practically had to drag him off!* I wrote about Andy, who was home with a cold at ten years old. When I gave him his medicine, he'd said, "No compliments to the chef."

Someday my sweet, nostalgic journals would be worth more to our children than shares of Berkshire Hathaway stock, I thought. That was before Burton started pulling his disappearing acts, and I had nowhere else to turn. Then my journal became my lifeline.

> ... I asked B. what has been going on during those eternal stretches of time when I haven't been able to reach him. He said, "Nothing's going on." I told him, "I want both of us to be happy, but I'm not willing to share your body or your soul."
>
> —Journal excerpt, April 1998

> ... Haven't heard from B. for almost 20 hours. It is 5:45 a.m. His portable phone doesn't answer. I haven't ever thought of myself as a divorced woman, but I have the sickening feeling that may be the prospect. I was up

all night crying. I hope if he does leave me, I'll have stopped allowing it to hurt so much.

—Journal excerpt, July 1998

ONE DAY IN MY CAR, I tuned in to Dr. Joy Browne, a sensible and sympathetic radio shrink. When a wife called in expressing doubts about her husband's fidelity, I turned up the volume. "Don't dwell on your suspicions," Dr. Browne said. "Spend your time trying to improve the marriage."

I took Joy Browne's advice. When Burton was around, I repeated jokes I thought he'd enjoy and gave him articles about farming or golf that I'd torn out. I kept the refrigerator stocked with his favorite fruits, Clementines and Fuji apples. I fluffed my hair and wore pretty colors. I'd have worn sexy underwear if I thought it would help, though I didn't think it would. Not with my flat chest.

One Friday morning I told my husband, "I'm planning a romantic evening for tonight." I set a table with our good white and gold Royal Doulton china in front of the living room fireplace, where we had never dined before. I added a Steuben crystal bud vase with a yellow rose. As a fire blazed, we savored lasagna, one of Burton's favorite dishes, sipped a Caymus Cabernet and listened to Frank Sinatra sing *All The Way*. After my second glass of wine, I suggested we squeeze into the Jacuzzi. We shared a bath by candlelight and talked about David's upcoming wedding. I told Burton how Amy and I had visited a store, put on headsets, listened to Pachelbel's Canon, agreed the music was perfect for her walk down the aisle. Though I initiated it, we made love that night.

The next morning when I woke up at 7:30 A.M., Burton's pillow was pressed down in the middle where his head had been.

FIVE YEARS AFTER OUR ANNIVERSARY PARTY, in 1997, we had spent Christmas vacation up north. Riding a chairlift with my girlfriend Lisa, I'd mentioned that Burton and I would travel to Africa on a safari in a few months. Burton was a trustee of the Detroit Zoo;

we planned to accompany the zoo director. For background on our trip, Lisa recommended I read *West with the Night* by author and aviator Beryl Markham, who had lived in Africa earlier in the twentieth century.

"Markham was one of those tough, independent, sexually aggressive women," Lisa said. "She was a lot like someone we both know—Jody Sommers."

The temperature that day reached the twenties, but I suddenly felt as though it had dropped below zero. I started to shiver. If Lisa had heard that my husband had a relationship with Jody Sommers, she didn't say. I didn't have the courage to ask.

Later, I told Burton about the conversation. "That's ridiculous," he insisted. "From what Jody tells me, she doesn't even like sex very much. Besides, she already has a boyfriend."

I didn't tell Burton how strange it seemed that he and Jody had discussed her sex life.

Four months later, I sat in my office working on a source sheet, the tedious part of my job. Regional editors needed to identify everything in a photograph—every lamp, table, chair, rug—what it was, where it came from, its style number. A transparency of a family room lay on top of my light box. I was scanning my notes to see if I'd jotted down anything about the sofa. When a shock occurs, you remember details about what you were doing at the time. I remember the sofa was taupe suede.

My phone rang. Burton's secretary, Denise, was reviewing our bills. "There's a charge here I don't understand. I thought you might be able to help," she said. "Who is Jody Sommers?"

My stomach lurched the way it does when you're speeding and a police car pulls up behind you, lights flashing.

"I'll be right there."

I walked down the hall. My mouth was too dry to swallow.

Denise sat at her desk, holding a piece of paper, frowning. I leaned over, hoping she didn't notice my trembling hands.

"There's a charge for a first-class ticket to Florida for someone named Jody Sommers," she said. "The ticket was issued for the same day Burt flew there to join his forum."

I peered at the bill, and noticed the date on which the ticket had been booked: April 9, the day after our thirty-first wedding anniversary.

A few years before, Burton had retired from YPO, as required on turning fifty. He had joined DPO, the Detroit Presidents Organization, and had become a member of another forum of thirteen men who met often and were as close as brothers.

"Jody Sommers is a woman Burton rides horses with once in a while in South Lyon," I said in the steadiest voice I could manage. "I don't know why he bought her a plane ticket. I'm sure there's a good explanation."

"I'm sure there is, too. Burt adores you," Denise said. Her cheeks flared red. "I'm sorry if I said something I shouldn't have."

"You were just doing your job."

THAT NIGHT WHEN I RETURNED from visiting my mother, Burton's space in the garage was empty. Again the house was dark. I walked into the kitchen and began attempting to sort through the mail. My heart pounded so hard I don't know how I heard the garage door open.

Burton walked in wearing jeans and worn leather boots and smelling horsy. He tossed his keys on the granite counter.

"How's your mom?" he asked.

"Okay."

He must have seen the look on my face.

"What's wrong?"

"Denise came across a bill for a plane ticket for Jody Sommers."

"Since when does Denise check with you on my bills?"

"She was trying to be responsible. She asked who she was."

"What did you say?"

"She's a friend you sometimes go riding with."

"Well, that's true."

"You flew to Florida with her?" I had felt nauseous all day. Seeing Burton avoid my eyes, I tasted bile.

"You know I'm friends with Jody. That's all there is to it. She was hard up for cash. I loaned her the money to visit her condo in Florida. Something came up, and she canceled. I don't know why the charge was still on the bill."

"But you planned to fly down there with her?"

"She was just going to be on the same plane."

"Sitting next to you in first class?"

"That's where I always sit."

"Was she intending to pay you back for this loan?"

"Yes."

"She's short of cash, but she's going to sit in first class and pay you back?"

"That's what I said," he snapped. "I told you she didn't go."

"But you intended to fly there with her. Anyone could have seen you together on the plane. How would that have looked?"

"I didn't think about it."

"What if I found out?"

"I guess it was pretty stupid."

"You say there's nothing wrong. I'm not there when you're with her, so I have to take your word for it. Do me a favor. Don't loan her any more money."

"I won't. I told you—don't worry about it."

His usual refrain.


In January, I had joined my friends Ginny and Cara on a ski trip to Vail. I did my best not to let worries about Burton destroy an otherwise lovely week. I tried out some shaped skis and settled on a pair of Olins. During the ski clinic I'd signed up for, I discovered how my new equipment helped me to turn more easily. I tried hard to appreciate the views of Colorado mountaintops etched against blue sky.

Burton had flown to Phoenix—alone, he'd said—and rented a

car. He told me he needed time to get lost in the desert. Although he wouldn't have an itinerary, he'd promised to phone from the road every day, and he had. When we spoke, we'd filled each other in about our adventures. He had sounded glad enough to talk to me that I believed he really might be alone.

In late April, a few days after the incriminating bill for the plane ticket, a statement showed up in the mail. It reported on Burton's recent account activity in the Hilton Hotel Honors program. Burton received more than 2,000 points for staying at a Hilton. I scanned the page for the date of this stay. January. There must be some mistake. We hadn't ever stayed at the Drake, though over the years we had dined there several times at the Cape Cod Room. Burton loved their lobster. I flipped back through my date book. On the day Burton supposedly visited the Drake in Chicago, he had claimed to be in Arizona.

I shoved the paperwork into a drawer, along with the note I had jotted down earlier about the airplane ticket charge. Exhibit A and Exhibit B. Evidence. Not that I wanted evidence. Some faint instinct for self-preservation told me I had better hang on to this documentation. Even with no-fault divorces, a lawyer might find it helpful someday. Compiling these sad bits of evidence against my husband made me feel sick. It also made feel a little less helpless. I might someday need to be shrewd and cutthroat as I had never been before, to protect my assets, to take care of myself. I had better start now.

Later I mentioned the Hilton reward points to Burton.

He shrugged his shoulders. "It's complicated," he said.

He didn't try to explain.

THREE OR FOUR MONTHS PASSED. No improvement. One day in summer, Burton told me he would fly to a small town in central Michigan to attend a horse auction. He hadn't returned home by dark. Didn't answer his cell phone. The Michigan State Police should know if a plane had crashed. I phoned. My husband was missing in his Cessna 421. Had any accidents been reported? No. I called Chris, the professional pilot Burton hired when he did not personally fly the plane. Ten minutes later, Chris called back. "I phoned the airport and had someone check Burt's hangar. His plane has been there all day."

It was about 11 when I heard the back door slam. I walked to the kitchen.

"I was worried," I said. "I called Chris."

"I can't believe you dragged Chris into this."

"I was afraid you were dead."

The rest of the conversation went the way many had of late. Burton apologized. Yes, he should have called. How was the auction? Didn't go. Took a drive instead. Where? Around. Nowhere special. Stop grilling me.

I choose to believe you, I said.

I had our son David's wedding to think about. The wedding would take place in early September, just a few weeks off. I'd lock away my doubts, keep going until then. I assumed Burton would, too. He'd try to get through the occasion without strife, for the kids' sake. After, I thought, he might leave me.

Meanwhile, I focused on what needed doing. I found the perfect gold bag to carry. Talked to the bandleader about dance music. Ordered toffee candies covered with caramel and nuts for the dessert table. And did my best not to think about life after the wedding.

My hairdresser had highlighted my brown hair with golden streaks; a makeup artist had stroked a peachy glow onto my cheeks. Richard Tyler's sage green silk jacket emphasized the curve of my waist. The night of David and Amy's wedding, I wore high, gold leather sling-backs with pointy toes, my first Manolo Blahniks— shoes that fashion mavens call CFMs, or Come Fuck Me pumps. For all the good they did. Burton looked as distinguished as ever in his new black Armani tuxedo.

As Amy walked down the aisle of a ballroom at the Detroit Athletic Club, I watched her smile through her simple white veil.

Pachelbel's Canon in D never sounded more beautiful. Burton and I stood beside David and Amy as the rabbi led them through their vows. I thought to myself: this should be one of the happiest moments of my life. I bit my cheeks.

Later in the evening, it was time for the parents' dance. I searched through the crowd and found Burton in a corridor. As popular Detroit bandleader Mel Ball announced our names, Burton led me, along with Amy's parents, Lynda and Bob, onto the empty dance floor.

*When I fall in love,*

I felt Burton's chest, so solid against mine. I felt the pressure of his hand on my back. A few years before, I had hired a dance instructor to give us private lessons. Burton worked so hard in those days that by night he was exhausted. He fell asleep on the sofa while I danced with the teacher. So I ended the lessons. Burton and I continued to dance the simple two-step we danced now.

*It will be forever,*

I rested my head against Burton's cheek, breathed in the minty smell of shampoo, closed my eyes, squeezed back tears.

*Or I'll never fall in love . . .*

As a baby, David had curly dark hair and thick eyelashes that everyone said were wasted on a boy. Twenty-six years later, in the blink of an eyelash, he had a wife of his own.

*And the moment I can feel that you feel that way, too,*

We had worked hard to raise David. Our son had grown into a sensitive, dynamic young man who had joined his father's business. He was proof of what was once so right about Burton and me.

*Is when I'll fall in love with you.*

David and Amy were lifted high on chairs held by groomsmen and bounced up and down to the beat of "Hava Nagila." Guests danced the hora in a circle around them. Burton and I were hoisted up next. Gripping the seat of my chair, I shrieked and pretended to giggle.

Being raised on chairs is a tradition at Jewish weddings. It stems from Orthodox Judaism, which requires men and women to dance on opposite sides of a curtain. During the dancing, the Orthodox bride and groom are lifted up to glimpse each other. As Burton and I bobbed, music blared and guests whirled and I felt as though a curtain hung between us.

That night, it took all my resolve to keep smiling. None of my friends, not even my sister, or my mother, who had enough problems of her own, believed I had a care in the world. For all I knew, not one of our guests would have thought anything mattered more to me than the flowers being fresh, the food hot, and the kids living happily ever after.

TWO DAYS AFTER THE WEDDING. Another one of those nights. Burton sat downstairs, hunched over his computer. He hadn't walked out on me after all, but nothing had changed. I could feel myself drowning. Despite the advice I had shared at our twenty-fifth anniversary party six years before, I found it harder and harder to keep paddling.

I propped up two king-sized down pillows, leaned into them, then propped and leaned again. I thought back more than forty years to the house in which I grew up—a white colonial with black shutters and a red door and a flagstone walk, a pleasant enough exterior. Inside, my mother lay upstairs in bed, reading. Downstairs, my father hunkered on the blue sofa in the den. Like a baseball through the living room window, a thought crashed into my belly: Burton and I were becoming my parents.

*Vogue, Architectural Digest, Traditional Home,* and other magazines had collected on my nightstand. To distract myself, I pulled out the thinnest piece in the pile—a newsletter from designer Donna Karan. I flipped through, expecting to pitch it straight into the wastebasket. Toward the back, I spotted an interview Donna had conducted with an author named Debbie Ford. Donna's headline jumped out at me: "I Discovered I Was Becoming My Mother."

*Chapter Six*

# CHASING THE LIGHT

———— ∞∞∞ ————

BEGIN TO WEAVE AND GOD WILL GIVE YOU THE THREAD.
*German proverb*

WHEN CLOSE FRIENDS JOHN AND TERRY INVITED us to join them in Italy, it had seemed an inspired idea. John was a good friend and investment partner of Burton's; I loved Terry's wisecracks. If the four of us were to have a good time together, my husband might remember how he enjoyed being part of a couple. Specifically, a couple including me. And if he did, was it such a leap to conclude that in Italy he might fall in love with me all over again?

A week after the wedding, John and Terry had led us through the Parma antiques fair. We roamed through warehouses as big as football fields, stuffed with Italian Baroque furniture. Our friends purchased iron beds and bronze urns for the home they were building in Palm Beach, Florida. I approved their choices and tried to make them glad they had asked us to come, pointing out a graceful Venetian glass light fixture here, a weathered gilt-framed mirror there. But strains of romantic arias sung by Bocelli and Pavarotti floated from CD players tucked among the busts and books and china, and my heart felt as cracked and fragile as old porcelain.

In Florence, our friends dropped us off while they visited a tile factory. I felt relieved to have a couple of hours free of the need to chitchat and pretend all was well. Burton and I walked toward a leather goods shop we had found years before on a happier visit. Burton thrust his hands in his pockets. His shoulders hunched forward. I slipped my hand through his arm. He stiffened. I took my hand away and hooked my thumbs around the straps of my backpack.

It was a sunny day in September. The Arno River, with its graceful curved bridges, stretched out ahead. It cut through the center of town, protected on either side by buildings standing shoulder-to-shoulder, hundreds of years old, proudly wearing their age.

We strolled along the Lungarno Corsini. Ahead of us, a young couple walked in the same direction. He stood slightly taller than she. She had the kind of hair the luckiest young women toss around—shoulder-length and silky, the color of a caramel apple. He slung his arm around her tanned bare shoulders. She circled his waist with her arm. They stopped. She smiled. He kissed the top of her head.

"Were we ever like that?" I asked.

"Like what?"

"Like that couple."

"What about them?"

I sighed. "If you don't see it, I can't explain it."

The pair turned right on the Ponte Vecchio and disappeared into the crowd. I thought back to the first time I had visited this narrow bridge. I was twenty years old, touring Europe with my college friend Judy. The trip was a pre-graduation gift from my world-traveling grandmother. I thrilled to discover a bridge lined with jewelry shops set side-to-side like tightly strung pearls. I had entered one of those little shops and, trying to seem blasé, as though I did this sort of thing all the time, negotiated for a narrow brushed gold necklace.

London, Paris, Florence, Rome—I visited them all on that trip. The world had welcomed me then.

As Burton and I walked across the bridge, I wondered if my young couple had entered one of these shops seeking an engagement ring. Maybe he was buying her a bracelet as a token of his love. The thought sliced through me. Burton wasn't buying me anything to celebrate our love. He was scarcely speaking to me. For months, his eyes had avoided mine like those of a child caught with his hand where he was told not to put it.

Stepping off the bridge, Burton turned left. "I want to stop at the river. I need to think," he said.

I followed him down to a low concrete wall at the top of the riverbank. He stared at the muddy water. I waited beside him, stealing glimpses of a man I had known for most of my life. He had become a stranger.

Burton was as handsome as the day we met. Six feet tall and stocky, he towered over me by eight inches. His once-black hair had turned a commanding silver gray; his face was scored with creases; his belly bulged more than he liked due to a love for kosher hot dogs and bridge mix. But he still had the hazel eyes and the rosy cheeks of the twenty-one-year-old man I'd fallen in love with.

"I feel numb. I feel empty," Burton muttered to the river. "I don't know what I want to do with my life."

More than two years had passed since I overheard that strange voice—"Hiiiiiiii"—on Burton's cell phone. Burton had talked about feeling numb and empty before. His mood would pass, I'd thought. He had every reason to feel good about himself, had all the trappings of success. He had parlayed a tiny company into one of Michigan's top real estate firms. His twin engine Cessna 421 bore his initials, Bravo Foxtrot, on its tail. He owned two Cadillacs, two trucks, more than a dozen horses. He had presided over clubs, been honored by charities. Two tuxedos hung in his closet—one for when he was dieting, one for when he wasn't. We'd traveled on first-class upgrades, had slept at the Plaza Athenée in Paris and Claridges in

London, savored foie gras in Michelin multiple-star restaurants. He had self-supporting sons and a wife who was his best ally.

But the mood hadn't passed. Whatever was wrong with him had pulled me down, too. It had stolen my confidence, made me question matters I'd come to feel sure about—my abilities, my decisions, my marriage. Whatever was wrong had trailed him all the way to Italy.

He gazed at the river. "When we get home, I'm going to head back out west and get lost for a while."

I fought the urge to tell him, for the thousandth time, how lucky he was, how grateful he should be. Instead, I did something entirely out of character. "Meet me when you're ready," I said and turned and walked away.

I found the leather goods shop and picked out some wallets and belts, amazed by my ability to discern between cowhide and pigskin. I handed over a credit card. After a few minutes, Burton showed up. A frown still marred his face.

We wandered back along the river toward our hotel. The dark water stretched out before us. A scent of spicy marinara sauce wafted from an open window.

The night before, I had finished the book I'd learned about in Donna Karan's newsletter. Debbie Ford's *The Dark Side of the Light Chasers* was the first self-help book I had ever read. I had begun it on the plane and continued reading as John drove our minivan through the grapevine-covered hills of Tuscany. The book had helped me to see something radical: the goal in life was not to be perfect, but to be whole. I had spent more than thirty years trying to live up to my version of the perfect wife. I had entertained Burton's clients, gone to hockey games instead of art openings, passed up foreign films I wanted to see. Yet perfection had eluded me. Perfect wives in perfect unions should not end up routinely sweating over their husbands' whereabouts. I was sure of that.

I heard myself say to my husband, "You're going to do what you're going to do. I have to start thinking about me."

Silence. There may have been chatting tourists passing on the sidewalk, or the sound of honking horns, but I heard only silence. Burton stared straight ahead, his jaw clenched.

More strange words emerged from my mouth. "I used to love life," I said in a voice steadier than I felt. "I don't know what happened to the girl who felt that way. Maybe while you're out west, I'll take some time for myself. Maybe I'll come back to Florence and study Italian."

Let my husband venture off on his own? Was I nuts? My world was falling apart, and I was making travel plans. Come to Italy by myself? Where would I start? The only native whose name I knew in the whole country was Maria, my saleslady from the leather goods store. She had given me her card.

Burton shot me a startled glance. In a voice so low I could barely hear him, he said, "You want to come back here by yourself? I'm not sure how I feel about that."

ON OUR LAST NIGHT IN ITALY, the four of us stayed at a villa on the outskirts of Rome. Years before, tycoon J. Paul Getty had converted an old post office into a private residence and named it Poste Vecchia. Now an elegant inn on the shore of the Tyrrhenian Sea, it was furnished with antiques, some chosen by Getty himself, and boasted an antiquities museum on the lower level.

Before dinner, I flipped back through the underlined and dog-eared book I had just finished. I came across an exercise I had skipped earlier: Name five adjectives you want to describe your life. I picked up a pad of paper and wrote: *loving, creative, productive, nurturing, appreciated.*

That night in the dining room, with its high ceilings and tall French doors, I read my list out loud. Burton didn't say anything.

John said, "'Appreciated' isn't something you can control. Someone has to feel it for you."

I had wondered the same thing but left the word in anyway. Now I knew why. "I can choose to be with people who appreciate me," I said.

On the plane home, I thought about my list. I didn't feel appreciated, not by the man who sat beside me, the man who mattered most.

I turned to Burton. "I don't like who I've become," I said. "Either I need some help or we need some help."

"If it's important to you, I'll go with you," he said.

If the plane had landed on the moon, I couldn't have been more surprised.

ARRIVING HOME IN FRANKLIN, I fell asleep that night feeling a stirring of hope. The next morning, I turned over in bed and opened my eyes. The blanket and top sheet on my husband's side lay thrown back. The bottom sheet glared at me.

"Burton," I called. No answer. I shot out of bed into the bathroom. Empty. I peered into my husband's walk-in closet. A dozen-plus dark suits, seldom worn any longer, hung as silent witnesses to his absence. I swung open the back door, looked into the garage. Burton's car was gone. After choking down three spoonfuls of yogurt, I picked up the phone.

Several weeks before, I had run into Lori Wagner, a close friend. We had stopped for coffee, and I'd told her about Burton's determination to retire. "I'm having a hard time with it," I'd said.

She must have sensed there was more to my concern. She'd lowered her voice. "A few years ago, Ronnie was out of control. I was ready to leave him. Before I did, I decided to make one last attempt. We went to a couples program together. It was the start of turning our relationship around." At the time, I had been so sure Burton would not agree to couples therapy that I'd never broached the subject.

Lori's answering machine responded.

"It's Suzy," I whimpered. "Call me as soon as you can."

About five minutes later, my phone rang.

"Are you okay?" Lori asked.

I burst into tears. "Burton keeps disappearing. He says nothing's wrong."

"Of all my girlfriends, you were the strong one," Lori said. "You and Burt seemed like such good partners."

"Tell me about that couples program."

Lori told me about a place called Onsite that ran crisis intervention programs. It helped couples and individuals deal with problems relating to families of origin and of choice. She and Ronnie had attended one program together, and each had attended one on their own.

I recall thinking Lori's husband was every bit as headstrong as Burton. "Ronnie cooperated?" I asked.

"Not at first, but they got him to open up. After what he told me, I needed to go back. A few days later, I participated in a Living Centered program, the best gift I ever gave myself. It gave me the strength to do whatever I had to do." Ronnie had picked her up at the airport and, on the way home, pulled off the road. He apologized for how he had treated her, turned on the CD to *Wind Beneath My Wings*, and pulled a small box out of the glove compartment. Inside were two gold wedding bands. "He put on a wedding ring for the first time that day. He's worn it ever since."

She gave me the number for Onsite.

Early the next morning, I phoned. The woman I spoke to told me the date for the next couples program, agreed to send a brochure, and advised me to call back soon if I were interested.

"I don't have to read the brochure," I said. "I'm interested."

The program was twenty-three days off. I had survived twenty-six months of uncertainty. I could survive for another twenty-three days.

That night, I told Burton I had signed us up.

"I can hardly wait," he said, rolling his eyes.

"This is about enriching our lives."

"It's about guilt."

I COUNTED DOWN THE DAYS. Burton didn't get home until 9:30 P.M. Twenty days until our couples program. He didn't answer his cell phone all afternoon. Thirteen more days. He didn't tell me he loved me for forty-eight hours. Seven days to go.

Faith sustained me for twenty-three days, but on the plane to Nashville my confidence in our approaching salvation began to waver. For starters, I didn't have much confidence in psychotherapy. I had watched too many people jump from shrink to shrink or spend years with the same one and remain as unhappy as ever. Now I'd have a paltry four and one-half days to figure out what was or wasn't going on between us and whether it could be fixed. True, we'd be guided by experts. But it was hard to believe a so-called expert who had just met us could figure out problems that had confounded me for more than two years.

Then there was Burton, a take-charge kind of guy. He had trained himself to keep his mouth shut the way Lance Armstrong trained himself to pedal. If word leaked out about a deal Burton planned, property could be bought out from under him or the price jacked up or a tenant stolen. I couldn't imagine his spilling secrets to a group of strangers. If, that is, he had secrets to spill. If he did, he hadn't shared them with me, the one person on the planet who knew him best.

RATHER THAN TAKE THE ONSITE VAN from the airport, Burton rented a car. "In case I need to escape," he said. We drove through pretty green hills to Cumberland Furnace, a town too small to rate a dot on our road map. On the way, I began to worry about the food we'd be served over the next few days, and we stopped at a supermarket. "Take all the time you want," Burton said. I bought raisins and apricots and pretzels, just in case. I didn't want to give Burton any excuse to bolt.

A long driveway led up a hill to a restored white Victorian home wrapped with a porch. We checked in at a barn behind the house. Wandering through the barn, we passed several small rooms.

"Torture chambers," Burton muttered. The rooms were paneled with pine planks and stocked with blackboards, pillows, and back jacks like the one Andy used for mountain climbing.

Spread out around the barn, several two-story log buildings contained guest rooms. Ours had two double beds and one twin, all covered with colorful quilts. Gas fireplace. Wood armoire. Friendly but spare. I wandered to the back window, overlooking a field. Dozens of what I thought were ladybugs hovered around the glass. I later learned they were Asian lady beetles, and over the years from then on, I'd associate them with the bittersweet experience of our couples program. Our room had no radio, television, or telephone—all banned as potential distractions. I wondered how Burton would survive without his beloved remote control and his cell phone, which he left in the car.

I sensed that while here, I'd need to share secrets I had never shared with anyone. I didn't know how honest to be, how honest I could be when I, myself, didn't understand what Burton was doing with Jody. We had been advised not to discuss our professions and to keep what we heard confidential. Our nametags bore first names only. Still, I hesitated to say what worried me.

THAT NIGHT, FORTY MOSTLY MIDDLE-AGED ADULTS in jeans and sweatshirts sat on chairs in a circle. We shifted our weight, fidgeted with our hands, and introduced ourselves.

"I'm Suzy," I said.

A man in a plaid sweater vest burst out, "Hi, Suzy!"

"Burton and I have been married for thirty-one years," I said. "I'm here to develop more truth and intimacy in our relationship."

Burton followed. "I'm Burt."

"Hi, Burt!" the man in the vest called.

"I'm here to keep Suzy company," Burton said.

Almost everyone, including two lesbians, had come to work on improving their relationships. One couple came with a different intent. Laura and Tom, who looked to be in their mid-forties, had been separated for six months. "We've decided to get a divorce," Laura said. "We're here to make the process easier."

"Laura speaks for both of us," Tom said.

I was still stunned by Laura and Tom's introduction when we returned to our cabins and went to bed. Within minutes, Burton snored gently. I switched my sound machine to "White Noise" and popped in earplugs. Still, I tossed and turned.

THE FIRST FULL DAY STARTED with what I hoped was a good sign. After some meditations were read out loud, a staff member stood up and called off dates. May 6, my birthday, was mentioned quickly, surprising me because I'm the last one whose raffle ticket ever gets picked. I jumped to my feet. "That's me!" I cried. I became the official birthday celebrant for the day. I wore a ribbon and received wishes and hugs. Silly as it sounds, it was nice to feel special again.

Burton and I were assigned to a small group with four other couples. All of us had previously sent in background information. Three couples were married and Caucasian, including Albert, the friendly greeter from the night before, and his wife, Marie. There was also an African-American man with his white girlfriend. Burton and I were the only pair on our first marriage.

Ted and Marjie, our facilitators, also married, passed out marking pens and sheets of paper. They asked us to draw maps of the important people and events in our lives up until we met our mates. We taped our sketches to the wall and explained them. One woman had been raped by her stepfather; one man's alcoholic father had abandoned him and his mother when he was still a baby. Albert and Marie had four prior marriages between them. Burton spoke about his father's death when he was eleven and his mother's remarriage two years later. I talked about my father's religious conversion, my parents' separation, my earlier broken engagement.

At the end of our first session, Ted and Marjie faced each other, held hands, and recited what they called the Couples Serenity Prayer. "God, grant me the serenity to accept what I can not change, which is you, the courage to change what I can, which is me, and the wisdom to know the difference, which is hard."

A day had passed. I knew our fellow group members better. But I hadn't learned anything more about Burton's behavior over the last couple of years. Nor had I voiced my deepest fear.

AFTER DINNER THAT NIGHT, we broke up into same-sex groups. I joined ten women in the parlor of the main house. Sam, a no-nonsense female therapist, led an informal chat.

Laura, who had announced her divorce plans the night before, sat near me on a high-backed, red velvet chair. When Sam invited comments, Laura spoke.

"Tom has been having an affair," she said in a firm, throaty voice. No hysterics. No scene. I envied her composure. "We've been married for twenty years. Last year, Tom fell for some young bimbo he met in a bar. Six months later he left our beautiful house and shacked up with this girl and her baby. He planned to live with her in her one-bedroom apartment for a couple of years, get her out of his system, then come back to me.

"When Tom first moved out, I sat home and cried for weeks. Then I found a therapist who has helped me to move on with my life. The day after we get home, I'm meeting with a lawyer."

"Good for you," Sam said. "He got you down, but he couldn't keep you there."

Words I had never uttered out loud now worked their way around gulps of air and across my tongue. "I'm afraid my husband is having an affair," I said. I blew my nose and kept going. "He disappears a lot. He has a female friend he horseback rides with. He says that's all there is to it. I don't know if he's telling me the truth. If I could just learn not to care, I could still have my career and keep our family together."

Sam's eyes locked on mine. "Bullshit," she said.

I whispered, "How do you know when it's time to end a marriage?"

"When it becomes toxic."

After, I thought about what Sam had said and about how suspicions had poisoned my spirit. I was afraid to share the conversation with Burton. I avoided confrontations as though they carried the AIDS virus. Nevertheless, back in our room, I repeated Sam's words.

"That sucks," Burton said. "They're supposed to help us make up our own minds. They're not supposed to make up our minds for us."

To my relief, he did not add: I'm out of here.

I DREW A CIRCLE FOR EACH IMPORTANT PERSON in my life—mine in the middle surrounded by a larger one I labeled Burton. I drew Mom's big circle below mine and connected her to me with jagged lines. Circles for David, Andy, and my sister rested above mine, close but separate. Dad's small circle floated by itself in a corner. Next to Burton's circle, I drew one for Jody, and then pondered how to connect them. Heavy lines seemed ominous. Dotted lines, safer. I settled for dotted lines.

I was surprised at how clearly a few strokes depicted my predicament. There was Burton's dominance, Jody's interference, my mother's dependence—all glaring back at me. The picture helped clarify our problems. It did not tell me what to do about them.

In our small group, we explained our diagrams. "Jody is someone who rides horses with Burton," I said. "He tells me that's all there is to the relationship." I looked at Burton for confirmation. He was busy studying the pen he twisted between his fingers.

Burton did a diagram, too. His consisted of our sons, his sisters, his late parents, and me.

TED AND MARJIE, THE DIRECTORS OF ONSITE, had suffered through as much as any of us—alcoholism, affairs, other marriages, troubles with parents, neglecting their own children. That night, after sharing their stories with the whole group, they pulled two chairs to the front of the room. They placed them seat-to-seat and climbed up.

Standing on separate chairs, they pressed their hands on each other's shoulders and swayed.

"You can see how unbalanced we are, clinging to each other while standing alone," Ted said. "What might give us more stability?"

"A third chair," an audience member called out.

Ted pulled over another chair, and then climbed back up on the first. He and Marjie each placed one foot on the third chair. This time, when they pressed on each other's shoulders, they remained balanced.

Audience members suggested what the third chair represented. "Common interests." "Mutual goals." "Communication."

"All valid," Ted said. "But for Marjie and me, the added chair represents something more. A support that's bigger than we are. It represents a spiritual foundation."

A spiritual foundation, I thought. I wonder what that means. I wonder if it's possible. I wonder if it would help.

THE NEXT DAY'S EXERCISE DIDN'T SCARE ME. Each couple was placed into the physical positions that best portrayed their relationship. Since Burton and I had survived thirty-one years of sickness and health together, way more than anyone else in our small group, I assumed we'd be depicted as the closest of all.

I was wrong. Our group placed us as far apart as possible. They directed me to one corner, sent Burton to the diagonally opposite corner, and gave him a companion. LeAnn played Burton's horseback-riding friend. She batted her blue eyes at my husband and tilted her chin back and forth in a nauseating display of overacting.

"Suzy seems stuck in an emotional box," someone said.

Marjie pulled a rope out of a chest, looped it around my arms, and knotted it.

"Burt's relationship with Jody is a mystery."

Ted posted people on either side of Burton and LeAnn and had them hold up a black veil, obscuring my view of Burton and his "friend."

"There's still some connection between Suzy and Burt."

"More like a tug of war," Marjie said. She gave me one end of a second rope, gave Burton the other, and directed us to pull it back and forth.

After LeAnn's stroking had almost worn through my husband's sleeve, Marjie asked Burton and me to step aside. Val and Bill replaced us.

"Stand back and see what your relationship looks like," Marjie said.

As if watching weren't torture enough, we had to listen, too. Marjie gave each player lines to repeat.

Val: "I helped you with your career. Now it's my turn."

Bill: "I want to play. You won't play with me."

LeAnn: "Your wife doesn't appreciate you. I do."

All-too-familiar messages I had played over and over in my head now screeched out loud like violins in a beginner class. I wanted to cover my ears. This discordant little scene was more than play-acting. It was my life. Me: despairing, alone, stuck in a corner. Burton: cold, far away, with someone else fawning over him. I had stumbled into a humiliating cliché, a rejection that happened to lots of wives. Not to me. And the only way out—if there was a way, if it wasn't already too late—was one I didn't want to consider: the choice between my husband and my career. A choice that wasn't fair.

Our group clearly sensed a close connection between Burton and Jody. I still didn't know how close.

"We bring emotional baggage to bed with us. We call such baggage our invaders," Ted said. "Invaders violate our bedrooms and disrupt our sex lives." They could include previous lovers, children, in-laws, workaholism, overeating, drinking, and childhood abuse.

Couples took turns lying on a sheet spread on the floor. As the rest of us suggested what each pair's invaders might be, Ted and Marjie piled pillows on them. Watching grown men and women pretend to lie in bed struck me as perfect material for *Saturday Night Live*. Miserable as I was, I fought the urge to laugh.

Pillows collected on Tommy's chest for his anger with his alcoholic father, his fury at LeAnn's efforts to control his drinking, his guilt over how his drunken binges affected their son. LeAnn received pillows for the way Tommy's drinking repelled her sexually and how it jeopardized his health.

"Are you ready to get rid of your invaders, Tommy?" Ted asked.

"Hell, yes."

Ted pressed down on the pillows stacked on Tommy's chest. Tommy reared up with a roar, pushing Ted aside. LeAnn did the same. Ted then helped them to negotiate one change they were each willing to make. LeAnn agreed to stop policing Tommy's drinking; he agreed to join AA.

Although I respected the courage Tommy and LeAnn had shown, I still felt a nervous urge to laugh. I dreaded our turn. I doubted I could take the exercise as seriously as Tommy and LeAnn had.

George and Pam volunteered next. George was a soft-spoken black man, never married, around forty. Pam was petite and fair-skinned, the mother of two young children. She had ended her former marriage when she caught her husband in an affair. Having dated for a year, Pam and George were considering moving in together.

We suggested their invaders. Pam's children, her mistrust of men, her fear of another failed relationship. George's mother's opposition, his reluctance to commit, his worries about racial differences. As pillows piled up on them, Burton passed me a note: I don't have any invaders. I wrote back: I have enough for both of us.

Tears streamed down Pam's face. George pounded his fist on the floor. Burton leaned over to me and whispered in my ear, "I figured out an invader."

I was glad he had started to relate to the exercise. I mouthed the word: Who?

He whispered, "Eddie Mae."

Eddie Mae Watson had been our housekeeper for almost thirty years. I pictured her invading our bedroom, unfurling clean linens, and I burst out laughing. I clapped my hands over my face, hoping my guffaws would be taken for sobs. When I couldn't stop laughing, I fled from the room.

After, Burton met me in the hall. "I shouldn't have done that to you," he said.

"Forget it. You've been a good sport. This isn't your thing."

"That's true. But it's important to you."

AFTER EVERYONE ELSE HAD TAKEN A TURN, Ted looked at us. I wasn't laughing anymore.

"Let's get it over with," I said.

Burton and I lay beside each other on the sheet. Pillows mounded on my chest. My suspicions about Jody. My responsibility for my mother. My reluctance to retire. Because Burton hadn't voiced any concerns, he lay unencumbered.

Ted pressed his weight into the pillows layered on top of me. "Suzy, this is a lot of baggage," he said. "You can get angry. You can push these invaders away."

I willed my limbs to move, my torso to rise up, my vocal cords to roar with rage as Jimmy's had. But I lay frozen, unable to budge. I shivered as the cold of the floor seeped into my arms, my legs, my back.

Ted pushed down harder. "Come on, Suzy. You don't have to take all this pressure."

My limbs felt paralyzed. All I could do was lie there, mute, miserable, and shaking.

Ted sat back on his knees. He took each pillow off my chest, one by one, and placed it aside. "Suzy," he said in a gentle voice, "what would you like to say to Burt?"

Later, I realized I should have shouted: *Take your disappearing acts and shove them.* But relationships are complicated. Understanding them is, too. Like many women of my generation, I wasn't taught to fight for myself. It would take many months of self-examination to come to terms with the ambivalence that plagued me. At that point, I only knew that as hard as I fought to maintain my independence, I depended on Burton with equal force. Not just for financial support. For my sense of self-worth.

Although the pillows were gone, the weight on my chest remained.

I said to Burton, "I can understand how you've withdrawn from me. I've been wrapped up in my own interests. I haven't been available for you."

Ted gazed at me like a parent whose child has fallen and bumped her head. "Suzy," he said, "you sound like you're taking eighty percent of the blame here. I've counseled thousands of couples. No relationship problem is ever eighty percent one person's fault."

I slunk off to the restroom. I was pathetic. I had let Ted down. Let the group down. Let myself down. Everyone else had made breakthroughs. George had postponed moving in with Pam. Val and Bill grieved together over the infant son they'd lost. Albert and Marie confronted how past failed marriages hampered their trust for each other. But I had claimed 80 percent.

I returned to our group room and walked up to Burton, expecting him to turn away. "I flunked bed," I said.

He put his arm around me. "You did fine."

*Chapter Seven*

# FACING FACTS

———⌾⌾⌾———

WHEN YOU ARE A BEAR OF VERY LITTLE BRAIN, AND YOU THINK
OF THINGS, YOU FIND SOMETIMES THAT A THING WHICH SEEMED
VERY THINGISH INSIDE YOU IS QUITE DIFFERENT WHEN IT GETS
OUT INTO THE OPEN AND HAS OTHER PEOPLE LOOKING AT IT.

*Winnie-the-Pooh*, A. A. Milne

BACK IN OUR CABIN. "I feel like I let us down," I said. "I expected you to be mad at me."

"Why?"

"When I do something you don't like, you blow up at me. Or stop talking. That's how you control me."

I'm asking for trouble, I thought. But Burton put his hands on my shoulders and looked into my eyes. "I didn't know you thought I controlled you," he said. "Maybe you've told me before, but this is the first time I've heard you."

The pleasant surprise that rippled through me lasted two seconds. The fact was, we had slogged through three full days of exercises, lectures, and conversations at the one place that was our last hope, yet our problems were no clearer to me than they were on the day we arrived. If we were going to resolve anything, we had twenty-four hours left to figure it out.

THAT NIGHT BURTON LAY DOWN in one of the two double beds. I took the other, hoping to avoid tossing or snoring and get some sleep. Lying alone, I prayed for understanding. The glow from the gas fireplace flickered on the walls, danced inside my eyelids.

About 4:30 in the morning, Burton put his hand on my arm.

"Come over to my bed," he said.

Glad he wanted to hold me, I climbed onto the still-warm sheet and curled against him. I inhaled his scent, a smell of cloves and old leather and the woods after it rains. For thirty-one years I had loved lying beside him, my thigh over his, my ear to his chest, grateful for the steady thump-thump of his heart.

"Being here has forced me to see the trouble we're in."

The low, controlled tone of his voice raised bumps on my skin. Up to this minute, I only suspected we had trouble. He could tell me I was imagining things, and if he sounded convincing enough, and if my hormones happened to cooperate that day, I could almost talk myself into believing him.

"I'm ready to tell you what's going on if you're ready to hear it," he said. "I warn you—up to now, you haven't been."

The air around us turned cold. I began to tremble.

"I've fought telling you the truth. With everyone else baring their souls, this place has gotten to me. There may only be one hope left—to be completely honest, right here, right now, while we can still get help."

"At this point, we don't have much to lose," I said.

I didn't mean it for one second.

From years of running a business, Burton had learned to get bad news over with, fast.

"I lied about my relationship with Jody," he said. "She did travel with me. We have been sexually involved, though that never was a big part of our relationship. At first we were just friends. She still is a good friend. I never meant to let it get this far."

Sexually involved. The words slammed into my gut. By themselves, words don't mean much. But when they're projected a certain way, one after another like bullets, they can start wars, destroy civilizations, break hearts. I wanted Burton to stop, to tell me he didn't mean what he said, to apologize for the sick joke. At least I wanted him to claim he'd made a terrible mistake. But his words lodged in my stomach. Jody still was a good friend. He used to call *me* his best friend.

"Should I go on?"

Go on? I only suspected one problem.

I swallowed. "Go on."

"Before Jody, there was a woman I did business with. That lasted a few months. No emotional involvement."

Probably around the time of his gall bladder surgery. He hadn't wanted to make love for a while after. Or a while before, now that I thought about it.

I took deep breaths, the way I was taught in the Lamaze class Burton and I attended while I was pregnant with David. The breathing hadn't helped much then; it didn't now. I stared at the dark ceiling, unable to look at the father of my children. My limbs shook.

Burton tightened his arms around me. "Are you okay?" he asked. "Can you handle this?"

I thought I'd come here to learn the truth. Now I realized I didn't want the truth after all. I wanted something safe and sanitized, not like what was shaping up as the truth, a grim reality that could force me to change my life. All I wanted was a simple fix—to put my marriage back on track like a little toy train, to count on my husband again.

I threw off the covers and lurched to the other bed. Wrapping a quilt around me, I felt myself grow smaller, as though I might tremble down to nothing.

"Is that all?" I rasped.

He sighed. "No."

"How many more?"

"One."

I groaned. "Get it over with."

"Remember the thing with Sally?"

"Oh, my God."

Sally Preston. The lawyer Burton dismissed from our account some fifteen years before when so-called false rumors about their affair spread around the office. I had put Sally Preston out of my mind the way I might have shoved a piece of lint under the Persian rug in our dining room.

"I don't know why it happened," he said. "I was crazy about you for so long. But we were both busy with our careers and raising the kids. You didn't seem very interested in sex."

I would have liked to declare him wrong. To protest that I initiated new positions from the Kama Sutra and lured him to bed with skimpy negligees. But the fact was I slept in flannel nightshirts. The heat of our courting days had cooled. Crying babies and kids' hockey games, meetings and movies can do that to a sex life. Though I never begged off with a headache, given a choice between intercourse and *The Tonight Show*, I'd have called "Heeere's Johnny" as often as not.

"My relationship with Sally lasted about two years," Burton said. "Breaking up was so hard on me I swore I'd never get involved with anyone else again. And I didn't—for a long time.

"Sally moved to the East Coast, got married, and had a family. We didn't speak for years. A few months ago, when I was already involved with Jody, you and I visited New York City. You went shopping with a girlfriend. I rented a car and told you I took a drive in the country."

"I remember."

"I drove out to see Sally. She had gotten in touch with me. She was having trouble with her husband and wanted someone to listen. That's all I wanted, too. I wasn't attracted to her anymore. I'm still not, but we've talked a lot since then. She understands what I'm going through."

That makes one of us.

A ray of daylight seeped through the window. The beginning of our last day at Onsite.

"Remember fifteen years ago when I got so depressed?"

"I remember."

"What really bothered me was breaking up with Sally."

"All my theories," I said. "How could I not have known?"

"You didn't want to know."

A more tuned-in wife, a wife with a shred of self-respect, might have cracked her husband over the head with the table lamp or thrown a chair at the wall. Pam, from our group, had shot a gun at her former husband when she'd caught him cheating. She had missed. But at least she'd shown some gumption. All I could do was sit and shiver.

The spaghetti I had eaten a few hours before backed up in my throat. I staggered to the bathroom, shut the door, collapsed on the toilet. I couldn't throw up, couldn't even cry. I had been faithful to this man my whole life, stayed a virgin until I married him. For what?

An Asian lady beetle landed on my leg. I couldn't muster the strength to flick it away. Your house is on fire; your children are gone. I was a fool. The man I'd been married to for thirty-one years wasn't who I thought he was. My house was burning down.

Burton knocked on the door. "Are you okay?"

"I'm alive."

Through the door: "Should I have kept my mouth shut? Are you sorry I told you?"

I opened the door. He looked at me with sad, droopy eyes. His soft, silver hair stuck out at angles from his head. I resisted the urge to smooth it. Better to scratch his eyes out. I folded my arms. "I'm not sorry you told me. I'm sorry about *what* you told me. I was going crazy not knowing what to believe. At least I wasn't crazy."

"In spite of the shit I've pulled, I love you very much. I hope you don't walk out on me. I won't blame you if you do."

He put his arms around me. I should have forced him away, but I couldn't. My arms folded between his chest and mine, I continued to shake. I understood why I couldn't push off a pile of pillows the day before. I couldn't fight invaders I didn't know. Now I knew them. I didn't know what to do about them.

I need to talk about this with our group, I thought. Burton will never let me.

Fear bubbled up in my chest. I took a breath to suppress it.

"I'd like to bring this to our group."

"Do what you need to do."

ON OUR FINAL AFTERNOON, Ted told our group I had requested their attention. I don't know what I'd have done if they hadn't agreed. I hoped they could help me find my way through this nightmare. I couldn't do it on my own.

Ted didn't put us back in the dreaded bed position. He placed two chairs in the middle of the room and asked Burton and me to sit facing each other. He and Marjie drew up chairs beside us. Everyone else sat on the floor. Val and Bob leaned against the wall. Pam and George folded their legs, Indian style. Albert and Marie slouched into back jacks. LeAnn lay with her head in Tommy's lap.

Looking at them one by one, I said, "Thank you for giving us a second chance. You've been so open with your problems you've given us the courage to face ours. This morning Burton told me some tough stuff. I hope you can help us deal with it."

I told them what Burton had said: about his current affair with Jody, his previous fling, the earlier affair with Sally. No one coughed or whispered or budged. My voice came out in a flat line. Looking back, I marvel at how calm I seemed. For someone who weeps over Folgers coffee commercials, I repeated the most hurtful words without a tear. It had been nine hours since Burton broke my heart. I hadn't been able to cry.

Burton sat still, without expression. Having negotiated hundreds of real estate deals, he had mastered the poker face.

Ted turned to Burton. "Did Suzy sum up what you told her?"

"She did."

"Okay, then." Ted clapped his hands on his knees. "Let's get to the bottom line. Suzy, what is the one change you must have and what are you willing to give?"

I was afraid to ask Burton to break up with Jody. Afraid he wouldn't. Or couldn't. Afraid half a marriage was better than no marriage. Without the people around me, I don't know if I could have forced out the words. I came up with something that sounded serious, like I meant what I said.

In my most convincing tone: "Burton agrees to end the affair immediately. Suzy will work to forgive him."

Thirty-one years. Two children. Grandchildren someday.

"You want me to end the affair," Burton said. "I'm prepared to do that."

My heart leapt. My skin prickled. There was hope. Then: they're only words. They don't mean anything. I pressed my lips together.

"You're in shock," Burton said. "I doubt you're ready to forgive me. Why not just say you'll be honest about your feelings?"

I am in shock. How can I ever forgive him?

"Burton agrees to end the affair immediately. Suzy will be honest about her feelings," I said. I sounded like a robot.

"I can't agree to immediately."

I didn't think immediately was soon enough. I clenched my teeth and waited.

"I've broken up with her before. We got back together. She won't believe I mean it unless I do it in person. And I need to pick up my truck and horse trailer. Instead of immediately, make it: as soon as possible."

"How long is that?"

"Within two weeks."

"Too long."

"By the end of this weekend."

We would arrive home on Wednesday afternoon. I ticked off the days on my fingers: Thursday, Friday, Saturday, Sunday. Four days to see if my husband would keep his word.

"It seems like a long time, but I'll live with it."

Albert jotted down our agreement in a notebook, tore out the page, and passed it to me. *Burton agrees to end the affair as soon as possible, by Sunday at the latest. Suzy agrees to be honest with him about her feelings.* Albert's choppy handwriting looked like the tracings of angels' wings.

I turned to Ted. "Can I ask another question?"

"Go ahead."

Burton sat with his running shoes planted on the floor, arms crossed, face blank. If he was upset or angry or uncomfortable, it didn't show.

"How will you get to South Lyon?"

"I'll have someone drive me."

"I don't want to involve anyone else in this. I'll drive you to her house and wait."

"That would be uncomfortable for you."

I'd manage, I thought. I've had practice.

"You could take a cab and call me when you're dropped off and again the minute you leave," I said.

"A waste of money," Burton said. "Jody lives an hour away."

I raked my fingers through my hair. "I could drive you to some-place near her house. You could call a cab from there."

"There are no cabs in the country, Suzy. I'll take one from home if it makes you more comfortable."

I exhaled with relief. We had gotten through the breakup night-mare. I felt exhausted. I looked at Ted, wondering if we were finished.

He spoke gently. "Suzy, things you're not thinking about may occur to you later. You might want to get some of them worked out now. For instance, when Burt goes to break up with Jody, how much time can he spend with her?"

Burton would need enough time to exchange a few pleasantries, say good-bye, and walk out the door. I didn't want to give Jody an extra second to dissuade him.

"Fifteen minutes seems reasonable."

Burton nodded.

"Is any physical contact acceptable?" Ted asked.

My stomach twisted.

"I guess it would be okay to kiss her on the cheek. Not on the lips."

The minute the words left my mouth, I wanted to take them back.

Pam looked away. Val coughed.

Kiss her on the cheek. How could I say something so inane?

At the end of our final small group session, Marjie turned on the tape recorder. Twelve of us stood in a circle, arms around each other's shoulders, listening to Garth Brooks' "The River." I had never heard the song before. One verse blew my heart wide open. For the first time that day, I began to sob.

*Too many times we stand aside and let the waters slip away,*
*'Til what we put off 'til tomorrow has now become today.*
*So don't you sit upon the shore and think you're satisfied.*
*Choose to chance the rapids, and dare to dance the tides.*

ON THE WAY BACK TO OUR CABIN, my legs wobbled. Burton wrapped his arm around my waist. How could I give my husband permission to kiss that woman on any part of her anatomy? I wondered. What was wrong with me? I thought about the day. My world had been blasted apart and cobbled back together within a few hours. I thought about how long it would take for Burton to live up to his promise. Four days from tomorrow. An eternity.

"Waiting till this weekend will be hard on you," Burton said. "I could go down to the car, call Jody on my cell phone, and break up with her right now. Would that make you more comfortable?"

I shouted loud enough to be heard all the way to Nashville: "YES!"

As I waited in the buffet line, Albert came up behind me, wearing a light blue sweater vest I hadn't seen before. He spoke into my ear. "I've been where Burt is," he said. "The lies, the sneaking around, the other women—I've done it all. More than once. That's why I'm on my third marriage. Marie and I came here because I don't want a fourth.

"I give Burt credit for facing his demons. He knows he screwed up. He wants your marriage to work. Years ago I should have done what you're doing. I wish I'd had as much courage as the two of you."

"Thanks, Albert. I needed that." Clutching my quivering empty plate, I gave him a hug.

After helping myself to roast turkey and mashed potatoes, I tracked down Val and Pam and asked them to sit with me. They picked up their plates and followed me to a free table.

"I have breaking news," I said. "Burton is in the parking lot on his cell phone. Calling Jody to end the affair."

"Right now?" they chorused. Their eyes bulged.

"Right now. He'll meet me here later." Under the mahogany table, my left heel bounced.

"I figure it could take twenty minutes," I said, checking my watch. "It's been fifteen."

Pam said, "I could hardly keep my mouth shut today. When you were talking about how he'd get to that woman's house, I was ready to jump up and yell that I'd come with you."

Val curled her lips. "He thought it would be uncomfortable for you to be there. I wanted tell him I was sure you could handle it. I'd have flown across country to join you, too."

"Perfect," I said. "You two could be my posse."

"As for that crap about physical contact," Pam said, "I'd have told him: A kiss on the cheek? *I don't think so*. While I gripped the knife in my pocket."

Remembering that Pam had pulled a gun on her unfaithful former husband, I burst out laughing.

"Kiss her cheek?" Val said. "I'd have told him: Kiss my ass."

I choked down two or three bites. My stomach was in no shape for food, not even comfort food. The energy from my bouncing heel could have roasted the turkey we were eating. I checked my watch again. Twenty minutes.

"He should be here soon."

"Assuming he reached her right away," Val said.

"If he couldn't reach her, he'd be back already."

Val and Pam chewed on their dinners.

"Now how long?" Val asked.

"Twenty-three minutes."

"What if the phone was busy?" Pam said.

I groaned.

Twelve minutes later. Still no Burton. Val and Pam had returned to their rooms. So had I. I yanked my duffel bag out of the armoire, flung it on the bed, checked my watch for the hundredth time. Thirty-five minutes since Burton headed for the parking lot.

I shoved a sweatshirt and a pair of jeans into my bag. What if Burton changed his mind? I smacked a T-shirt on top of the jeans. What if he couldn't bring himself to break up with her? I stuffed in a pair of hiking boots. What if she talked him out of it?

I sat on the bed, stuck out my left hand, and stared at my narrow gold and diamond band. I had been proud to wear a wedding ring; it meant someone wanted me. It protected me against advances from other men—not that I attracted that sort of attention, but also an explanation for why such advances didn't occur more often. Burton had never worn a wedding band. A ring would interfere with his grip of a tennis racket or a golf club, and if he had to keep taking one on and off, he would lose it. He'd said that when we first married. Hadn't changed his mind.

I slipped the ring into my pocket and held out both bare hands. One age spot on the left, three on the right, all too big to count as freckles. Cuticles on both thumbs chewed red and ragged.

I checked my watch. Forty minutes.

I can keep the damn ring in my pocket.

We had been assigned to write commitment statements to read out loud at an assembly that evening, a declaration of how we wanted our relationships to change. I propped some pillows against the wall, picked up a pen and a legal pad, and sat back down to begin writing. My hand would not budge.

Flinging the blank yellow pad to the floor, I grabbed my journal off the nightstand. *Early this morning Burton admitted he was involved in an affair with Jody,* I scrawled. *He has gone to the car to break up with her on his cell phone. It has been forty-five minutes. I can't imagine what is taking so long.*

The door to the cabin opened. Burton walked in. I held my breath.

"It's over," he said.

Jody's phone was busy. He sat in the car waiting, tried several times before getting through.

"I told her she and I were finished. I told her you knew everything."

"Good," I said.

It was all I dared to say.


BURTON AND I SAT IN THE ASSEMBLY AREA of the barn waiting for the final program to begin. I gazed around the room. Conversation buzzed. Faces smiled. I already missed the people surrounding me. We had shared so much, yet would probably never see each other again.

I was curious about two couples who weren't in our small group. We had dined the first night with Eddie and Ann, who appeared to be in their early sixties. This was a second marriage for both. Eddie had a habit of double-blinking his eyes. Ann seemed as cool as Eddie did nervous. She wore a strand of pearls around the neck of her pale pink cashmere sweater. The day before, I had asked Ann how things were going. "Eddie has worn me out," she said. "I don't think I have the energy for the changes they want us to make."

Scanning the audience that night, I spotted Eddie. Alone.

I also wanted to know about Laura and Tom, who had attended in hopes of making their divorce easier. Earlier, Laura had flashed me a thumbs-up. Now she and Tom walked to the front of the room.

"Tom and I have decided to get back together," Laura said. The audience applauded. Laura smiled at Tom. "I'll be glad to have you home again."

Tom said, "I commit to you that I'll move back in right away. I'll give you the time you deserve."

"All right," I whispered.

As for me, realizing that Burton had really and truly broken up with Jody, I felt giddy, as though I'd drunk just the right amount of champagne. When our turn arrived, I strode to the front. Burton came with me.

"When we first got here, our relationship was rocky," I said. "Now I feel like playing the theme song from the movie *Rocky*. Burton, I'll keep fighting for our marriage."

"Suzy," Burton said, "I have always loved you. I will try to make up for the pain I've caused you."

As we returned to our seats, I raised my arms above my head and waved my hands in "V for Victory" signs.

THE NEXT MORNING, I rolled my duffel bag across the gravel parking lot to the car. I could no longer remember the tune from *Rocky*. I was no prizefighter. I was an aging woman with a husband who had betrayed her, a bag of dirty clothes, and a chin that had started to sag.

Walking into the barn to drop off our room key, I ran into Ted.

"Burton made the call," I told him. It was hard to get the words out. "He broke up with her."

"I'm glad," he said. He wrapped me in a hug. I'm sure he felt me trembling.

I stepped back, gazed at him through blurry eyes, took his hands in mine.

"Thank you," I said.

As I headed for the door, Ted called, "Suzy?"

I turned to face him.

"Keep breathing."

*Chapter Eight*

# TO HELL AND BACK

THE DISCOVERY OF YOUR PARTNER'S AFFAIR FORCES YOU
TO REDEFINE YOURSELF IN THE MOST FUNDAMENTAL WAY.
"IF YOU, MY LIFE PARTNER, ARE NOT THE PERSON I THOUGHT YOU
WERE, AND OUR MARRIAGE IS A LIE, THEN WHO AM I?" YOU ASK.
*After the Affair*, Janis Abrahms Spring, Ph.D.

BACK HOME, I FELT AS DAZED AND SHAKEN as if I'd lived through a
hurricane. Questions dangled over my head like broken tree limbs.
Was I crazy to take Burton back? Did I have the courage to leave?
Would I ever feel good about myself again?

The morning after we returned from Tennessee, I made plans
to go back. I signed up for a weeklong Living Centered program
for individuals in early December. Burton decided to attend a program, too.

"You go first," he said. "I'll go in January."

I'll believe that when I see it, I thought.

I longed to hear *The River* again. Garth sang about mistakes and
uncertainty and hope. I wanted to memorize every word. Burton

drove me to Birmingham, a few miles from our home, to pick up a CD. Through the glare of my new knowledge, everything we passed looked different. Banks and shops and galleries I'd seen a hundred times stood out in garish relief. Turning south off Maple Road onto Old Woodward, I noticed teenage girls slouched in front of Starbucks, smoking cigarettes. They should know better, I thought. I should have, too. We passed the art deco Birmingham Theater, where Burton and I had been guests at the reopening a couple of years before. We'd had fun that night. Or had we?

At Borders, a voice from my mouth requested the CD. Someone else seemed to unsnap my Gap backpack, dig beneath the sunglass and reading-glass cases for my wallet, withdraw my credit card, sign my name. Someone else seemed to climb back into the car with Burton, clutching a small plastic bag.

Getting through the last day of our program had taken more courage than I knew I had. Being home again would take even more. We had returned to our cars, to our phones and computers, to a life in which Burton had too much free time. There were no smart psychologists or sympathetic group members to keep us headed in a positive direction. I wondered what would stop my husband from running back to South Lyon the first time we got into a fight.

I had to say something. I only hoped whatever that something turned out to be, it wouldn't chase Burton farther away. Our program had taught me to start with "I feel" and "I need." Strange to be told how to talk to someone I had talked to for most of my life.

In the car on the way home, I choked out the words. "I feel insecure," I said. "I'm afraid you'll go back to Jody."

He frowned. "I told you it's over."

"I need to know I can trust you for a while."

He took his eyes off the road and looked at me. "I'll give you a commitment. I won't go back to Jody before I finish my Living Centered program."

"Jody or anyone else."

He nodded.

He had deceived me before. He could do so again. But if he made it to a program of his own, anything might happen. I'd try to have faith. Faith was the first part of faithful. I took a pen out of my bag and wrote on the back of an old sales receipt: *Burton agrees to be faithful to Suzy at least until he completes his Living Centered program.* I read the sentence out loud.

Burton said, "I want something back—a block of time for us to go away together."

I wrote again, being more specific about the faithful part. I read out loud: "Burton agrees to be faithful to Suzy, physically and emotionally, at least until he completes his Living Centered program. Suzy agrees to go away with him for two weeks this winter."

"Three weeks."

"It's a deal."

We shook hands.


Despite our agreement, I kept comparing myself to Burton's ex-mistress. I felt as though I were competing with Jody Sommers in some bizarre Ms. Michigan pageant. Was I as pretty as Jody? No. As athletic as she? No. Smarter than she? Yes. Nicer than she? Obviously. Did Burton still think about her? Probably. Would the crown of his affections go to Mrs. Franklin or Ms. South Lyon?

Dim light filtered through the wood blinds of our library. I lay for hours, alone on the sage green wool carpet, punching the button for our CD player, listening to Garth over and over: *Trying to learn from what's behind, and never knowing what's in store/Makes each day a constant battle, just to stay between the shores.*

While I floundered upstairs between the shores, Burton retreated downstairs. He hunched over his laptop computer at his desk or reclined in the dark on the guest room bed. Avoiding me, I thought. Missing her.

When Burton and I crossed paths in the hall or sat together at dinner, we attempted courtesy. "Good chicken." "I'm pooped." "TV sucks." At one point, as I lay on the library floor, Burton walked through. He looked at me and shook his head. "I shouldn't have told you everything," he said. "You'll never forgive me."

Having tucked Burton's promise into my journal, I took it out and studied it. He would not race back to Jody—the piece of paper said so. The words seemed concrete and hopeful. I wanted to believe that little yellow slip was an official, binding document and not just a crumpled sales receipt.

AFTER FOUR DAYS OF OUR TIPTOEING around each other, I realized I wasn't tough enough or smart enough to handle our problems on my own. I needed help. Finding a marriage counselor wasn't as simple as, for example, finding a dentist. I could ask a dozen friends who took care of their teeth. They all knew I had teeth. They didn't know I had marital problems, at least I didn't think so, and I wanted it that way. Onsite recommended a psychologist in our area named Jim Rowe. On Sunday morning, I punched the numbers for his office and left a message. That night he called back.

"I think I can help you, Suzy," Jim said. "I hear from your voice that you're in a lot of pain. You may find this hard to believe, but now that things are out in the open, there is hope. One word of advice: this is no time to make any decisions. For now, your job is just to get stronger."

His words soothed like ice to burned skin.

DURING AN AIRPLANE FLIGHT YEARS BEFORE, the pilot's voice came over the loudspeaker. The landing gear signals hadn't lit up, he said. We'd prepare for a possible crash landing. As the plane circled over the airport, I looked out the window. Fire trucks waited below; foam covered a section of tarmac. The burly guy sitting next to me threw up in a bag. When we descended, I did as the stewardess instructed. Dropped my head to the pillow in my lap, wrapped my arms around my knees. We landed safely that time. Now that same sense of terror rushed back at me.

If my marriage crash-landed, my whole world would change. I'd have to leave my beautiful new home, with the swing on the screened-in porch. Living there alone, I'd fear each creak announced the Franklin Strangler. I'd have to swat every moth myself. I'd dine at the Bangkok Hung Café with a magazine for company and no one to tell me when I needed a breath mint. I dreaded having to get a bikini wax to go on a date, exposing a stranger to my bulging inner thighs. Considering the competition for decent men, liposuction seemed inescapable. I didn't want to read *Cosmo* again or make new single girlfriends who didn't already have boyfriends. We would spend nights on the town, hunting for prospects. Where would we find them? Temple socials? Parents Without Partners? I was too old for the bar scene, and I never attracted attention in a pick-up joint, even at my dewiest. The list stretched on. Rooting around Burton's pockets for incriminating evidence. Snooping through his e-mail. Conspiring against him with an attorney. Running into him with his arm around another woman. Walking down the aisle alone at Andy's wedding.

Beneath the fear of change was one simple fact: I still loved my husband. I had loved him for almost two-thirds of my life. I loved the way he brought up a topic like variable rate financing as though I understood what he was talking about. I loved the way he gave me the first bite of his Tootsie Roll. I loved how he provided me with extra cash when I needed it without asking why. How he started my car and cleared off my windshield in winter. How at Christmastime we shopped at Somerset Mall and reclined in the massage chairs at The Sharper Image, bought a new CD of carols and listened to *Oh Holy Night* as we drove around town to view holiday lights. How when I was attacked by no-see-ems in Florida, he got up at four in the morning to find a twenty-four-hour pharmacy that sold some potion to take away the itch. I loved the guy things about him—that he never missed our sons' baseball games, that he ate Red Pelican mustard from the jar with a spoon, that he wiped his hands on his jeans and drove out of his way to save ten cents on a gallon of gas. I loved that he knew the names of Roy Rogers' and Gene Autry's horses and could quote almost every line of *Lonesome Dove*. I loved how he purchased new gadgets, even the tacky plastic glass with chemicals in the sides to keep your drink cold, which I spurned until I tried it. I loved that his breath smelled like Cream of Wheat, except when he smoked cigars. I even loved that he counted on me to check his spelling and that he'd mispronounce names, like Deepak Opera and Regis Philmore. I loved what we had created together—our children, our business, our friendships. Our history.

I treasured the memories we shared. Like the day Andy, age four, insisted he be allowed to carry a cherry pie into the kitchen. He tripped, and the pie spattered into a puddle of red goo. As I exploded and Andy sobbed, Burton calmly withdrew four forks from a drawer. We all sat down on the (relatively clean) tile floor to eat dessert.

Or the winter night not long after. Burton pulled our shiny new Cadillac into our driveway at the end of an evening. He started to push the remote control button for the garage door when we heard a sharp rap on his side window. A man in a ski mask pointed a sawed-off shotgun at our heads, gestured for us to get out of the car. Burton roared *Noooo!* "Calm down," I said. "Do what he wants." Burton hollered *Nooo waaay!* louder than I had ever heard him yell, so loud I feared he would cause himself a heart attack. The assailant smacked his gun against the driver's side window again. "Honk the horn," I said. Burton pressed down, making enough noise that inside the house our baby sitter turned on the light and came to the window. The attacker fled into the car waiting behind ours and took off. *I'm gonna ram the fucker!* Burton yelled, shifting into reverse and backing out of the driveway. Our wheels spun on the ice as he tried to pursue the getaway car. "He has a gun," I hissed. "Go home and call the police."

The next day, we learned on a newscast that two masked men with a sawed-off shotgun had hijacked a Cadillac after first forcing their way into the owner's house and raping his wife. That same day Burton completely lost his voice.

I treasured the memory of meeting Papillon together. Burton and I had both read his bestseller about his daring escape from Devil's Island. (The book later became a hit movie starring Steve McQueen as Papillon and Dustin Hoffman as his sidekick.) We traveled to Caracas, Venezuela, where author Henri Charriere lived. I arranged to interview him. Burton joined me in asking questions through an interpreter. Our irascible but charming subject chain-smoked Cuban cigars and flicked the burning butts out the open window of his upper floor office. He showed us shelves lined with copies of his book translated into every language. Charriere spoke no English and we, no Spanish. When our interpreter proved unavailable for the second day, I tried to make do with my high-school French. Charriere took us back to his apartment, introduced us to his wife, and muttered something I did understand: "Elle parles Français comme une vache Espagnole." She speaks French like a Spanish cow.

Then there was the memory of one glorious afternoon in Nassau years ago when we snorkeled for the first time. A couple invited us to split the cost of a private boat captain. I objected to the $100 price, but Burton insisted we go. We thrilled to see the glowing, Technicolor beauty of the coral reef below us. Our captain dove down, speared lobsters, ferried us to a deserted island, and grilled his catch. He produced locally grown limes and a bottle of wine, and on that pink sandy beach we savored the most romantic lunch I'd ever enjoyed.

I cherished the silly memories, too. The night I won an award from the Great Lakes Chapter of the American Society of Interior Designers, Burton and I dined at the Dearborn Inn, surrounded by dozens of Detroit's top decorators. The chapter chairman praised my efforts to raise awareness of good design, and then invited me to the podium. Earlier that day Burton had purchased a pocket-sized gadget that shrieked out insults when pressed a certain way. As I walked to the front of the audience, Burton must have shifted in his chair. Through the quiet room, a voice screeched: Screw You, Asshole!

I couldn't forget the fun I'd had with Burton. The friends we'd made together. The places we'd been. The times he'd made me laugh. The times he had protected me. Memories all the more indelible from sharing them.

Try not to come to any conclusions, Jim had said. That would require a new sort of positive thinking. I'd get a mosquito bite and figure it was something terminal. When my son was late for dinner, I'd visualize his car twisted around a telephone pole. For lack of a better plan, I focused on a short-term goal. I would keep myself together until I returned to Tennessee. Two and one-half weeks. One day at a time. One fear at a time.

On the way to Lapeer, you pass The Palace arena in Auburn Hills, where the Detroit Pistons played and where I'd seen Michael Jackson and Barbra Streisand perform. The Palace was the extent of the action in this part of town, north of Detroit. Lapeer consisted of industrial and office buildings, strip centers, a Burger King, and a McDonald's. There wasn't a trendy restaurant or boutique within miles—which was fine with me, because that meant I'd never run into anyone I knew, anyone who'd ask what I was doing there.

Burton and I drove separately to Jim Rowe's office. The small sign outside his door advised that our therapist had MSW and CSW degrees. I didn't give his credentials much thought. On the phone, Jim had seemed kind and empathetic. Those were all the credentials I needed.

The empty waiting room had just enough space for three chairs, a small table, and a broken heart. Burton and I sat without speaking. A brochure on the table read: Coping With Divorce. Despite Jim's advice on the phone, I shoved it into my purse. The Girl Scout motto was Be Prepared. I was once a Girl Scout.

A door opened. Jim stepped through. He had thinning brown hair and eyes the color of strong hot tea. His cheeks drooped just enough that I guessed him to be in his mid- to late forties. Old enough, I decided.

If I were to write a decorating article about Jim's office, which I would not, I'd use the term "modest." A lone window overlooked the parking lot. There was an old-fashioned, bulky oak desk. Jim sat in a high-backed, pseudo-brown-leather armchair, Burton on a stained tan upholstered chair with a metal frame. I collapsed into a sagging beige tweed love seat. The table beside me held a box of tissues. I used at least a dozen of them getting through our history.

"Once our kids were grown, Burton started cutting back," I said. "We were in our early fifties, too young to retire. The economy was strong; the company could have gone national. Or international."

I turned to Burton. He eyed me warily, the way a buck in a clover field watches a car in the distance. "You weren't interested," I said. "You wanted to play."

Burton shrugged his shoulders. "I needed something different. You weren't ready."

After Burton left, I stayed behind to talk to Jim on my own.

"Burton didn't care about working on a national level, but I did," I said. "Better Homes and Gardens wasn't the New York Times, but it was a start. Burton took his career as far as he wanted. He wouldn't give me the same chance. If I tell him how I feel, I'm afraid I'll chase him farther away."

"Don't be afraid of your feelings," Jim said. "When you deny yourself the chance to grieve, you give away your power."

"I hate feeling so weak."

"You've put up with Burt's unpredictability for thirty-one years. A bomb has exploded around you. You're just dealing with the fallout. Most women in your position would already be in court. You don't know how strong you are."

I DID WHAT JIM SAID. I grieved the sense of safety I once felt in my marriage. I grieved the chances I had lost—living in Chicago, taking that job with *W*, marrying a man who might have been true. I mourned the prospect of growing old alone, of someday needing surgery with no spouse to pace the waiting room as I had during

Burton's kidney stone and gall bladder operations. Jim recommended being honest about my feelings with Burton. My self-help books did, too. But when, I wondered, did honesty turn into nagging? When did grief slide into self-pity?

As we drove north to our vacation home, I flipped through *Vanity Fair*, looking for an article that might distract us from our problems. I found one about Y2K concerns, crises that could occur at the millennium, a year off. By the time I finished reading the article aloud, we pulled into the driveway. Outside, winds gusted. The late November sky was the color of ashes. Inside, our house felt soothing. Its red brick fireplace, nutmeg-stained oak shelves, my collections of tramp art and cottageware gave me a sense of history, of happier days.

Burton and I sat side by side on a sofa in the library, gazing at the fire. We had enjoyed so many good times in this room. We had warmed up here with mugs of hot chocolate after our kids sledded on the hill in front of our house. Slurped homemade turkey lentil soup after days of skiing or snowmobiling. Put milk and cookies on the mantel for Santa and, despite our being Jewish, opened presents on Christmas morning.

Now Burton and I sipped vintage port from Waterford crystal goblets we had acquired on a trip to Scotland several years before. As usual, at the time I had protested that the glasses were too expensive. As usual, Burton bought them anyway.

"The house feels as cozy as ever," I said. "We're wearing the old sweatshirts we always put on when we get here. Later, Jill will wait on us at Terry's; I'll order whitefish the way I always do. Everything seems the same. But everything has changed."

Burton heaved a sigh. "You think every aspect of our lives is affected by our problem."

"Let's see if you know what I think. Driving here, I asked if you wanted to get involved working on the Y2K problem. I didn't say what I really thought."

"I know what you thought: if I got involved trying to prevent a worldwide disaster, I'd be too busy to focus on other women."

"Not quite."

"What did you think?"

"If the world came to an end, there wouldn't be any other women left for you to fuck."

Strange as it seems, we both laughed.

OUR PROGRAM HAD TAUGHT US to talk about our expectations ahead of time. One night, home in Franklin, we decided to work together researching our winter vacation. Instead, Burton disappeared downstairs to pack for a hunting trip. Over the years, I'd grown accustomed to his last-minute impulses. He'd initiate a phone call or start to wash his car, delaying what we had planned. But now we were trying to establish new patterns. He obviously had no respect for the changes we needed to make. I banged around the kitchen, slamming pots into drawers.

When Burton came back upstairs, I glared at him. "We agreed to work on our trip," I said. "If you changed your mind, you should have let me know."

He narrowed his eyes. "I just decided to get some packing out of the way. You're driving me crazy with this scheduling. I feel trapped. I'm not a programmed person."

"I'm just trying to follow the guidelines."

"This is never going to work. You're going to monitor me forever."

AS I WROTE IN MY JOURNAL one night, the telephone rang. It's hard to come up with a cheerful greeting in the midst of tears.

"Hello," I quavered.

"What's wrong?" my twenty-three-year-old son demanded.

"Hi, Ander Bander."

"What's wrong, Mom?"

Andy has bullshit radar. No point in faking it.

"You might have sensed Dad and I have had some problems. We went to a couples program a few days ago."

"Stop right there." Andy's voice registered alarm. "Don't tell me any more. I want to hold on to my own ideas of romance, whether they're realistic or not. Most of my friends' parents are divorced or splitting up. You and Dad were the ones who gave us hope."

"You caught me at a bad time," I said. "Dad and I are trying to work things out. Don't worry about us. It's not your problem."

Hanging up, I clutched my stomach and rocked back and forth on the bed. Burton worshiped his sons. How could he have let them down? Let all of us down?

The next day, I talked to my friend Lori, who had referred me to Onsite. "At eleven years old, I started counseling my mother," I said. "If I tried hard enough, I thought I could fix things, turn my parents into a regular Ozzie and Harriet. I'm glad Andy won't make that mistake."

"Give yourself credit," Lori said. "You raised your son with the confidence to set boundaries."

The next night Andy checked in again from his office in New York. He worked sixteen-hour-plus days for Lazard Freres, an international investment-banking firm.

"I haven't been sleeping," he said.

"Something bothering you?"

"No."

Andy hadn't had trouble falling asleep since he was about five years old and developed a fear of monsters. At the time, Burton gave him a plant mister he'd filled with water and marked Monster Spray, then twisted a wire hanger to resemble a pistol for a monster gun. Despite the weapons, night after night our younger son continued to cry, cling to us, and beg us to inspect his closet. Desperate for sleep, I came up with an idea. I suggested Andy invent special magic words to repeat every night. He decided on a phrase for each of us, and his monsters disappeared.

Andy and I said our secret words for several years. In his fifteenth summer, his father and I drove him to a parking lot to meet the campers with whom he'd spend the next month mountain climbing and kayaking out west. Just before he boarded the van, I whispered our phrase into his ear. "Ditto, thirty times," I added.

"It's okay, Mom," he said, and he patted my shoulder. "We don't need to do that anymore."

Andy had slept soundly ever since he came up with our secret words. Now that he was a young adult working grueling hours, I could not imagine his being unable to sleep. Unless he was troubled by a new form of monster.

BURTON ACCOMPANIED SOME FRIENDS on the overnight hunting trip about which we had fought earlier. In his absence, I listened to classical music and took a bubble bath by candlelight. As I lay soaking, I thought about what I'd been going through. I wondered if any of our friends suspected our marital problems. I wondered if I should keep up the pretense of our so-called enviable life. In any case, I decided I cared too much about what other people thought.

The next morning, Burton called from the car.

"How are you feeling?" he asked.

"Better."

"Is that good for me?"

"I don't know what's good for you. It's good for me."

That night we drove to the airport to pick up Andy, who was visiting for Thanksgiving.

"Did you have fun hunting?" I asked.

"Yeah."

"Did you shoot many ducks?"

"Some."

Burton took short, audible breaths, the way he did when he was aggravated. I had never learned how to deal with his bad moods. Typically, when he stopped talking, so did I. But he was tougher than I was. I'd eventually start crying, and he'd eventually come around. Our program had taught me a better way to deal with these episodes. I was afraid to ask. I asked anyway.

"How are you feeling?"

"I feel like shit," he said. "You're growing away from me. You don't care about me anymore."

I was learning to stay calm. Or at least, when my heart pounded as it did now, to simulate calm. "Why do you say I don't care about you anymore?"

"This morning I asked how you were feeling. You didn't ask me."

"I was afraid you'd say you were thinking about Jody."

"I wasn't thinking about her, but I see what you mean."

From the way Burton's breathing slowed, I realized that a technique I'd learned at Onsite had actually worked. I tried another one. "Can we bookmark our problems while Andy's home? Talk about them after he's gone?"

"Good idea."

Burton reached across the armrest. He pressed his hand on my knee. "I want you to know something. In spite of what I've done, you're the most important person in the world to me."

I didn't say a word. That was as close as I could come to graciously accepting the compliment.

ANDY HAD THE BROAD SHOULDERS and thick neck of a weight lifter. He was a strong, silent type who only talked when he was in the mood. From the way he tapped his knuckles on the stainless steel kitchen range, I guessed he was in the mood.

"Dad," he said, "you've always told us you loved us unconditionally. You may not like something David or I did, but you'd love us anyway."

Sitting at the breakfast table, Burton said, "That's how I feel."

"I used to think I was so lucky that my mom and dad got along. Knowing things were okay back home allowed me to push myself. I could put in long hours and focus on my work because I didn't have to worry about anything else. I can't concentrate anymore."

I sat on a stool at our kitchen island and rubbed my hand over cool green granite, waiting.

"I'm glad you told us how you feel," Burton said. "Mom and I aren't perfect. We're very different from each other. We've grown farther apart than we should have. Neither of us wanted it to happen, but it did. We love each other, and we're trying to work things out. I believe we will." Burton looked at me. "Don't you, Suzy?"

"Yes," I said, hoping my response was more than wishful thinking. At that point, I just wanted to make it through Thanksgiving.

Andy pulled out a chair, flipped it around, and straddled it backwards, facing his father.

"You know, Dad, when I choose a wife, I want her to bring something to the table. I hope she'll be more organized than I am, or more creative, or more intellectual."

"I hear you, pal," Burton said. "When the time is right, you'll find her."

Andy exhaled a breath that puffed out his cheeks, then checked the stainless steel watch we'd given him for his graduation from the U of M. He stood up and slid the chair back under the table. "Time to catch up with the gang," he said. "We're meeting at a bar in Royal Oak."

I walked up to my younger son and noticed for the first time that tiny lines grooved the space above his nose. "How about a hug?" I asked.

Andy folded his arms around me, and then stepped back to look into my eyes. His hands on my shoulders, he said, "Whatever has been going on, Mom, remember one thing: Dad is a good man."

"I know that, honey," I said. Part of me still believed he was right.

Andy wrapped his arms around his father. His voice came out husky. "I love you, Dad. Unconditionally."

SOME WOMEN WERE BORN TO BE MOTHERS. As little girls, they dressed up dolls and held tea parties, serving vanilla wafers and lemonade under a tree in the yard and pretending to be mommies. I played with little girls like that and acted as though I was one of them. I wasn't. On my own, I pretended I was a doctor, or an actress, or a businesswoman. Having babies was not part of my fantasy. I grew up with the same desire I held as a kid: to pursue my own dreams.

Then I had children. I probably should have looked at motherhood as my career, but I never did. Careers were something other people paid you to do, and you dressed up and went to an office and received a paycheck and more recognition than you did for just being a mom.

But there were times I loved being a mom, times I was knocked out by our kids' brains or their talent or their grit. Like our older son's bar mitzvah. I had urged David to practice his candle-lighting ceremony in advance. I offered to help him write poems or messages about the people who would light the candles on his thirteenth birthday cake. "Just give me the names," he said. "I'll handle it." And he did. He brought our guests to tears remembering Burton's late mother and to laughter recalling how he'd steal his brother's shoelaces. A few years later, David won the C.S. Mott regional high school tennis tournament and dazzled me again with his deadly serve and focused attitude.

Talking with Andy that night provided another such moment. Later, I thought about what my son had said. And about what he didn't say. He loved his father. Unconditionally.

Lying alone in bed, I replayed the conversation in my head and felt a warm rush in my chest. Andy had given me a message, too. When he described the traits he hoped to find in a wife, he described his mom.

I LOVED THANKSGIVING. You didn't need to worry about whether the video game you purchased for one child equaled the skateboard you bought for another or whether your mother needed another blue blouse. It didn't matter if you were Jewish or Christian. Thanksgiving was for everyone. It was purely about family, gratitude, and pigging out.

Thanksgiving had been our official holiday since Burton and I first married. Normally, I enjoyed basting the turkey in my late mother-in-law's roasting pan, inhaling the smell as the bird browned, and setting the table, arranging gourds and votive candles down the middle. This year, these simple tasks seemed almost more than I could handle. Trying to keep up a happy front took all the energy I had. I couldn't worry about whether I had seasoned my chestnut-laced stuffing right or whether the Jell-O mold would collapse. I just hoped *I* wouldn't collapse.

Dinner turned out well. Burton carved the turkey his special way, removing the white meat first. His sister Lenore brought noodle and green bean casseroles; his sister Anita, her chocolate cheesecake pie. Everyone agreed, as we did each year: nobody on the planet enjoyed a feast more delicious than ours.

We were one big happy family. Or so we seemed. Burton helped himself to seconds, complimented me on the meal, played Ping-Pong with the kids after dinner. I busied myself fussing over my mother, removing plates. It was, all considered, a fine evening. As fragile as I felt, I had stopped dodging the truth. Burton had sworn off other women, at least for a while. I had resolved not to make any decisions. My family was healthy and whole. I still had a lot to be thankful for.

The tranquility didn't last.

TWO DAYS LATER, BURTON SLUMPED into one of the two chenille sofas in our library. They were cinnabar in color, a shade that flattered my skin. Burton propped his feet on the caramel travertine coffee table. Smudges marked the bottoms of his white athletic socks because he persisted in walking outside in them. He aimed the remote control at the TV, jumping from one channel to another. Andy had left the house to visit friends. In two hours we would host an engagement party for Burton's nephew at our country club.

Sitting next to Burton on the floor, I sorted snapshots into piles, organized by months, on the coffee table. I always brought our albums up-to-date before Christmas, when dozens of friends' photos flooded in with the holiday mail.

I dabbed rubber cement on the back corners of pictures and

pressed them right side up onto black paper inserts. The process felt routine and peaceful, as though putting order into our album could restore it to our lives. My Living Centered program would take place in less than two weeks. I was trying to stay sane until then.

Snapping off the television, Burton said, "Why don't we run away for about ten years until my libido dies down?"

That's when it hit me: Burton wouldn't stay faithful to me. He couldn't. He'd as much as said so. I wanted to scream.

He ranted on. "I miss being with Jody. I don't feel like I broke it off the right way. I should see her and straighten that out. She was a very good friend."

I burst into tears.

Burton's voice grew louder. "I've been so stupid. Your name's on deals I suffered with for years. I'll be forced to split everything with you and to pay a shitload to some greedy damn lawyers."

Our marriage was collapsing and all my husband cared about was real estate. As if that wasn't bad enough, he wanted to see Jody again. I could not think of a thing to say that wouldn't make matters worse.

"What . . . about . . . our bookmark?"

"Fuck the bookmark. Fuck your phony rules. You're going to end up with properties I killed myself to save."

He kicked the table, scattering my piles.

"We're falling apart," I gasped, grabbing for photos, pulling them toward me. "How can you worry about stuff?"

"I worked my ass off for that stuff! If you want that stuff so bad, you take it. Take the houses. Take the companies, too. You figure out how to run them. You can have all the fucking stuff. And all the fucking problems."

He seized the remote control and began flicking, his eyes riveted on the TV. His nostrils flared. His face turned cold and rigid. My eyes burned; I gulped air.

"Go to the party without me," I said. "I'd spoil everything."

"It would spoil things worse if you didn't come."

And so I carried on. I pressed a damp washcloth to my red eyes, patted on makeup, slipped into a black wool pantsuit. The color suited my frame of mind. Burton and I did not speak as we drove to the party.

Guests in bright silk and sequins milled around the fireplace room sipping drinks, munching cheese straws. My husband and I had been married in front of this limestone-framed fireplace thirty-one years before.

I did my best to fake the role of gracious host. I kissed cheeks. I cooed over cousin Judie's new mega-diamond ring, something I never wanted even when I might have talked my husband into buying one for me. I had always tried to spare him from any extra financial pressure. In retrospect, my concern seemed to have been wasted. I audited a conversation on laser dermabrasion, wondered if it might improve my marketability.

I welcomed Sheila and Alan Felstein. Sheila and I had met years ago when we served on a museum board together. Alan, a divorce lawyer, was known for winning hefty settlements for the wives of wealthy, errant men. I had last seen the Felsteins at our son's wedding.

"Suzy, that wedding was to-die-for," Sheila said. "You looked drop-dead gorgeous."

"It only takes a couple of hours with the right experts," I said. I turned to her husband. "Speaking of experts, how is my favorite champion of the walking wounded?"

"Better than ever," Alan said. He waved a thumbs-up. "There's an inexhaustible supply of son-of-a-bitch husbands in this town. It warms my heart to take them on."

"I salute you, sir." I touched my hand to my forehead.

When I joined Burton a few minutes later, he muttered, "I saw you with your friends, the Felsteins. What was that all about?"

"I told him he was the hero of every wife in suburban Detroit."

"That creep makes his money ripping off guys who've worked their whole lives to build up a business. He's a leech and a pig."

"I think he's Robert Redford."

Burton came up with a toast. I, for whom gracious toasts were once a specialty, stayed in my seat. What was I going to say? "Kristin and Robbie, we're gathered here tonight in the same room where your uncle and I were married thirty-one years ago. We hope you're as happy as we've been"?

When you hear advice from couples who've been married a long time, they seem to agree on one thing: they never go to bed angry. That night Burton and I didn't go to bed angry either. We went to bed furious, separated by our own shells of silence. I prayed for patience. I prayed for clarity.

Before my marriage collapsed, I had enjoyed less contact with any sort of higher power than I did with my mailman, and I was rarely home when mail was delivered. I didn't have to see our mailman to know he existed. God was a different story. If I couldn't see Him, He didn't exist. I was in charge of me.

I grew up as a Reformed Jew. The Fuchs family had a Christmas tree in the living room and a menorah in the kitchen, which we often forgot to light. Sunday School bored me, except when I managed to sneak out of services to buy Sugar Babies at the candy store down the block from Temple Beth El.

Religion separated me from others, and I felt separate enough. At Kingswood, my private girls school, I saw myself as an outsider. Most of the cool clique had entered the Cranbrook school system through Brookside, the elementary school, and formed alliances years before. I began in seventh grade and did not catch up socially. I was never sure whether I wanted to identify with the cool girls or the smart ones anyway. Our class of sixty, including six Jewish members, attended chapel every week. Prayers spoken out loud or hymns sung made me more aware of my difference. Under my breath, I would edit the end of a blessing: "in the name of *their* Lord, Jesus Christ."

When I was fifteen, my father changed religions. He made his decision five years after the death of his father, Walter, and his father's second wife, Stella, in a mid-air United Airlines plane collision over the Grand Canyon. Dad worked for Walter at the time of the crash, and he inherited a failing company. As he struggled to rebuild the business, he longed for support Judaism didn't provide him. When he told me he was considering changing his faith, I figured he'd turn to something neutral, like Unitarianism, something that wouldn't embarrass my mother or me. Instead, Dad turned Catholic. Full-out Catholic. He attended mass every Sunday. He joined a weekly prayer group. I'd find church pamphlets on the seat of his car. I avoided touching them.

Dad converted during the year I was confirmed. I was one of a few girls selected for the Rose Ceremony, a special part of the confirmation service. Accepting my long-stemmed red rose from the rabbi, I felt proud to belong to a family that merited such recognition. My mother's father, sitting up front, was a past president of Temple Beth El. I also felt shame over the presence of my newly Catholic father, who sat farther back in the sanctuary. Worse, I was ashamed of myself for feeling ashamed.

I told myself to give my father credit for having the courage to do what he did. But I couldn't help viewing Dad's conversion as weakness. Mom told me that before he turned Catholic, Dad had seen a psychiatrist and begun to share his feelings with her. After converting, she said, he'd shut her out again. Mom sensed that in rejecting Judaism, Dad had rejected her. Since I generally sided with my mother, Dad's conversion widened the distance between him and me as well. It also further turned me off to organized religion.

Four decades had passed since my late father turned Catholic. I had become a woman with marriage problems of my own. Having lived for more than fifty years thinking I was controlling events, I no longer thought so.

I had no idea who God was. Or if He would answer. Or whether I would recognize an answer if it did show up. Prayer was not a skill I had honed, as though by bowing my head over a lifetime I had racked up points with the Lord, and He owed me. But I was desperate. Without any clergy to guide me, I came up with something that sounded the way I thought a prayer should. I admitted I was confused. Asked God to show me the way.

At first I wasn't sure God was listening. I did not feel better overnight. But slowly, I began to receive comfort from praying. I was not in this mess alone.


PRAYER GOT ME THROUGH THE NIGHT of Burton's blowup. The next morning I awoke to a different husband.

"I had no right to treat you like I did yesterday. I'm feeling really insecure," Burton said. He suggested we drive to South Lyon together to pick up his truck and horse trailer where he'd left them at Jody's friend's farm.

Over the past two years, I had offered to visit South Lyon with Burton. "You'd be bored," he'd protested. "You're just trying to humor me." He was right. I hadn't wanted to visit. I wanted to investigate. Now his invitation seemed a hopeful sign, the purple tip of a crocus after a long, cold winter.

"Sounds like a plan, my man."

We sped west on I-696 that cold but sunny afternoon. My stomach churned as though it were stuck in the wash cycle. "Help me to survive this day with grace," I prayed.

Burton drove me around South Lyon. Sun glistened on nearly naked trees. Dirt roads cut through deep woods. Rolling pastures lay napping. The benign indifference of the universe.

Jody's friend Ellen lived in a pale blue clapboard-sided farmhouse. As Burton and I walked up the mossy brick path, I felt the hairs on my body stand away from my skin. I expected to be offered a cup of tea laced with rat poison.

Ellen had pulled her graying brown hair into a ponytail. Her face was lined, free of makeup. She guided me around her restored home, with its antique pine furniture and eyelet curtains. She asked if I liked the yellow shade of paint she was considering for the foyer.

(I did.) She escorted us to the barn, where Burton's truck and trailer were parked, as casually as if she were showing us the eggs her chickens had laid. She never mentioned Jody.

Burton got into the truck, backed it up to the trailer, hooked the trailer on the hitch. I walked to our car.

"Don't be strangers," Ellen said, waving as we both drove off.

Heading for home, I thought about how surreal the last couple of hours had been. I had actually enjoyed a pleasant visit to the setting of my worst nightmares.

My cell phone rang.

"Are you okay?" Burton asked.

"I'm fine. How are you?"

"I'm fine, too."

I WASN'T FINE FOR LONG. Soon I found myself again stumbling through a minefield of emotional traps. There was the self-pity trap: I didn't do anything to deserve the way Burton treated me. There was the vengeance trap: If I were killed in a car crash, it would serve the bastard right to feel guilty for the rest of his life. There was the past trap: What if I can't get over what has happened? The future trap: Will I ever trust a man again? The insecurity trap: I'm not enough for my husband.

Getting through the days was tough, through the nights—all but impossible. I'd lie in the dark flopping back and forth like a dying fish. I'd wonder if the man I had slept with for most of my life now lay beside me wishing I were someone else. Or wishing he were someplace else. Images of Burton and Jody in bed together flashed through my brain. He lay on top. She lay on top. She slipped down beneath the sheets. He slipped beneath them. The more I tried not to obsess, the more I obsessed.

Once I was merely hard on myself. Now I turned ruthless. Despite Burton's obvious treachery, without realizing what I was doing, I remained stuck at the 80 percent Ted had talked about. I couldn't do anything to change my husband, but maybe I could do something about me. I sat as judge and jury of myself, issuing decisive verdicts. Defensive: guilty. Jealous: guilty. Undesirable: guilty. Every day I rooted out some new flaw. I spent all the energy I had visiting Jim or voicing my grief to his answering machine, writing in my journal, devouring self-help books. Fortunately, my magazine responsibilities slowed down in the winter. I couldn't have focused on them if I had to. Learning to like myself again was a full-time job.

Author Debbie Ford claimed that to escape being dragged down by my negative traits, I needed to recognize their gifts. She presented a helpful technique—to visualize my personality as a bus, with each of my traits represented by a different passenger.

Lying in bed, I climbed aboard my crowded imaginary bus and picked out whoever represented what I hated most about myself that night. I escorted that passenger off the bus and talked to her. All my passengers had different names, ages, and appearances. I met Insecure Annie, Doris Dukes, Judgmental Joan, and Guilty Greta. The next morning I wrote about our encounters in my journal.

What bothered me in someone else tended to be something I didn't like about myself. One day, talking to Jim, I said, "I hate it when Burton tries to control me. I don't see where I am controlling."

"Self-control?" he said.

That night, I visited my imaginary bus again.

> Controlling Connie
> What she feels: Exhausted from maintaining my reputation as a nice person, guarding against my being too open, exposed, or vulnerable
> Her gift to me: My sterling image
> What she needs from me: Compassion
> —Journal excerpt, December 1998

"YOUR HEAD IS A DANGEROUS NEIGHBORHOOD. You shouldn't go there alone," a psychiatrist at Onsite had said. I realized that I had considered my head the desirable, high-rent district. I had lingered there for a lifetime, avoiding my heart as though it were a slum. Jim helped me to venture into the neighborhood I had shunned, to appreciate what my heart had to offer. Take my Sally dilemma ...

At Onsite, Burton told me he had reconnected with Sally, his ex-mistress. I explained to Jim how they had been in touch on the phone or through e-mail. "Burton says he isn't physically attracted to Sally anymore. He just likes having someone he can talk to, someone who understands him."

"Interesting," Jim said.

"He says Sally's on my side in the Jody situation."

Jim stroked his cheeks.

"Sally told Burton, 'This is the first time you've lived without deception. You're going through withdrawal.'"

"Interesting." Jim nodded.

"I figure giving up Jody was hard enough on Burton, so I didn't ask him to stop talking to Sally. But I have to admit: their relationship makes me squirm."

"If it makes you uncomfortable, don't try to talk yourself out of it."

"That's not all." I grimaced. "Sally recommended a movie to Burton. We went to see it. We didn't like it, so we left early. When we got home, I said, 'Call Sally and find out how it ended.' Burton asked, 'Are you sure you want me to do that?' I said, 'Why not?' So he called her while I listened, sitting across from him at the kitchen table."

Jim's eyes had grown wider. When I got to the part about the phone call, my calm and unflappable psychotherapist groaned. "I don't believe it," he said. He clapped his hand to his forehead and rolled out of his chair and onto the floor.

IN JIM'S OFFICE, I TALKED TO BURTON about problems I wasn't brave enough to bring up on my own. Problems like Jody's mortgage payments. The morning at Onsite when Burton confessed to the affair, he had added another complication.

"You aren't going to like this," he'd said, "but I figure I'd better get everything out in the open. I agreed to give Jody enough money to cover some mortgage payments on her house. I've already given her half of what I promised."

"How much was that?" I'd asked, knowing that any amount was too much.

"Twenty thousand dollars. I owe her another twenty grand."

Forty thousand dollars. The number sent a bead of sweat trickling down my spine. For forty thousand dollars, I could send some inner city kids to college or buy a lovely necklace of South Sea pearls or rent a villa in Tuscany. But Burton never reneged on a business deal, and that's how I'd decided to view the matter. I had swallowed hard, because pride is a hard and bitter pill to swallow. "Do what you think is right," I'd said.

Although Burton and I were lucky enough to have grown able to afford luxuries, I still watched our spending. Thrift was in my genes. I grew up with a father who complained about the cost of electricity or a steak dinner as often as some people gripe about heartburn. As a girl, I had trained myself to do what I could to spare the family budget. I split cotton balls in half to apply skin toner, and stuck the remnant of an old soap bar to a new one. I still maintained these frugal habits.

As a cotton-ball-splitting soap-sticker, I loathed the idea of enriching a mistress, even an ex-mistress. I tried to frame the outlay in a more positive light. If several thousand bucks was the cost of getting rid of her, it was a cheap price to pay. At least that's what I'd told myself.

In Jim's office, I admitted my true feelings.

"Burton," I said, "the thought of giving Jody all that money makes me sick."

"I'm not thrilled about it either."

"She's bound to call to thank you. When she does, I'm afraid she'll try to win you back."

"You don't have anything to worry about."

I was not convinced. "Don't worry" was his mantra the whole time he cheated on me.

"There's something else," I said.

Burton eyed me with the sort of look he reserved for a delinquent tenant.

"It's about Sally. Someday she may want to dump her husband, get a facelift, and start over with you. I know you need someone to talk to. I'd feel better if that someone didn't have a personal interest. Maybe you could stick around and talk to Jim after I leave."

Although Burton and I had seen Jim a few times together, I'd mostly visited him on my own. Burton had declined to do so. Now he shrugged. "I'll stick around if it makes you more comfortable."

I left Burton with Jim and drove off on my own, feeling relieved.

EARLY THE NEXT MORNING, Burton and I set out on a walk through our neighborhood. I felt happy to be outdoors, spending time with my husband again. We had walked together most days since our kids had been old enough to leave them alone. Our walks had always given us time to talk. In recent months, Burton had preferred to exercise at home in front of the television. He claimed the stationary bike and free weights gave him a better workout.

I could not wait to hear about Burton's session with Jim. I was sure Jim's wise counsel would help Burton to understand his restlessness and strengthen his resolve. Jim's support would make Burton less likely to run back to South Lyon in a couple of days when I returned to Onsite. Jim would help Burton see what a lovely and loyal wife he had, maybe even cause him a tinge of guilt for betraying someone so lovely and loyal.

Burton and I hiked up and down rolling hills. We passed the bare branches of forsythia and lilacs, cotoneaster and burning bush. We marched by dozens of farm colonial and Cape Cod homes. Not a word about his conversation with Jim.

I adopted my breeziest tone. "So what did you and Jim talk about?"

"Jim answered something I really wanted to know, something that's been bugging me."

There was a spring in his step. His face did not look contrite.

"What's that?"

"I keep thinking what I did wasn't so abnormal. I wanted Jim's professional opinion. I told him I hang out with a bunch of Type-A high achievers. Lots of them consider it normal to cheat on their wives."

"And Jim said?"

"He tried to duck the question. Finally he admitted what I figured all along: many successful men consider cheating to be normal."

"Is that all he said?"

"No. He said you and I have a chance for something better, something special. But he told me what I wanted to know. I don't need to feel guilty. I was just being a guy."

On their own, my feet advanced, one after the other, along the bumpy dirt road back to our house. Jim was my friend, my support, my best hope. How could he have let Burton leave his office thinking this way? I ran to the kitchen, grabbed the phone, and stabbed out the numbers.

"I need to talk to you," I begged Jim's answering machine. "Am I crazy to expect Burton to be faithful? Am I beating my head against a wall?"

Minutes later, Jim phoned. "I'm obliged to keep my conversations with both of you private. I'd like you to come back together right away to clear the air."

In Burton's opinion, clearing the air meant taking another dose of medicine. The next day he postponed a meeting and came anyway.

"Burt," Jim said, "you told me that many men consider cheating to be normal. 'Common' might be a better word. It's also common for a herd of buffalo to fling themselves off a cliff. In some satanic cults, it's common to impregnate women and sacrifice the babies."

Jim paused, tapped a pen against his hand. "Because something may be common doesn't mean it's good for you or morally right. You both need to decide what changes you're willing to make to have a higher commitment to each other.

"And Suzy," he said, turning to me. He emphasized each word, as though I were hard of hearing. "You are entitled to your own expectations. Including monogamy."

*Chapter Nine*

# LEARNING TO LIVE CENTERED

—————◯◯◯◯—————

GRACE IS . . . THE HELP YOU RECEIVE WHEN YOU HAVE
NO BRIGHT IDEAS LEFT, WHEN YOU ARE EMPTY AND DESPERATE
AND HAVE DISCOVERED THAT YOUR BEST THINKING AND
MOST CHARMING CHARM HAVE FAILED YOU.

*Traveling Mercies: Some Thoughts on Faith*, Anne Lamott

I DUG THROUGH MY TOTE BAG, among the Kleenex, the contact lens fluid, the magazines, and the vial of calcium and vitamins and the Xanax I had in case I couldn't sleep. I pulled out a small object covered in a scrap of gold paper that Burton must have found in my closet and torn off the roll. He had folded the ends at jagged angles and taped them. He'd handed me this misshapen little bundle the night before, telling me to open it on the plane.

As my flight headed to Tennessee, I unwrapped Burton's gift: a gold ring shaped into his initials, BDF. A handwritten note fluttered into my lap. "I wanted you to have something of mine to take along for luck. This was a bar mitzvah present from my parents." I traced the initials with my finger, touched the ring to my lips, then zipped it into the makeup bag in my purse.

*117*

In the restroom, I studied myself in the mirror: Beside one ear, a couple of uninvited spots that tactful cosmetologists called hyper-pigmentation. Friendly brown eyes, crinkles around them. Thin lips in which I took pride as a girl, before a fuller, more ethnic mouth came into style. A nice face, surgically altered only by a nose job at age eighteen. A face that had held up well, considering the strain of recent months.

"It's you and me, girl," I said to the mirror. "We're in for an adventure."

"ALL ABOARD," THE DRIVER CALLED in a tone so convivial you'd have thought he was taking us to Disney World instead of to Dante's *Inferno*. Hilary sat next to me in the van. She had dyed black hair and wore a sweater woven with black and white cow designs. I asked what brought her here. She'd been married for twenty-five years, she murmured. I strained to hear her over the chatter from the front and back rows. Four years ago, her husband, whom she adored, admitted he was gay and introduced her to his lover. They had stayed married and kept his secret from almost everyone, including their son, who was failing in school, and their anorexic daughter.

I held out my arms. "You need a hug," I said. She clung to me, her hair soft against my cheek.

And I thought I had problems.

MY ROOM SAT DIRECTLY ABOVE the one Burton and I had occupied three weeks earlier. Its pine-paneled walls rose into a peaked ceiling. Thinking about the week ahead, remembering what I'd been through downstairs, I stepped inside and started to cry.

Heaving my bag onto one double bed, I undid the zipper and found Amy's gift. The night before, my daughter-in-law had stopped by our house to give me a Beanie Baby beagle. In case you need company, she'd said. I pressed the little stuffed dog to my cheek and collapsed on the bed.

After soaking my Beanie beagle with tears, I sat up, blew my nose, and leafed through some papers I had received when checking in. The headline of one handout flashed at me like warning lights around a pothole.

Relationships: Intimate vs. Addictive

Intimate:

My dedication to you is based on my true interest in your spiritual path, even if it takes you away.

Love is always an act of self-love.

Addictive:

Love is wanting someone to love me at all costs.

THREE WOMEN SAT ON BEDS BEYOND the open door of my old room. They welcomed me.

"On the morning of our last full day here, right in this room, my husband confessed to an affair he had denied for more than two years," I said. "He broke up with his mistress that night. I've come back here to get my bearings." After keeping silent for so long, I was surprised to hear the truth spill out of my mouth.

"I can imagine how hard it's been," a woman named Joanie said. I guessed her to be near my age.

Ginger, a forty-something brunette from Ohio, handed me a paperback book. "Do you read affirmations?" she asked.

"I don't know what they are," I said. Flipping through the pages, I noticed messages about love and forgiveness, one for each day of the year. "This looks inspiring."

"Keep it for the week," she said. "I have others."

Later that night, I lay in bed, skimming through the book. One title stopped me: "Letting Go of Those Not in Recovery." I read every word of the message that followed. When I glanced at the date, I caught my breath: February 12, Burton's birthday.

Today, I will move forward with my life, despite what others are doing or not doing. I will know it is my right to cross the bridge to a better life, even if I must leave others behind to do that. I will not feel guilty, I will not feel ashamed.

*The Language of Letting Go*, Melody Beattie

The door to my bedroom flung open and banged against the wall. A woman with dark wavy hair and olive skin dragged in a suitcase. In accented English, she said, "I'm Maria. From Colombia." She threw herself onto the other double bed and groaned. "I'm dying for a cigarette. I agreed not to smoke while I'm here. If I feel this bad tomorrow, I'm going on the patch."

"How much did you smoke?"

"Three packs a day. And I'm still coming off a cocaine addiction I gave up eight months ago."

Oh, great. I'm sharing my emotional crisis with a drug addict who's facing a nicotine fit. I handed Maria some dried apricots I had stored in the armoire. "Thank you," she moaned as she tore open the package.

I pulled a ladder-back chair close to Maria's bed. "Tell me about yourself," I said. "Are you married?"

"I was for ten years. Now I'm separated from my husband, Julio. Two years ago, Julio found out I was having an affair and went crazy. I broke up with my lover, and he left the country. I never saw my lover, or cheated, again. Julio and I have a six-year-old daughter. I wanted our marriage to work." She popped another apricot into her mouth.

"Julio kept checking up on me with my friends. He'd follow me. I'd be at a café for lunch with a girlfriend, and I'd catch him peeking in the window. I couldn't stand it anymore. A few months ago, I told him to move out."

"In my case, my husband had the affair. I'm the suspicious one."

"I'll give you some advice. Let it go, or it will destroy your marriage. There's a verse I learned as a little girl: 'If you love him, set him free. He'll come back if it's meant to be.'"

"Set him free?" I said. "I don't know how. Maybe I need a patch."

ON MY FIRST FULL DAY OF LEARNING TO LIVE CENTERED, I asked Jake—tall, broad-shouldered, around fifty—to play Burton. I cast Emmy as Jody. At twenty-two, Emmy was the youngest member in my small group of five men and three women. She had white teeth and a big smile and the pep of a cheerleader.

Dee, our group leader, taped a name card to the chest of each character and directed the action. Jake stood on a stool while I knelt on the floor in front of him. Emmy stood beside Jake, holding his arm. Carla, as my mother, loomed over me from behind, pressing her hands on my head.

"Does this feel about right?" Dee asked.

Burton above, Jody beside him. Me, below. Mom on my back.

"Yes."

After a few seconds, Dee had Jake and me stand face-to-face. "Suzy, what would you like to say to Burt?" she asked.

Looking at Jake, handsome like my husband, I felt overwhelmed with sorrow. All I could think about was the mess I'd made of my marriage.

"I understand why you left me," I said. "I was busy with my career and preoccupied with my mother. I wasn't there for you."

Dee frowned, stepped forward, put her hand on my shoulder. "That's enough," she said. "Listening to you, I feel sick. Where. Is. Your. Anger?"

We sat down on the floor in a circle. My legs buckled beneath me. I had failed again. First I had screwed up my marriage. Now I was screwing up my chance to fix it. A sense of ambivalence had dogged me for most of my life. Now it blocked my working up a decent case of anger, even when it was justified. The same uncertainty had struck when Burton proposed, when we got married, when I became pregnant. I wished I could make clear decisions, experience pure feelings. I wished I could be like my old friend Trudi and know when something was right.

The rest of my group had no problem with clarity. At least where I was concerned.

Carla: "As Suzy, I felt demeaned."

Jake: "As Burt, I felt guilty about what I was putting my family through."

Emmy: "Burt's selfishness pissed me off."

Dee: "Suzy, you seem so stuck."

Verlon, a southerner in a soft plaid flannel shirt, spoke with a drawl as thick as hominy grits. His words skewered my heart. "Suzy," he said, "I felt your loss of pride."

WE WERE ASSIGNED TO WRITE LETTERS to our addictions. I sat on my bed trying to figure one out. I had given up smoking years before. I ate and drank and shopped in moderation. I loathed gambling. Picking my cuticles did not seem worthy of a letter. On her bed, my roommate wrote intently.

"Maria, can you be addicted to a person?" I asked.

She put down her pen and paper. "An addiction is something you think you can't live without. You'll do almost anything for it, even if it's bad for you. Like nicotine." She pulled back her shirtsleeve, showed me the patch on her upper arm.

"Can you live without Burton?" she asked.

My stomach collapsed in on itself. "I don't know."

That night, sitting among the whole group, I debated about whether or not to read my letter out loud. The debate brought back painful memories. As a young teen at Camp Fernwood, I was one of the last to be picked for the volleyball team. Other girls in shorts and T-shirts bounded over to the side of the girl who called their names. I pretended I didn't care, but my face grew hot as I waited. At Kingswood, my prep school, the popular girls received frequent letters from boys at Cranbrook, our brother school. During mail distribution, dozens of young women stood around the green tile floor of the lobby, hoping to hear their names called. When mine was, I strode forward to accept my envelope as though it were an Academy Award. When I wasn't called, I bent down to tie my saddle shoe, hoping my disappointment didn't show. In college, I was dropped from D Phi E before the final dessert of sorority rush. I'd rather be in SDT, I said. And I meant it. But more than thirty years later, I still remembered the girl who had shepherded me through my last visit to the house that turned me down.

With a successful career, a successful husband, and what had seemed to be a successful marriage, I thought I'd outgrown my problems with rejection. I had chaired events for our art institute, our historical museum, our zoo. Burton and I had attended fancy parties. Social acceptance was good for business. And for my morale.

Now I sat in a circle of attendees, each holding a piece of paper. If I read my piece of paper out loud, forty-plus people would know a shameful thing: my husband had rejected me. Eighty-plus eyes would shoot looks at me, from pity to revulsion.

A slender man with fine features, young enough to be one of Andy's friends, went first. "Dear Sexual Addiction," he began. I looked at my lap in embarrassment, but he read with a steady voice. "You have been part of my life for more than twenty years. You have cost me jobs, friends, girlfriends. You have damaged my family. You came into my life when I was five years old. It felt good when my cousin touched me, but I knew it was wrong. And when I touched my baby sister, that felt good, too. I knew it was bad.

"Because of you, I masturbate many times a day and don't enjoy normal sex with women. Because of you, I have sought therapy, attended countless groups and meetings. You bring me some pleasure but much more pain. I will no longer let you control my life."

I lifted my eyes. This troubled young man looked so normal. He could have been my next-door neighbor or the guy in the office down the hall. I no longer felt embarrassed for him. I respected his courage.

When my turn came, I read my letter.

Dear Marriage,

You have dominated my life for over thirty years. You rewarded me with wonderful children, with love and financial comfort. You also restrained my freedom and limited my growth.

For the past two years, I looked the other way as Burton became unavailable. Living with deception almost destroyed me. Now that Burton has broken off his affair, I must make changes, too. I must respect my own feelings and needs as well as his.

I have appreciated you and suffered from you. I will turn you into a relationship of mutual support and commitment. Or I will say good-bye.

I raised my eyes to look at the people around me. No one glanced away. I had admitted a terrible thing out loud. And I had survived.

We carried our letters to the center of the circle and placed them on an empty chair. When everyone had read, we jumped up and grabbed papers from the pile and tore them into shreds. We threw the pieces in the air and whooped out loud as our painful revelations turned into harmless confetti, sprinkling our heads and drifting to the floor.

ONE NIGHT THE WHOLE GROUP at Onsite played kids' games. Burton loved any sort of game, be it Red Rover or Monopoly or bridge. He made a game of getting our sons to eat green beans when they were toddlers or guessing a stranger's occupation in an airport. Goal-oriented as I was, I considered most games a waste of time—other than Scrabble, which improved my vocabulary. But I had come to Onsite to grow and to challenge myself. If playing games could help loosen me up, I'd join in the so-called fun.

One person stood in the middle of a circle and called out a description. Everyone born in June. Everyone wearing jeans. Everyone with brown eyes. As music played, those to whom the description applied stood up and walked in a circle, darting for a chair when the melody stopped. As with children's musical chairs, one chair was removed each time.

I actually found myself having fun when I discovered I could invent creative descriptions. "Everyone who likes sex," I said. "Everyone with chemically-addicted hair." "Everyone who wishes Tom Cruise were here."

A good-looking man with clipped graying hair laughed loudest at my wisecracks. After the game, he introduced himself. His name was Joe. He and some others were headed toward the main house. He asked, "Why don't you join us?" As we walked from the barn, Joe told me he was a stockbroker from Atlanta and had flown helicopters in Vietnam. We hung out with a group that night and the next, reading from a book of cowboy poetry and telling jokes. When I caught Joe looking at me across the room at morning assemblies, I felt a little flutter in my chest. But that's all the excitement there was. Joe and I never spent time alone together. Upon arrival, attendees had been cautioned against being alone with anyone of the opposite sex. That made sense to me. I was confused and vulnerable enough.

TIME FOR ONSITE BATTING PRACTICE. When our sons were in Little League, Burton and I drove them to the batting cages at Thirteen Mile and Woodward in Royal Oak, near our home in Huntington Woods. For fifty cents, a machine pitched baseballs at them, and they whacked away.

Batting practice at Onsite did not require athletic talent. It required a skill I had never developed—the ability to let go. Hitting a pillow could help you confront and release pent-up feelings. That was the theory, anyway. Since I was a child, emotional outbursts had made me want to run and hide. My mother's occasional bouts of temper had frightened me. My father harbored resentment. Like him, I locked my feelings inside. I had locked them away for so long, there were some I didn't recognize anymore.

Jake and Emmy took turns smacking a pillow with a plastic bat and screaming with abandon. Jake was torn between his wife and his mistress, and he yelled at both of them. Emmy, a shopping addict, hollered at her emotionally distant parents. Meanwhile, I cowered in the corner by the door, clamped my hands over my ears, and squeezed my eyes shut. I knew I'd be expected to carry on like Jake and Emmy, too.

That night, I wrote in my journal: *Dee says I'm supposed to feel anger. I don't know if I can.*

When my turn came the next day, I again chose Jake and Carla to represent Burton and my mother. Dee posed Carla on the stool in front of me; Jake stood behind, tugging on my sweatshirt. Dee had them repeat messages.

Carla/Mom: "I'm unhappy. You succeed for both of us."

Jake/Burton: "Pay attention to me."

Jake and Carla switched positions—Jake above me, Carla behind. Dee handed Jake a wad of Kleenex, and asked him to tear up the tissues and toss the pieces at me.

"Is this what you want, Suzy? Crumbs?" Dee asked.

"I want more than crumbs," I said.

Jake continued pelting me.

Dee demanded, "Are you satisfied with crumbs?"

I forced more air through my vocal cords. "No. I deserve more."

"You've put up with crumbs for years. Is that okay with you?" Dee looked indignant.

"No, it's not okay."

Shreds of tissue wafted through the air and clung to my sweatshirt.

"It looks like you're willing to settle for crumbs." Dee's eyes bored into me. She wanted me to get angry. I wanted me to get angry. That's why I was here. Still, I held back.

Dee gestured for two group members to hold a pillow in front of me.

You can do this. You'll never see these people again.

"Why aren't crumbs okay?" Dee demanded.

I pushed more air through my diaphragm, produced a sound loud enough to be heard in the next room. "I deserve better!"

Dee handed me the bat. "Put it on the pillow."

I struck the pillow. It barely budged. I hit harder. "I deserve more than crumbs! Keep your fucking crumbs!" I brought the bat down with force and the pillow bobbed. I began whacking and yelling for real. "Fuck you, Burton! I've been loyal to you! I've been faithful to you! I deserve better!"

After more than a dozen whacks, Dee stepped forward. "Good work, Suzy. What do you need to say to Mom?"

"It's *my* life, Mom. I can't lead it for you. It's *my* life!"

I pounded the pillow until my arms ached. When I slowed to a stop, my fellow group members crowded around, hugging me. I had done it. I had unlocked some anger. Shown a little self-respect. I had begun to fight.

Verlon touched his fingertips to my cheeks. "Suzy," he said, "you look luminous."

WITH LONG, BLACK HAIR and dark, downcast eyes, Carla resembled a young Angelica Huston, yet she seldom spoke or smiled. She seemed wary, like a beaten animal. In her mid-thirties, she lived with a man who physically abused her. She hadn't been able to leave him.

Carla stood by herself on one side of the room. She directed the rest of us—her family, friends and bosses—to the opposite wall. She screamed, over and over, "You're mean to me! I hate you all!"

In a calming voice, Dee said, "Carla, if there were anyone you could trust, you wouldn't feel so alone. Can you ask someone to stand with you?"

Eyes streaming with tears, Carla looked at us. Slowly, she lifted her arm. She pointed to me. "Suzy," she whispered.

I walked across the room and took her hand in mine.

"What do you see in Suzy?" Dee asked.

"Strength," she said. "And wisdom."

"You can only see in another what you have in yourself," Dee said.

One at a time, Carla invited the rest of the group to stand with her. When we had surrounded her, I noticed a brightness in her eyes I hadn't seen before.

As I walked back to my cabin, I reflected on how hard it had been for Carla to ask for support. I felt honored that someone so vulnerable had singled me out, had seen a strength and wisdom I didn't see in myself. I thought: If I'm so strong and so wise, what the hell am I doing here? But then I had a second thought. When I first came to Onsite, I had looked at myself and the others as the weak ones, the lost ones, the ones who couldn't straighten out our lives on our own. Now I realized Carla was right. We weren't the weak ones after all. We, all of us, were strong enough and wise enough to realize we had problems. And brave enough to get help, to try to make a change.

DESPITE THE PAINFUL SELF-EXAMINATION we went through at Onsite, there were moments of levity. One day on a break between sessions, Jake said, "Society makes too big a deal of sex. Society looks at sex like it's this important." He spread his arms wide. "In reality, it's only this important." He put his thumb and forefinger close together in front of his nose.

"Right, Burt," I said.

Jake laughed. So did I. Laughing again felt as refreshing as jumping in a lake on a hot summer day.

When our session resumed, I repeated Jake's remark to the group. "Jake, I give you credit," I said. "In a discussion of sex, you are the first man I've ever met who turned this," I spread my arms wide, "into this." I compressed my fingers.

On our last night, each group performed an original act. One did a riff on a reporter interviewing some nutty people about their Onsite experience. Another composed and read a limerick. Our group wrote and sang a takeoff on "I'm Henry the Eighth I Am." I remember the first verse: "I'm a co-dependent wreck, I am. A co-dependent wreck, I am, I am. The van dropped me at the Onsite door. I've been here seven times before . . . "

When the applause subsided, a staff member spoke about what we'd encounter on returning home. "Whenever you try to bring about change, expect a backlash," she said. "Whatever your addiction may be, the same forces that created it are waiting for you. When you get back to your daily lives, problems will come up. Don't let yourselves lapse back into your habitual reactions. It will be hard work. Remember: the addiction wants to take over again."

"IF YOU HAVE A MINUTE, I'd like to talk to you," Joanie said.

Although I hadn't seen much of Joanie since meeting her in my old room soon after I arrived, that afternoon I had noticed her carrying a vase of flowers. She placed it on a table in the barn. "My husband sent these," she'd said. "I wanted everyone to enjoy them."

After the final assembly, I followed Joanie past her daisies, irises, and alstroemeria. We sat down on a trunk in a deserted corridor.

"I haven't shared my story with anyone outside my small group, but I think it might help you to hear it," she said. Joanie had rosy cheeks and a serene manner and a husband who obviously adored her. I was intrigued. "My husband is an entrepreneur like yours. He built a successful business. He's well known and respected in our community. We've been married thirty-five years. I thought our lives were fine.

"A year ago, my husband phoned in the middle of the afternoon. He had been arrested in a prostitution sting. I was horrified. I had no idea he'd been seeing prostitutes. If the case became public, it could jeopardize our reputation and his business. We knew we had to tell our children so they didn't hear about it from someone else."

"What a nightmare," I said.

"At first, I didn't know how we'd get through it. But my husband agreed to do whatever it took not to lose me. He began seeing a therapist for sexual addiction. We went into counseling together.

He's become more in touch with himself and much more thoughtful. When I got here, I found he'd put several cards in my suitcase, one for each day. And you saw the flowers."

"I'm glad to hear there's hope," I said.

"Right now you'll find this hard to believe. If your husband gets help, you may someday look at this whole experience as a gift. Not wrapped in a very pretty package, but still a gift."

Back in the main room, attendees milled around, saying their good-byes. I ran into Jake. He gave me a hug. "You tell Burt his wife is hot stuff," he said.

"Thanks, Jake. I consider you an expert."

A staff member handed me a fax. Burton had sketched a big heart with our initials. *I can't wait to see you,* he wrote. *I feel like a teenager on a first date.*

After the first night, the telephone had been removed from the kitchenette. This small room had served as our canteen during breaks, providing comfort in the form of coffee and tea and big glass jars filled with pretzels and raisins. Now, on my final night at Onsite, I walked into the kitchenette for the last time. The phone had reappeared, our link to the outside world. I picked up the receiver.

It had been almost a week since I last spoke to Burton, longer than we had ever gone without speaking since the day we met. I rewarded myself with a handful of raisins. I had survived six whole days without obsessing over where Burton was. Now I wanted to know. I punched the numbers for home.

Please let him be there.

"Hello?"

"Hi, hon. It's me."

"Well, hi. I'm so glad to hear your voice. How are you?"

"It's been a good week. I've gotten a lot of insight. I did a number on you and my mother."

"I bet you did."

Trying to sound unconcerned: "So what have you been up to?" I held my breath.

"I had dinner with one of our executives one night and with David a couple of times and with Terry and John and with a few guys from my forum. I spent some time in the office."

Safe enough. I exhaled.

Earlier that day he had met with his forum of fellow DPO confidants, he said. "I told them what we've been through."

"Everything?"

"How I told you about the affair. How I broke it off. How we're trying to work things out."

My mouth went dry. "What did they say?"

"Most of them thought I was crazy to admit anything. I said I wanted to clear the slate. I hoped our relationship would be better than ever someday. Are you upset that I told them?"

"I trust the process."

"What does that mean?"

"We each have to do whatever we need to heal." Could I have come up with a more contrived answer?

"If you say so." He sounded as though he didn't know what I was talking about. I didn't.

"We'll discuss it tomorrow when we're together," I said. "A bunch of people are waiting to use the phone. Can't wait to see you. I love you."

"Love you, too."

I knew this wouldn't be easy.

THE NEXT MORNING, before climbing into the van, I ran across Ted. The last time I left Onsite he had reminded me to keep breathing.

This time, he offered different parting words: "Kick butt."

*Chapter Ten*

# BACK TO THE REAL WORLD

⚬⚭⚬

THE PROCESS OF SPIRITUAL GROWTH . . . IS CONDUCTED AGAINST
A NATURAL RESISTANCE, AGAINST A NATURAL INCLINATION TO KEEP
THINGS THE WAY THEY WERE, TO CLING TO THE OLD MAPS AND
OLD WAYS OF DOING THINGS, TO TAKE THE EASY PATH.
*The Road Less Traveled,* M. Scott Peck, M.D.

ONSITE HAD ADVISED US to spend the next few days in quiet reflection, processing what we had learned. I did just the opposite— flew straight from Nashville to Manhattan to celebrate our son's birthday. Arriving at the Sherry-Netherland Hotel, I let myself into our room and noticed a note on the chest near the door: *Having lunch with Andy. Back soon. Love you.* Tucked behind a lamp on the same chest was something more significant, something that caused my heart to race—a small turquoise Tiffany bag. A little turquoise box, tied with white satin ribbon, nested inside.

The gold wedding band I had given my husband for our ceremony had spent that one night on his finger and then retired to our safe. It had emerged three months ago when David wore it for his wedding ceremony, after which he, too, put it away. Now I remembered what Lori had told me. Ronnie had never worn a ring before. Following their couples program, he bought matching bands for the two of them. They slipped them on then and had continued to wear them. "That plain little band means more to me than the biggest diamond ever could," Lori had said. I had repeated her words to Burton.

Hoping Burton had taken my none too subtle hint, I waited for his return. I picked up *New York* magazine and flipped to the art gallery listings, but they failed to tempt me the way they usually did. I paced from the window to the bathroom and back again, leaned against the glass to look down at Christmas shoppers swarming along Fifth Avenue, tapped my fingertips on the cool surface.

The doorknob clicked. The door opened. Burton walked in. Held out his arms.

"I missed you," he said.

He wrapped his arms around me. His lips felt soft on mine, the way they used to.

"Tell me about your week."

I swallowed. "I learned a lot."

"Such as?"

"I need to share my feelings with you."

"Share away."

"I wrote about the week in my journal. I could read it to you."

"I'd be honored," he said. He kicked off his shoes and flopped on the bed.

I switched on the lamp beside the window, sat in the armchair, and put on my reading glasses. I read about arriving and breaking into tears, about meeting my roommate, about learning that I was addicted to our relationship, that I needed to establish boundaries. I read about Jake and Carla and their roles as Burton and my mother.

When I looked up, Burton's mouth pressed into a straight line. My biceps tensed.

"Have you heard enough?"

"Keep going," he said in a voice that could freeze alcohol.

I had practiced honesty for ten minutes, and I was already in trouble.

"A guy with a cute sense of humor seems attracted to me," I read. "His name is Joe. We hung out together with a group of people in the main house on a couple of nights."

I glanced up again. Burton's foot twitched. He stared out the window.

"You look uncomfortable," I said. "Should I stop?"

"Go. Ahead." His words hung in the air like two thick icicles.

A few more sentences would help him see the truth. "I was never alone with Joe. Never even learned his last name. But it was nice to have a man show interest in me again."

Burton glared at me. "You obviously had a great time with your boyfriend."

"Nothing happened. It just felt good to have a man admire me. I'm trying to be honest with you."

"I'll be honest, too. When I got to town, I bought us matching wedding bands. After what I just heard, I don't know if I'm ready to wear one."

*The addiction wants to take over again.* I took a deep breath. In what I hoped passed for a steady voice, I replied: "If you're not comfortable wearing a ring, we'll take them back."

A CRUSH OF CHRISTMAS SHOPPERS lined up in front of Tiffany's the next morning. Burton's salesman had recommended entering through the side door when we brought our new rings to be sized and engraved. We walked right in.

The day before, I had opened the little turquoise box. Inside were two gleaming platinum bands. Just the right weight. The essence of simplicity. From the place immortalized by Audrey Hepburn. With Tiffany's steep retail prices, I had never owned a piece of jewelry from the legendary store. Now it looked as though I still wouldn't. If Burton wouldn't wear his ring, neither would I.

"They're beautiful," I'd said. And I had sighed, snapped the box shut, and returned it to the bag.

I carried that little turquoise bag into the store. The happy strains of holiday music and the glitter of Christmas lights made me feel disconnected, even sadder. If only I hadn't read my journal to Burton, I thought. But then we'd be right back where we were, dancing around the truth, sparing each other's feelings. And, whatever Burton believed, I had done nothing to be ashamed of.

Burton spotted his salesman standing behind a counter, concluding a sale. While we waited, I said to Burton, "We'll put the charge back on our credit card."

"No," he said. "We'll have the rings sized and engraved and just hang on to them. I've made worse investments."

Hmm.

"You must be Mrs. Farbman," the salesman said. "Your husband told me you've been married for thirty-one years. That's something in this day and age. Do you like the bands he picked?"

"They're beautiful."

He beamed. "I knew you'd think so. Let's measure."

He produced a loop of small metal circles and slipped several of them on our fingers. Finding ones that fit, he wrote down our sizes.

"I assume you've decided how you want your rings engraved," he said.

"Suzy's should read: Love you," Burton said.

Our salesman wrote down the words.

"And you, Mrs. Farbman?"

"I'll always love you."

He looked at Burton. "She should have gone first."

Burton shrugged. "She's the writer."

Our salesman smiled as brightly as if he'd just sold us a significant diamond brooch. "I can't tell you what a pleasure it's been," he said. "How inspiring to see a couple still so devoted after all these years."

I HAD BOOKED A MASSAGE for the next morning, requesting a masseuse. There was a knock on the door. I opened it to find a masseur holding a large black case.

"Hellooo," he sang.

At the moment Burton was downstairs having breakfast with Andy. He would return soon. He had already misunderstood what seemed to me a minor reference in my journal. I did not think he would thrill to discover a male working on his naked wife's flesh. Not even if that flesh were discreetly concealed beneath a sheet. Not even if that male were clearly gay. If by some chance this slender young man in the tight navy and white striped sailor shirt did not make Burton uncomfortable, I would be uncomfortable anticipating the possibility. That alone would prevent my enjoying the massage.

"I'm sorry," I said. "I requested a woman."

"Well," he snorted. He swung around his table and strode off.

I called the massage service. "The record shows you did request a woman," the receptionist said. I felt relieved to hear it—tending, as I did, to blame myself for screw-ups. "Would you feel better to know the therapist we sent was gay?"

"My husband and I have been having problems," I said. "Under the circumstances, I don't want any male here, whatever his sexual preference."

Hanging up, I thought: There you go, justifying yourself again. You did not owe that woman an explanation.

When the masseuse arrived, I lay down on her table and smelled the fragrant oil she spread on my back. As she pressed on my shoulders, muscles that had been rock-hard for months began to release. It had been a long time since someone had taken care of me. A very long time. I had been so focused on Burton's needs that I had forgotten my own. As strong hands began to break up the tension in my back, I realized how lucky I was. Despite months of holding my feelings in, my body had remained healthy. The terry cloth ring beneath my face grew moist from grateful tears.

My sense of gratitude lasted no longer than the massage oil on my skin. Back in Michigan, I felt insecure and adrift once again. I trudged through the December cold into the office and stared at my computer screen, not comprehending a word. Editors called to remind me of deadlines. I dragged out paperwork but couldn't get myself to care which manufacturer made which table. At home, the stack of self-help books beside my bed grew taller. Authors Melody Beattie, Harriet Lerner, and Iyanla Vanzant became my new best friends.

I began each morning by reading an affirmation for that particular date. One morning I said to Burton, "I just read something powerful. Would you like to hear it?"

"How about we take a break from that today?" he snapped.

I retreated to my closet, dressed for work, and drove to the office. An hour later I sat at my desk, feeling hurt, desperate to hear a friendly voice. I picked up the phone.

"Hi, Verlon. It's Suzy, from Onsite."

"Hey, Suzy. Good to hear from you."

"How are things going?"

"Not great. My wife moved out. She filed for divorce."

I wished there were something I could say to make the pain in his voice go away. I knew there wasn't.

"I'm sorry," I said. "How are you holding up?"

"I found a therapist I like. She's helping me cope."

"Good for you. You're a great guy, Verlon. Sooner or later, you'll be fine."

"I'll survive. How are you doing?"

"Up and down. Today is a down day. That's why I wanted to hear your sweet southern drawl."

"I met you at your lowest point and watched you pull yourself out of it. You're an amazing woman, and stronger than you think."

Hanging up the phone, I felt happier, calmer. Verlon appreciated me; Verlon cared. My stomach settled down as though I'd taken a swig of Pepto Bismol. Seconds later, the effect wore off. My gut kicked back in. I had asked Burton to stop calling his old friend Sally, yet I had turned around and called my new friend Verlon. I had never slept with Verlon. A significant difference. Still, I was flooded with guilt.

That night Burton and I sat in our library. I sipped a cup of herbal tea and flipped through the newspaper, trying to focus on the problems in the Middle East, on the obituaries, on anything other than what I had done. Confession was the only remedy I had ever found for guilt. But if I told Burton about phoning Verlon, he might storm out of the room to console himself with a call to Sally.

My teacup rattled as I set it on the table and turned to my husband. "When you shot me down this morning, I felt really hurt," I said. "I needed to talk to someone. I called Verlon, one of the guys from my group at Onsite. He made me feel a little better."

"I'm a loser either way," Burton muttered. "I can't be happy with you anymore, and I'll be more unhappy without you. I remember something John Wayne once said—in each of his marriages he was good for about ten years."

Burton's response stunned me. Here he was sitting in our cozy library with family photos on the shelves and memories of our couples program still fresh in his mind; we had thirty-plus years behind us, and he was thinking about John Wayne's record of ten. I switched into internal pep-talk mode. This is his problem, I told myself. Your job is to be honest about your needs. Period. Fake it 'til you make it. What you resist persists. My new respect for platitudes would have caused several of my English professors to break out in hives.

Fake it 'til you make it. That was the goal. I folded my hands in my lap and put on my best Mona Lisa smile. "I hope you'll figure out some answers for yourself at your Onsite program next month," I said.

"I plan to go, but I don't know if I have the personality for it. I don't trust authority figures the way you do."

A COUPLE OF MORNINGS AFTER JOHN WAYNE stampeded through our library, Burton woke me early.

"I just want to hold you," he said. He stroked my hair and kissed my forehead the way he used to do on lazy mornings. Then he said, "I've been thinking."

Something in his voice made my skin prickle. "Thinking. About. What?"

"About the kids. If anything happens to us, estate taxes could destroy their inheritance. It may be time to start putting more assets in their names."

As with many traditional marriages, I handled our houses, our social schedule, our travel plans; Burton earned most of our income and made the business decisions. This arrangement had worked for a long time. Lacking a talent for numbers, I appreciated not having to deal with our complicated finances. Under normal circumstances, I accepted Burton's fiscal decisions. He understood how to make money better than I and would want what was best for the family. But circumstances had veered beyond normal. Adultery infiltrates the deepest channels of your heart, the ones where trust resides.

Your job is to be honest about your feelings, Jim had told me. As I lay in Burton's arms, I wondered if my husband's affections were meant to disarm me, to foster some scheme to siphon away funds. I hated to risk disrupting one of the few tender moments we'd shared since I returned from Onsite, but I owed it to myself.

"If you and I don't make it, how would turning over assets to the kids affect me?"

He did not jerk his arms away and lunge out of bed. He continued to hold me. "It wouldn't change anything. We'd both continue to receive income."

"I'm feeling really vulnerable," I said. "I wondered if you were being so nice to me to get me to agree with something that's not in my best interest."

He sighed. "I hope you don't start second-guessing my business decisions, but I understand your concern. I wasn't setting you up. I just felt like holding you."

ON CHRISTMAS AFTERNOON, Burton went horseback riding in an indoor arena near our farm. As he circled barrels and picked up speed, his saddle slipped over and flung him to the ground. An x-ray later showed eight fractured ribs. For the remainder of the holiday, I cooked chicken noodle soup, propped up Burton's pillows, and helped him on and off the sofa. It was good to feel needed again. And after living through two years of my husband's mysterious absences, I appreciated knowing exactly where he was.

One day, as we played gin rummy, Burton said, "I think this accident might be God's way of telling me to take better care of myself." I wanted to suggest that a fine start would be to give up his wandering ways. I refrained. He would participate in the next Living Centered program at Onsite. He could figure it out for himself.

Burton's ribs healed slowly. Two weeks before his program, his chest still hurt. He protested that he wasn't in shape for the physical activity at Onsite—getting up and down from the floor and banging on pillows.

"You could sit in a chair," I urged. "You could bat one-handed."

When Burton phoned, a staff member assured him Onsite could cope with his disability. What's more, she offered to grant his request for a single room, which, she cautioned, she couldn't guarantee in the future. Nonetheless, Burton canceled, reserving a space in the next month's program.

"Are you disappointed?" he asked.

Now that Burton was getting back on his feet, those feet could again carry him to South Lyon. Although his recuperation had helped bring us together, our future remained uncertain. If Burton understood what had driven him to cheat before, there was a chance he might not cheat again. A small chance, maybe, but one worth hoping for. If not, all bets were off.

"Yes, I'm disappointed, but it's your call. I need to know we're still trying to move forward. Will you go back to see Jim with me?"

"If it matters to you."

BURTON AND I HAD LAST VISITED Jim together a few weeks before to clear up their "cheating is normal" conversation. Since then Burton hadn't wanted to pursue a relationship with Jim, and I had continued to see him on my own. On a cold and dreary January day, Burton and I drove to Lapeer.

"How do you feel, Burt?" Jim asked.

"How do I feel? I'll tell you how I feel." Burton's words picked up speed as he spoke. "I hate the fucking winters. I've shoveled enough snow and salted enough ice to last me a lifetime. I don't care if I ever see another damn snowflake. I've worked my ass off since I was a kid. I'm sick of the responsibility. I'm tired of the bullshit at the office. I don't have to take it anymore. I want to go someplace warm for the winter. I'm only sticking around here for Suzy."

He turned to me. "I invite you to run off and play with me."

I loved my job. I had waited so long to work for a national magazine group. I enjoyed visiting beautiful homes, meeting homeowners, figuring out what editors wanted, styling pictures that jumped off the page, collaborating with a talented photographer. I delighted in having readers across the country. At fifty-four, I wasn't ready to run off and play.

Burton and I had carried on this argument for over two years. I had voiced my objections to retirement until I was blue in the face, and blue was not my best color. I had also found that trying to talk Burton out of his feelings only made him more defensive. As Burton ranted on, I felt myself wilt like an old rose.

When Burton stopped for breath, Jim said, "You talk like someone who's single."

That night, confused and unable to sleep, I flipped back and forth in bed. Burton seemed determined to take off, with or without me. I worried about what would happen if I didn't go with him. And what would happen if I did. I resented feeling pressured to give up my work.

Before dawn, I slipped out of bed, padded into the library, and wrapped myself in a chenille blanket. The moon cast slanted beams through the window blinds. Sitting alone in the dark, I thought about a vow I had made. Before I left Onsite for the second time, I had promised myself to attend a workshop with Debbie Ford in La Jolla. Why hadn't I followed through?

A small voice inside me spoke. You don't want to make Burton mad. He thinks you're too carried away with psychology as it is.

Is that all?

If you're not around to keep an eye on him, you're afraid he'll get into trouble.

"Bad reason," I said out loud. "You're going to California."

Listening to my heart, I realized I had neglected someone important. I needed to take care of myself. I also realized I had completed most of my current assignments. My workload would not gear up again until spring. If I weren't ready to ride off into the sunset with my spouse forever, maybe we could take a shorter trip. If you don't go within, you go without—another of my new favorite platitudes. Going within, I had found a tiny opening to an impasse.

Tiptoeing back to the bedroom, I slid between the covers. Burton slept peacefully. Soon, so did I.

The next morning I said to Burton, "I realized I can take a month off with you later in February, after your program. Your ribs should be pretty well healed by then."

Burton grinned. "Great! Let's go to Florida and play golf."

"I also realized something else. I need to go to California later this month to attend Debbie Ford's workshop."

"If it will help, go."

OVER THE LAST FEW WEEKS, my mood had careened up and down like Burton's plane in turbulence. This Saturday morning, my stars— more likely my hormones, or what was left of them—must have been perfectly aligned. I felt surprisingly calm, considering our plans for the evening. A friend had invited us to his sixtieth birthday celebration. John belonged to Burton's forum—the group in which he had confided while I was at Onsite. His party would mark the first time I had seen these men since they'd learned the truth about us. At least since I knew they knew.

At Roz and Sherm, a favorite boutique, I tried on peach sand-washed silk elastic-waist trousers and a matching shirt—an updated version of the loose, sporty style I preferred. Perfect for our upcoming trip to Florida, I decided. I imagined wearing the outfit to dine alfresco with Burton at a romantic little trattoria on some balmy night. I could almost hear the violinist playing "O Sole Mio" while we sipped our Chianti.

Leaving the store with a plastic bag over my arm, I thought about how good it felt to shop for pleasure again. Recently, what shopping I had done, I had done for other reasons—to counterbalance my husband's extravagance, to console myself, to find the one special outfit that would make me appealing again to Burton, to build a wardrobe for the day he walked out and I ended up back on the market. This was the first time in months that I had shopped just for fun.

When I returned to the car, my mobile phone was ringing.

"Where have you been?" Burton demanded. "I've been calling and calling." His voice sounded urgent, the way mine did all those times I left messages on his unanswered cell phone. "Come home. I want to talk to you."

When I walked in the door, Burton wrapped me in a long, tight hug.

"I was afraid something had happened to you," he said. "I was afraid I couldn't tell you how much I love you. I've been thinking about what a wonderful wife you've been, about how you've done everything I ever asked of you."

Say what?

Several months before, I had told a girlfriend I was concerned about Burton's state of mind. She had given me the name of a psychologist, Al Katzman, who happened to specialize in Attention Deficit Disorder. Burton went to see him. Al diagnosed my husband as having A.D.D. I had rushed out to buy a book on the subject. I chose one by Edward M. Hallowell and John J. Ratey.

*Driven to Distraction* contained a questionnaire. I read it out loud to my husband. Are you left-handed or ambidextrous? Burton wrote and played tennis left-handed, golfed right-handed. Are you impulsive? Easily distracted? Do you procrastinate? Have a hair-trigger temper? Tune out a lot? Yes. Yes. Yes. Yes. Yes. The book said people with A.D.D. tended to be disorganized. Burton's financial statements, minutes from board meetings, golf tees, and ball markers piled up on counters in our kitchen. His reading glasses and cell phone cords collected on the floor of his car. Keys, equestrian magazines, and pilot supply catalogues swamped his desk. Spare camera lenses, packs of developed photographs, extra rolls of film, and pocket change landed on his dresser.

When I finished reading the questionnaire, Burton had said, "Now I understand my problems with school. My father's friends would brag about their sons' grades. My father would say, 'Burt has big hands.' My parents and my teachers thought I was lazy and stupid. I guess I wasn't after all. I was just different."

Although the psychologist had suggested Burton try Ritalin, my husband had declined and, after a few sessions, stopped seeing him. His depression, and his disappearing acts, had continued.

Burton's unexpected attention that afternoon struck me as what the book called an A.D.D. ability to hyperfocus. In business, my husband battled through insurmountable obstacles. He placated nervous bankers, ferreted out legal loopholes, secured nonrecourse financing—all with unyielding focus. Now, a few weeks after our couples program, Burton turned that focus on me. He held my hand and led me into the living room. Sitting in his favorite armchair, he patted his knees. As I sat in his lap, he put his arms around me and held me tight.

"I spent the last couple of hours thinking about how I've treated you," he said. "I realized that I'd never deliberately do anything to hurt you. I asked myself: If I wasn't trying to hurt you, who was I trying to hurt? It must have been me."

Though my heart darted about like a goldfish, I sat still and listened. I did not console Burton or make excuses for him, as I had so often. Earlier, Jim had described Burton as "emotionally shut down." For this glorious moment on this glorious afternoon, my husband was emotionally wide open.

"I am so sorry for the pain I've caused you," he said. With my head on his shoulder, I felt his tears on the back of my neck. My heart flitted back and forth as though gobbling flakes of hope that his repentance would last and flakes of fear that it wouldn't.

"When friends want to see our new house, I tell them to ask you for a tour. The house was your baby. I realized I've never had the complete tour. Sometime would you give it to me?"

"How about now?"

I held Burton's hand and guided him around the house I had named Acorn Hill, the place where we had lived, together but apart, for the past two years. I related how I had encouraged our architect to combine Shaker details with contemporary spaces and to balance walls for art with windows for view. I described the fun of collaborating with artisans on acorn-inspired hardware and tiles. Burton paid full attention. Of all the tours I had given, he proved my most appreciative audience.

Earlier, I had purchased marking pens and foam core board. That same afternoon, Burton sat beside me at the breakfast table and helped create a birthday poster for John. We searched through magazines for funny pictures and headlines, which we cut out and pasted into a collage. We had not shared a craft project since we were first engaged and had sanded and refinished his parents' old oak kitchen table. It was fun to work on a project together. More than fun. It was remarkable.

John paraded our poster around his house that night, showing it off to other guests while Burton and I sat on a sofa and savored beef tenderloin. I sang along with the pianist and small-talked with some of Burton's forum members. Not quite three months after our visit to Onsite, I made it through a potentially difficult evening, feeling good about feeling good.

As HARD AS IT WAS to find and express my voice, I continued forcing myself to speak out. One night while Burton and I shared a bag of low-fat popcorn in front of the fire in our library, he turned to me. "I did what I did because I was lonely and wanted a playmate," he said. "You know men are led by their dicks."

I chewed slowly to avoid choking on an unpopped kernel or on my husband's words. Like many women, I had once privately accepted the double standard, the male tendency to stray. Then it happened to me. After the anguish I'd been through, I could accept it no longer. As reluctant as I was to risk upsetting Burton, I needed him to understand how I felt.

"You say you were lonely and wanted a playmate," I said. "Did you ever think I might have needs that aren't being met by our marriage? How would you feel if I had an affair with a man who enjoyed escorting me to galleries or lectures?"

He stroked his cheeks. "I don't think I could handle it."

"Why not?"

"I want you to give me one hundred percent."

"How does that differ from what I'm asking of you?"

He chewed on his lip. "I guess it doesn't. I see your point. I'll try harder to give you all of me. I'll try to enjoy something like visiting a museum with you, instead of just going through the motions."

My heart spun. I kissed Burton's cheek, and considered sharing Joanie's prediction with him. Then I thought: he shamed me. He deserves to suffer.

I went ahead anyway. "A friend at Onsite told me something hopeful. She said if we really work at our relationship, we might someday be grateful for what we've gone through. We might come to consider our problems a gift."

"A gift, eh?" Burton grinned. "Shall I get you my mistresses' addresses? You could send them thank-you notes."

I laughed. "I'm not that grateful."

*Chapter Eleven*

# A NEW AGE NEW ME

—⟨⟨⟨∞⟩⟩⟩—

IN THIS THREE-DAY WORKSHOP YOU WILL UNMASK THE ASPECTS
OF YOURSELF THAT CAN LITERALLY DESTROY YOUR RELATIONSHIPS,
YOUR INNER SPIRIT, YOUR SUCCESS AND YOUR DREAMS. IT IS
CALLED THE SHADOW. FIND THE GIFT OF YOUR SHADOW
AND YOUR LIFE WILL TRANSFORM.

*From the Chopra Center for Well Being program*

IN THE MIDDLE OF A TYPICALLY GRAY midwestern winter, the
California coast proved a bright and shining relief. If I hadn't gained
a single new insight from Debbie Ford's Shadow Course or spotted
a seagull or felt a ray of sun, the weekend would still have been
worthwhile. I had shaken off my doubts and taken action. Despite
my worries about leaving Burton unsupervised, I had packed my
bag and flown across country, just for me.

I checked in at the Empress Hotel in downtown La Jolla, and
then wandered off past boutiques and real estate offices in search
of a flower shop. Debbie Ford's book had nudged me out of an
emotional paralysis that had gripped me for too long. I wanted to
show her what she'd meant to me.

Among masses of pink azaleas and orange birds of paradise in a flower shop, I spotted a bucket of individual stems of tiny yellow roses. They were bright but simple, just the effect I sought. I had one sprig wrapped in clear cellophane and tied with a yellow ribbon. I purchased a card. Inside, I wrote:

> In my personal pantheon of heroes, you are up there
> with:
>> My parents for giving me life,
>> My husband for giving me my children,
>> And my plastic surgeon for my new
>>> and improved nose.
> You helped show me the way to a better me.

I DINED THAT NIGHT WITH KATHY, a friend I hadn't seen in a decade. She had since divorced Peter and moved to California. Talking to Peter in Manhattan fifteen years before had helped Burton overcome a previous depression, the cause of which I now understood. I told Kathy why I'd come to town.

She said, "That night when Peter and Burt went out for drinks, Burt told Peter about the affair he'd had, and Peter told me. I got the sense you didn't want to know, so I never said anything."

"You were right. I didn't want to know."

"Most women don't. But since Burt pulled that trick before, I'm not surprised he did it again. Boys will be boys and all that crap. I had as much of it as I could take. That's why I got out. At least this time you're dealing with it."

I raised my glass of wine. "To truth."

She touched her glass to mine.

INSIDE THE MOORISH-STYLE Deepak Chopra Institute, the lobby smelled of herbs. The young receptionist told me she had taken the Shadow Course recently and found it life-changing. "Life-changing sounds good to me," I said.

The receptionist directed me to a carpeted room large enough to hold about forty people. In front, a bright blue paisley wool shawl draped across the back of a carved, dark wood armchair. Nearby, a wood chest was topped with a group of candles and a colorful framed image of a mandala, or Buddhist symbol of the universe. The next day, the stem of yellow roses I'd give Debbie would appear on the chest as well.

Our group of about thirty mostly middle-aged men and women helped ourselves to back jacks. For someone whose previous notion of proper seating ranged from Chippendale to Eames, I was becoming surprisingly comfortable with this crude form of support. We arranged our back jacks in a semicircle. I planted mine front and center.

Debbie Ford glided in, wearing a slim black top and pants. She sat down on the carved wood chair and flung the shawl around her shoulders. She was slender, striking, forty-ish, with short-cropped dark hair, large brown eyes, and cheekbones to kill for. Her manner was relaxed yet intense; her gaze penetrated. On first impression, she seemed too young and too hip to be much help to a conventional, sadder-but-wiser woman like me. But I knew from her book she had done a lot of living and offered lessons worth learning.

Debbie asked us to introduce ourselves. As I listened to others speak about what had brought them here, I realized that many of us, males as well as females, were relationship casualties.

Carol, a middle-aged woman who looked to weigh over three hundred pounds, sat on a chair in back. Her thighs overlapped the seat. All I could see was how overweight she was. I couldn't possibly have anything in common with her. Then, in a throaty voice, she said, "Believe it or not—I used to be thin. My first husband abused me, physically and emotionally. I divorced him and married a second time, and then that husband started abusing me. I could live with what he did to me but not with what he did to my daughter. I divorced him, too. Then I guaranteed I would never make the same mistake again. I gained so much weight that no man would ever be attracted to me. Now I realize something that hurts most of all—I've abused myself worse than either of my husbands did."

Tears sprang to my eyes. I found myself relating to this obese woman. My husband had had an affair, and it had practically destroyed me. Given Carol's experience, I, too, might have chucked my low-fat diet and exercise regimen and eaten myself into isolation.

My response surprised me. Until the last few months, I had prided myself on being the competent entrepreneurial wife, part-time career woman, volunteer, and mother. There was no room for humility on my résumé. But life had kicked sand in my face. I had learned what humility meant.

WHEN NOT PARTICIPATING in the program, we were encouraged to avoid such distractions as television, books, and conversation. Instead, we remained "in silence." Deepak Chopra proposed that most people were "object-referral"—their sense of self depended on their credentials and on the people and things around them. The Shadow program aimed to help us become less dependent on outside influences. Our goal was to be more authentic, or "self-referral," in touch with our own ideas and feelings.

I had spent most of fifty-four years avoiding silence. To me, down time had meant wasted time. In California, I began to see what I'd been missing. In simply being rather than doing, I reached deeper understanding and experienced fleeting moments of serenity.

I had continued to imagine my traits as passengers on a bus. Along with Controlling Connie and Guilty Greta, I had met Jealous Julie, who tried to teach me to be less self-righteous. Her gift to me: my competitive nature. Doubting Dottie took credit for my determination to seek the bright side of a situation.

One night in La Jolla, I thought back to a time when I was eleven. Attuned to my mother's moods, I had noticed that Mom seemed to sigh more than ever and spend more time buried in books. One afternoon, she sat down in a small blue club chair in my bedroom. She had let me pick out my own furnishings, and I had chosen a blue color scheme. Blue was her favorite, not mine. From a young age I was more focused on her needs than my own.

I asked Mom what was wrong. She didn't want to drag me into her problems, she said. You need someone to talk to, I insisted. And so she told me what I had sensed. She and Dad were fighting. When she encouraged him to open up, he accused her of criticizing him. When she became upset, he called her emotional.

"I shouldn't say these things," she said. "You need to have a good relationship with your father. Especially if you're going to grow up and be able to relate to men."

I remember her words. And mine. And the way my stomach nosedived when I said them. "If you're so unhappy with Dad, don't stay with him for my sake."

MORE THAN FORTY YEARS LATER, lying in bed in a La Jolla hotel, I met a new passenger. As she played out in my head, tears streamed down my cheeks. The morning after, I wrote about the encounter in my program workbook:

> Stuck Sue was me at eleven, in a striped T-shirt, jeans, and sneakers. Her brown hair was straggly. Tears ran down her face. She held a stone in her hand.
>
> "Why are you crying?" I asked.
>
> "I tried so hard to help my mother. I couldn't make her feel better," she said.
>
> "What is your gift to me?"
>
> "Your stubbornness. Your ability to hold on."
>
> "What do you need from me?"
>
> "Appreciation for how hard I tried. The chance to be playful, a chance I lost by growing up too soon."
>
> Sue and I walked over to a stream. I urged her to throw in her stone, to let go of the resentment she carried. She clutched the stone to her chest. "It protects

me," she said, but in a while, she tossed it into the shimmering water.

I hugged her and thanked her for looking out for me. "I have a special gift for you," I said. I presented her with a silver I.D. bracelet and fastened it around her wrist. The bracelet was engraved with her new name: Shining Sue.


I WALKED TO THE BEACH early the next morning, searching the clean sidewalks for a stone. Nearing the ocean, I came across a small construction site and spotted, in the dirt, a gray stone about the size of a plum. I picked it up, and I discovered it had the heft of the stone I had imagined the night before. I held it close to my face.

"Thank you for bringing me this far," I whispered. "You made me stubborn. You made me tough. You saved me from being consumed by my mother's neediness."

Fortunately, I had worn sunglasses because I was crying again. The sight of a grown woman in jeans and a sweatshirt mumbling to a stone while tears streamed down her cheeks might have caused passersby to wonder. Then again, maybe not. This was California.

Other mornings, I had stopped to marvel at seals playing in the surf. This morning, I headed for a deserted stretch of coastline. Black volcanic boulders pressed against each other, shouldering waves that ranged from friendly pats to solid punches. I climbed down to an outcropping of large rocks. Water surged below. Overhead, puffy clouds glowed peach and gold in the early morning light.

Looking out to sea, I spoke to my rock. "You helped me survive for many years. Thank you for bringing me this far. It's time to move on. I return you to the universe. Someday someone else may need you." I touched the stone to my lips and tossed it into the waves.

Heading back, I felt a buoyant sense of release. As I walked along the sidewalk skirting the shore, two lean and handsome young men smiled at me and said good morning. I nodded in reply, thinking: it *is* a good morning.

During the weekend, our group engaged in exercises that the workbook promised would help us reclaim our "power, creativity, brilliance and dreams." We identified fears that held us back, thought about what we needed to become whole, analyzed our negative emotions. We wrote letters of forgiveness to others and commitment to ourselves.

In one of my favorite exercises, we came up with the word that best described our sacred selves. My word was "luminous." Walking around the room, we introduced ourselves. "Hi, Ravishing. I'm Luminous." "I'm Luminous. Pleased to meet you, Powerful."

Creating lists of negative characteristics, we divided into groups of three. One member of each threesome admitted to a negative trait from his or her list; the others concurred. We tossed the claim back and forth until it lost its sting.

As the room filled with chatter, I declared, "I am a manipulative bitch." The two men sitting with me repeated, "You are a manipulative bitch." I insisted, "I really am a manipulative bitch." They concurred. Meanwhile, Debbie and her assistants circled the room, making suggestions. Listening to me blast into myself, Debbie volunteered, "Try old manipulative bitch."

How had she known? Old wasn't on my list, but it should have been. Old, as in life was passing me by. Old, as in having squandered my best years chasing after a bull that had roamed off in search of new cows and greener pastures. Old, as in too tired and beaten up to compete with the hordes of young predatory females swarming about any remotely available male, not to mention any handsome and remotely available male with a few bucks in his pocket. Old, as in stuck in a relationship too long to start over. But after I practiced "old manipulative bitch" long enough, the words began to seem comical. I stood up and announced them to the room.

Others proclaimed their vilest opinions out loud as well. "I am mean and hateful." "I am petty and devious." "I'm a mother-fucking asshole." Each pronouncement drew laughter and applause.

Most of us have parts of ourselves we try to hide, traits of which we're ashamed. At some point in our lives, we were criticized or punished for being too loud, too selfish, or too whatever, and we internalized that criticism. There was a liberating release in being able to voice your worst opinions of yourself, let them go, and know that you survived.

We also composed lists of positive traits we longed to believe about ourselves. I worked on the word "sexy." My partners, a male entrepreneur and a female schoolteacher, called me sexy with such conviction that I almost began to believe them.

One of Debbie's assistants suggested I work on the word "content." "I am content," I said. The phrase tasted like medicine sweetened to disguise the flavor, something you swallow because it's supposed to be good for you. My partners traded "content" back and forth with me. At last I said, "Okay, I own it." But in my heart, I knew I had claimed it simply to avoid hogging the rest of the exercise.

Later I wondered about the trouble I'd had accepting what should be a pleasant concept. Did I equate contentment with monotony? Was I afraid to feel content? Undeserving of it?

JEANIE JEWELL AND I BECAME INSTANT FRIENDS when we realized we were both struggling to cope with the aftershock of husbands having broken off affairs. Tall, with the kind of thick dark hair that never knows a bad hair day, Jeanie was in her mid-forties. She was a radio talk show host, formerly a professional dancer.

On our last night in La Jolla, we shared a cab to a small dinner party hosted by Debbie's sister Arielle, a publicist for clients including Dr. Deepak Chopra. On the way, I asked Jeanie how she had come to her new career. She told me her knees had given out and she was looking for something meaningful to do. She heard about a local radio station that was starting a program about women's issues and decided the job would allow her to do interviews that could make a difference in her listeners' lives.

"I prayed to know my highest creative good," she said.

An electric current ran through me. "Your highest creative good," I repeated.

At the party, I turned to the woman sitting next to me on the white sectional sofa. She had finished eating a chicken drumstick and licked barbeque sauce off her fingers. I noticed gold and silver rings on a few of those fingers.

"What are you interested in?" I asked.

"I help put people in touch with their spirit guides," she said.

Oookay.

"What are spirit guides?"

"People who come into our lives to teach us things we need to know."

"Do they have a physical presence?"

"They do."

"Does everyone have them?

"Yes, though they may not know it. One just left me—Native American, handsome, muscular. He said he had taught me all he could, said I didn't need him anymore."

"Do you miss him?"

"Yes. But it's time to move on. There will be others."

In my old frame of mind, as your basic, down-to-earth, midwestern conservative, I would have pronounced this woman a couple notes short of a full octave. In my new frame of mind, I wasn't so sure. Later that night, lying in bed, I closed my eyes and sent out a message: If any spirit guides are listening, I'm ready to meet you. I followed up with a prayer to know my highest creative good.

JEANIE AND I SHARED A CAB to the airport the next morning. I walked her to her departure gate, where we split a scone and exchanged e-mail addresses and hugs. After she boarded her plane, I headed to my gate, passing a wall hung with several framed photographs. One of them drew me back—a portrait of the late Mexican artist Frida Kahlo. Although Salma Hayek would not play Kahlo in the movie *Frida* for two more years, I recognized Frida because of her Detroit connection. In the 1930s, her husband, Diego Rivera, had created a powerful mural, *Detroit Industry*, at the Detroit Institute of Arts. Since I was a child, I had loved gazing at the heroic men and women painted in fresco on the walls of the Rivera Court. During their lifetimes, Rivera was far more acclaimed than his wife. Since, Frida's artistic reputation had soared.

In her portrait on the airport wall, Frida wore a long peasant skirt and several beaded necklaces. Her black eyebrows merged in the middle. She stood beside a pedestal supporting a mirrored reflecting ball. What did that ball reflect? I wondered. And why was I so attracted to this image? In my head, I posed a question: If you are meant to be a guide for my spirit, what is your message to me? In my head, a clear voice replied: Although you're married to a successful, domineering man, pursue your own art.

It is often said that everyone has at least one book in her. I didn't think I did. I had given up trying to write the Great American Novel soon after David was born and hadn't attempted anything so ambitious again. My life was too conventional for nonfiction, my imagination too limited for fiction. I lived in the flyover zone, in a provincial factory town far from the east and west coasts, where the real action took place. I didn't have a story to tell, not a story anyone else would want to hear. Other people, places, and things were more interesting than I was. That's why I wrote about them.

Suddenly I tasted a new thought. I did have a story to tell—the story of my struggle to reclaim myself and my marriage, although at that point reclaiming the marriage was far from a sure bet. When I finally stopped running from our problems, I had searched for such a story. I looked for a book by one wife who had slogged, day-by-day, through the same kind of heartache. I longed for an honest, first-hand accounting of how one woman survived the nightmare of infidelity and how her marriage survived, too, despite the odds.

Just looking for such a book proved a challenge. I felt too humiliated to slink up to the information desk at Barnes & Noble and ask the clerk for the section on Betrayed Wives. Even if there were a Web site called www.cheaterswives.com, I wasn't computer literate enough then to locate it. Loath to stir up suspicions about my suspicions, I visited bookstores outside of my immediate neighborhood. Glancing around to be sure no one familiar lurked in a nearby aisle, I wandered over to the self-help section and paused in front of the shelves marked "Relationships." I looked for a title like *Diary of a Betrayed Housewife* or *I Stayed with a Man Who Strayed*. If I had located such a book, I don't know where I'd have kept it. If I'd slipped it into a shelf in our library, any random visitor might have spotted it. And if one night I forgot to hide this potential literary lifeline in my underwear drawer, Eddie Mae might come across it on my nightstand. She might divulge my reading interest to the gardener, who might in turn mention it to the housekeeper across the street. Before you knew it, my tribulations would be the talk of the Oakland County canasta tables. I grant you this line of thinking sounds excessively paranoid. Infidelity does crazy things to an otherwise sane wife.

At any rate, I found inspiring books by marriage counselors with brief mentions of their anonymous clients. I found accounts by women who had recovered from divorce. But I didn't find what I was looking for. Could I write that story for others who sought what I had? Assuming my marriage were to survive, could I capture the truth of the experience? Explain how hard and scary it was to try to save yourself and your marriage all at once? Did I dare reveal my innermost secrets? Would my husband ever accept my exposing such revelations? Could this be my highest creative good?

I only knew one thing for sure: writing my story would be therapy. Aboard the plane, I took out my Shadow Process workbook. Several pages were blank on the reverse side. I drew a pen from my backpack. And I began to write.

*Chapter Twelve*

# BLOSSOMING OUT

———— ❈ ————

THOUGH NOTHING CAN BRING BACK THE HOUR
OF SPLENDOUR IN THE GRASS, OF GLORY IN THE FLOWER;
WE WILL GRIEVE NOT, RATHER FIND
STRENGTH IN WHAT REMAINS BEHIND.

"Ode: Intimations of Immortality
from Recollections of Early Childhood,"
William Wordsworth

ON THE PLANE TO FLORIDA, my friend Brenda wore a microfiber black pantsuit, a white T-shirt, and black leather slip-on shoes. Jil Sander designed the suit; the T-shirt came from the Gap, the shoes from Prada. I know because I asked. I gave up staying abreast of fashion when I stopped writing about it. My girlfriend Brenda loved clothes as much as she did when she worked full-time, traveling the world designing women's fashions for department stores and partying with Bill Blass and Gianni Versace. Though retired from retailing, she still wore the current trends, kept up on the latest beauty tips, and helped her friends do the same.

Brenda and I had planned our visit to South Beach to coincide with Burton's rescheduled trip to Onsite. But when Burton called to check on his accommodations, he learned the program was full and that he would have two roommates. He backed out again. Referred to a similar program where he could stay off campus by himself, he called and booked a reservation. That program, at The Meadows in Wickenburg, Arizona, would not take place for two more months. I hoped his pledge of fidelity would last for two more months.

Just back from Debbie Ford's workshop in La Jolla, I hated to leave Burton alone so soon again. But Brenda and I had looked forward to our journey, and I needed her help. Flying south, I told Brenda the secret I had guarded for the last two years. I filled her in about Burton's disappearances and my suspicions, about our couples program and our attempts to reconcile. She flipped back the armrest and put her arms around me. "You didn't have to go through this alone," she said.

I also told Brenda about my weekend with Debbie Ford. "You know how self-conscious I am about my body," I said. "I worked on trying to think of myself as sexy."

Her amber eyes glimmered. "Sexy? I can help you with sexy."

And so we had our objectives. We would improve our golf swings with the pro at Fisher Island. And we would develop my sex appeal. If there were a way I could become more desirable, I wanted to discover it. In case my marriage failed, I needed to discover it.

WE HAD BOOKED A SUITE at the Bentley, a new small residential hotel, a junior version of the nearby popular Delano. Our accommodations, all white with a low sofa and chartreuse throw pillows, looked cool enough to appear in *Met Home* magazine.

On our first morning in South Beach, Brenda and I brewed coffee in the sleek glass-and-chrome appliance in our kitchen and carried white china mugs out onto our balcony. Across the street, the ocean licked the empty sand beach.

I handed Brenda a pen and a pad of paper and encouraged her to join me in my homework. Debbie Ford had assigned our group to write a list of twenty things for which we were grateful. "Do this every day for one month, and it will change your life," she'd promised. The exercise had helped me start to focus on what I had, not on what I lacked.

I whizzed through my list. My good health. My revived sense of humor. My courage in facing the truth. My independent children. Brenda's pen hung in the air. Involved in a relationship crisis of her own, she mumbled, "I can't think of twenty things I'm grateful for."

"You can include anything," I prompted. "Your great hair. Your sense of style. Your chocolate fudge cake. Your straight putts."

She began to write. Her list numbered twenty within minutes.

PALM TREES RUSTLED. PEACOCKS ROAMED. Bougainvillea climbed the walls of Spanish-style apartment buildings. Fisher Island was so exclusive you had to know someone's name just to board the ferry to shuttle you there. We had a name—Kelly, the golf pro. Brenda and I had scheduled a lesson.

There's something manly and irresistible about golf pros and ski instructors. Kelly fit the mold. Not much older than my son David, Kelly walked with a lanky grace. His biceps strained the cuffs of his navy short-sleeved shirt. On the range, he watched as I hit several balls with my driver. Most landed near the 150-yard flag. Kelly suggested that teeing the ball higher would add distance to my drives. He advised me to slow down and sweep the club back. "Take the time to enjoy your back swing," he said. I followed his instructions. Several balls sailed past earlier shots.

Although I had played golf on and off since my teens, I did not understand how hard to hold my club. I extended my right hand to Kelly.

"Show me your grip."

He took my hand with what felt like the perfect handshake— firm but relaxed, the kind of handshake I had taught my sons. I had expected more of a bone-cruncher.

"Here's what I've been doing," I said. I doubled the pressure on his hand.

"Holding on too tight interrupts the flow," Kelly said. "Learn to trust your swing."

IT WAS THE KIND OF BALMY EVENING when all you needed was a light sweater tied around your shoulders. Brenda's friend Evelyn met us at our hotel. We headed for the China Grill, a few blocks away. A professor in her sixties with swingy blonde hair, Evelyn was shorter and rounder than I was. Yet she exuded intelligence and wit. And—for someone shorter, rounder, and older—surprising sex appeal.

Brenda said, "You can learn a lot about sexy from Evelyn. She owns sexy."

I turned to Evelyn. "Our mission down here is to help me develop sex appeal."

"I guess I'm lucky that way. I've always felt sexy," Evelyn said. "Men seem to be attracted to me. Take today. I was walking on campus when a good-looking professor tried to pick me up. He was from a different department, considerably younger, and very persistent. He tried to talk me into having lunch with him. I turned him down, but I enjoyed the attention."

"What is sex appeal?" I asked.

She cocked her head. "I'd say it's a state of mind. It's more about how you feel than how you look. Having a sense of humor. Feeling good about yourself."

"Evelyn even walks sexy," Brenda said.

I stopped. "Show me."

As I stood watching, Evelyn paraded down the sidewalk. She swiveled her hips back and forth with a cute little clip, then turned and walked back toward Brenda and me. I studied the effect. She wasn't dressed in anything seductive. She wore a bright yellow cotton cardigan sweater, loose-fitting yellow pants. But there was something about the way she walked. Confidence, I guessed.

"Your turn," Evelyn said.

I mimicked her gait.

"Too stiff," Brenda said.

I swung my arms in a wider arc.

"Too exaggerated," Evelyn said.

I eased up.

"Better." Brenda nodded.

"Keep practicing. You'll catch on," Evelyn said.

I worked my hips back and forth all the way to the restaurant. After cocktails and very fresh sushi, we departed. As the handsome young doorman held open the glass door, I spoke to him. "Watch this," I said. "Does this look sexy?" I demonstrated my new walk, to the curb and back.

"Very sexy," he said. He clapped his hands. "Can you teach me?"

"Oh, no," I replied. "It takes years of practice."

If this charming young man with the slim black T-shirt and the perfectly gelled hair were not clearly gay, I might not have been so brazen. But I was pleased by his response. I've always believed gay men were more observant.

THE NEXT NIGHT BRENDA SAID, "It's time you got rid of those baggy, old lady clothes."

At the moment I had on what I considered a perfect travel ensemble—black tumbled-silk elastic-waist trousers with a black leather belt. I had tucked in a loose-fitting black shirt and rolled the cuffs to a jaunty elbow level.

"You have a darling little body," she said. "You should show it off."

I once read in a magazine that about 80 percent of females were dissatisfied with their bodies. I belonged to that majority. Darling was one of the last adjectives I would have picked. Less-than-darling wads of flesh adhered to my upper thighs no matter how many leg lifts I executed. My stomach served on continuous advance patrol. My breasts might have been darling on a twelve-year-old. But if Brenda believed I had a darling little body, I decided to give the concept a go.

Young women with thick, dark hair and burnished skin strode along Ocean Drive, legs thrusting from tight miniskirts. Store windows vibrated with tiny tube tops in fluorescent colors. South Beach abounded in sexy clothing. Brenda decided to start me out gently with black, flat-front stretch pants. I never wore flat-front pants. I was as devoted to pleats as a robin was to worms. Nor had I ever purchased a pair of pants without enough room to tuck in at least a blouse or a sweater and an extra pound in case I succumbed to a slab of baby back ribs or a Sanders Hot Fudge sundae.

Brenda marched me in and out of several stores. I tried on pants in miniature fitting rooms. One pair proved short in the crotch. Another, Brenda ruled out as chintzy. One pair wouldn't have fit an anorexic. With the patience of a Zen master, Brenda viewed every stretchable black pant in the neighborhood. At a boutique crowded with racks and pounding with Latin music, I emerged from a curtained cubicle. The pants into which I had squeezed did not have room for an extra bite of celery, but I had zipped them up.

Brenda beamed. "Ta da."

She seized a black tank top from a rack. "Try this with the pants," she commanded. I retreated to my phone-booth-sized staging ground and slipped into the clingy garment. Personally I believed looser tops added fullness that helped balance my more ample bottom half. Nonetheless, I lifted my head high and ventured forth with a shimmy of my bare pale shoulders.

Brenda clapped her hands together. "Perfect."

The shop owner looked me up and down with piercing brown eyes. "She's right," he said, lifting a dark eyebrow.

Of course you're all admiration, I thought. I am about to plunk down $75 for a piece of elastic I may never have the nerve to wear in real life. But I smiled graciously and said, "Muchas gracias, señor."

"Why don't you two join my buddy and me at a dance club tonight?" the shopkeeper asked.

"Sounds tempting," I replied, in a voice so flippant you'd have thought I received pickup lines as often as third-class mail. "Maybe some other time."

It was close to midnight. I planned to head back to the hotel to phone my hopefully lonesome husband, who might be wondering why he hadn't heard from me sooner. Far be it from me to jeopardize what delicate progress we had made. Or to provide incentive for retaliation. I didn't think he would take to the notion of sitting home with the TV for company while I hip-hopped the night away with a new admirer, to whom I had paid retail.

Brenda and I headed back out into the tropical air. I carried the pink plastic shopping bag with my new miniature garments. Brenda took my arm.

"That guy tried to pick you up," she said. "He was cute, too. I told you—you have a darling little body."

"You did," I conceded. We sauntered along, arm-in-arm, with matching grins on our faces.

A threesome of lusty young women strode past in high-heeled, sling-back shoes. As I watched their tight little bottoms disappear into the crowd, my concept of myself as a late-in-life hot number evaporated.

"Do you think this new top brings too much attention to my less-than-buxom bazoom?"

"That's next," Brenda said.

She steered me into another boutique, toward a rack of flesh-toned brassieres. The cups protruded on their own.

"What size?"

"34A," I whispered.

She lifted a plastic hanger from the rack and handed it to me.

I retired behind a curtain. Hooking on the padded bra, I leaned forward to better arrange my limited assets as I had learned to do while a young teen at Selma Bonheim's lingerie shop in Detroit. Standing up, looking in the mirror, I did see an improvement.

It makes me sad to think of the years I spent maligning my small breasts. All they ever did was sit there and be healthy—thank God!—and mind their own business. As a girl, I waited for them to grow, and waited and waited as my friends began to swell around me. Early on I wore a padded bra. During college in the 1960s, I decided this deception represented false advertising. If some guy should try to get to second base with me, not that I was giving it away so fast, I didn't want him to discover that the base wasn't all he had expected. I talked myself into the Natural Is Better/Get Over It school of thinking and purchased an unpadded bra. When other women burned their brassieres in the 1970s, I resolved not to be confined by this symbol of female repression either. I put my bra in my dresser drawer and left home without it, hoping the gesture might help me to better accept my body. A breeze blew and my nipples peeked out to see what was what, and I felt so conspicuous and vulnerable that I retreated to my dresser. I had worn an unpadded bra ever since.

While other women got breast implants and flaunted them like diamond necklaces, I was frightened to risk the procedure. Lawsuits over silicone poisoning from broken implants multiplied. Because they were directed against a Michigan-based company, I could scarcely open a *Detroit News* or *Free Press* without reading about the problem. And Burton had insisted, "I'd rather see you small and natural than big and fake." Ultimately, I resigned myself: perky was as good as my chest would get.

I spent insane time and energy coping with my measurements. I prowled through stores seeking dresses with higher necklines. Climbed countless stairs to reduce the discrepancy between my northern and southern hemispheres. Scolded myself for envying other women's more copious décolletage. Avoided Victoria's Secret catalogues. Shunned *Playboy* magazine. I reminded myself to be thankful my breasts were healthy and to focus on other blessings such as my trim waistline. I rationalized that tits were only oversized mammary glands anyway. I concentrated on the fact that smaller breasts appeared more youthful and would sag less in my old age, lobbied to convince myself that brains mattered more than boobs.

As hard as I tried to love my flat chest, I never escaped my adolescent yearnings. I still longed for the kind of bosom that cried out for a Versace gown, for a cleavage that would bring a man to his knees.

Now, thanks to two chunks of rubber foam, pretty little mounds popped up on my chest. I held the curtain in front of me, poked out my head, and invited Brenda into the fitting room.

"Screw natural," I said. "It's an improvement."

"I told you so."

The nice thing about Brenda was she only said "I told you so" when you were clearly pleased she had.

Carrying the bra out of the fitting room, I glanced at the price tag.

"Forty-five dollars!" I shrieked.

Cool as a Cosmopolitan martini, Brenda reminded me, "You're the one who wants to own sexy."

I walked out with three.


IN THE CAB TO THE AIRPORT, I wore my new bra and tank top underneath an unbuttoned denim shirt. Feeling very risqué, I was sure I caught the driver staring through the rearview mirror at my inflated chest.

"We need to discuss your hair," Brenda said. "The style looks dated. It doesn't go with your younger, sexier image."

"I'm already perming my hair and adding streaks and using a curling iron," I wailed.

"You're still perming your hair?" Brenda groaned. "No wonder it looks so dried out. Silky, straight hair is the style right now. Look at Gwyneth Paltrow. Look at Cameron Diaz. You have the hair everyone wants today, and you have it naturally. When we get to the airport, we'll buy some magazines and find you a new look."

At the Miami International Airport gift shop, Brenda pulled *Vogue, Bazaar, In Style, Allure,* and others from the rack. I had never understood how so many beauty magazines stayed in business. Now I knew. She handed me the pile.

"Pay," she commanded.

"Six magazines? That's more than twenty-five dollars."

"We don't know where we'll find the right style."

I handed over enough cash to feed a Third World orphan for days.

On the plane I discovered once again: my beauty guru knew best. One by one, we flipped through magazines. Cindy and Elle, Claudia and Naomi and other single-name examples of human or surgical perfection gazed back at us. Brenda analyzed their hairstyles with the focus of a microbiologist examining cells in a petri dish. "Too long." "Too hard to maintain." "Too butch."

The last magazine we perused was *In Style.* "There it is." Brenda pointed with a short, pale pink lacquered fingernail to a coif that curved around a delicate shell-shaped ear hung with a diamond drop. Golden blonde streaks haloed the face of a beauty whose long neck rose from a low-cut black top. The caption bore the name of this dazzling young stranger: actress Charlize Theron.

"That's the look," Brenda said with as much satisfaction as if she'd just found the cure for cancer. She tore out the picture with a flourish and pressed it into my hand as though it were a treasure. It was.

"With bangs, if you want. And more blonde streaks. You must be much, much blonder."

The slew of magazines I purchased came with a bonus—an article, written anonymously by an American woman. Brenda and I took turns reading it out loud. When the author was about forty, her husband of several years took up with a younger female. They separated, and the writer moved to Paris. She allied herself with the city's leading madam and studied the ways of the most popular French escorts. After several months of this unique apprenticeship, the author returned home. Applying her new skills, she soon won her husband back.

Her sojourn abroad had taught the writer lessons. She learned that the top Parisian call girls, like the famed courtesans of old Venice, were not simply charming and intelligent. They were also attentive to and fascinated by the man they were with.

I thought about my relationship with Burton. Yes, I knew how to pour on the charm. Yes, I was blessed with above-average intelligence. But was I always attentive and fascinated? Or could I be distracted and impatient and judgmental more than I cared to admit?

THE NEXT DAY I SHOWED MY MAGAZINE CLIPPING to Judith, my stylist of many years. "I want high lights and low lights," I said, repeating Brenda's words. Judith scrutinized the picture and nodded. She stroked chemical potions on sections of my hair, folded them in foil and sat me under the dryer. Rinsing away the eye-burning, smelly concoction, she snipped off my permed ends and manipulated a hot air blower. My completed hairstyle looked soft and bright—much like that of my new idol, Charlize.

Superficial as it seemed, Brenda was right. After I had lightened and restyled my hair, padded my chest, and put on slimmer, hipper clothing, I looked better and I felt better. At fifty-four, having sped from zits to crow's-feet without ever experiencing sex appeal, I began to feel a tiny bit desirable. At a point when many of my contemporaries lamented their physical declines, when I acknowledged laugh lines that no longer disappeared with my smile, I began to feel good about my appearance. Every girl recovering from a broken heart could use a Brenda in her life.

I was grateful for the help I'd gotten—from Brenda and so many others. I was also grateful for the ability to pursue that help. If I hadn't had the time or money to devote to a crash course in reclaiming myself, I'm sure the process would have taken longer.

As it was, whatever lay ahead, whether my marriage revived or faltered, I had started to believe I would survive. I could take care of myself. With my husband, if he proved willing to make changes, too. Without him, if he didn't. My brighter new look reflected my brighter new outlook. I was beginning to heal, inside and out. I was learning to trust my swing.

# Chapter Thirteen

# REBUILDING

———— ∞∞∞ ————

FEELING FUZZYHEADED, INARTICULATE, AND NOT SO SMART
ARE COMMON REACTIONS EXPERIENCED BY WOMEN AS WE
STRUGGLE TO TAKE A STAND ON OUR OWN BEHALF. IT IS NOT
JUST ANGER AND FIGHTING THAT WE LEARN TO FEAR; WE AVOID
ASKING PRECISE QUESTIONS AND MAKING CLEAR STATEMENTS . . .

*The Dance of Anger*, Harriet Lerner, Ph.D.

I WOULD BE AWAY FROM MY WISE and sympathetic therapist for a whole month. For a last-minute boost of confidence, I visited Jim shortly before we left for our vacation.

"I've been thinking about something. It seems so self-indulgent and narcissistic I'm embarrassed to admit it," I said.

What I was most uncomfortable telling Jim was what he most wanted to hear.

"Go ahead," he said.

"Okay." I swallowed. "Here it is. I keep having this sense that I want to feel adored."

Jim beamed me a smile that felt like a hug. "That doesn't sound self-indulgent or narcissistic, Suzy. If that's what you need, that's what you need. You've been out of touch with your own needs for so long you don't even know what they are. Because your mother seemed so needy to you, you equate being needy with being weak. It's just the opposite. Being in touch with your needs is a sign of strength."

"But I'd feel stupid telling Burton to adore me. I can't make him adore me. He can't pretend to adore me. If he adored me, he'd act like it."

"You're trying to make changes in a long-term relationship," Jim said. "You've built up habits for over thirty years. Breaking old habits takes time and hard work. If you need to feel adored, that's your right. But you owe it to Burton to let him know how you feel. He's not a mind reader. He won't understand your needs unless you tell him."

"I guess I see your point," I said, admiring Jim's ability to shortcut through my mental traffic jam. "It's my responsibility to let Burton know what I need. It's his to decide what to do about it."

OUR APARTMENT ON LONGBOAT KEY, Florida, turned out to be a standard issue rental. Matching pastel floral print sofa and love seat. Glass-topped rattan coffee table. Laminate entertainment cabinet. We could see the bay above the tops of palm trees and, as a bonus, the CD player was equipped with Vivaldi's *The Four Seasons*.

Although Burton had asked, I hadn't told him what Jim and I had talked about two days earlier. I had been searching for the perfect words. I was still searching. I couldn't figure out how to tell my husband about my need to feel adored in a way that wouldn't cause the opposite effect. However I framed the words in my head, they sounded pathetic.

Hoping alcohol might spike my courage, on our first night in Florida I poured vodka and fresh orange juice over ice into two highball glasses. Burton and I sat beside each other on the sofa, drinks in hand. The strains of violins swept through the room. Outside in the eastern sky, orange puffs of cloud reflected the sun setting on the other side of the globe.

After several swallows, I said, "I'm ready to tell you what Jim and I talked about."

Burton looked at me with friendly eyes. He didn't punch the remote control or thumb through papers. Having waited for the right moment, I had his attention.

"I told Jim you and I were doing pretty well, but there was something I was embarrassed to admit."

I paused, still wondering how to phrase my pitiful admission.

"Go on," Burton said.

I forced myself to look into his eyes. His gaze seemed benign as he raised his glass for a sip. "I told Jim I couldn't talk myself out of wanting to feel adored." I waited for the familiar body language. The impatient twitch of his foot, the flare of nostrils. But he sat placid and unruffled. "Jim said I owe it to you to tell you how I feel. He said you and I are trying to change habits we've built up over thirty years."

Burton jiggled the ice in his glass, but more in a thoughtful than an exasperated sort of way. "That makes sense," he said.

"Here's what doesn't make sense to me. I can't force you to adore me. If you don't adore me, I can't blame you for how you feel. But I deserve to be adored. And you deserve to adore somebody, even if it isn't me."

Somehow I'd managed to say exactly what I wanted to say. Without even a catch in my voice. And it didn't sound pathetic at all. It sounded like the sentiment of a woman with some dignity. Even self-respect.

Burton put his arm around my shoulders. "I do adore you," he said. "I don't know why I don't show it more. But I get the message." With a tender hug and a kiss, he proved it.

I had begun to learn an important lesson. It was like learning to walk, only different. When you learned to walk, first you crawled, then pulled yourself up on a table, then fell down when you ran out of table, then wobbled to your mother's hands. Once you learned to walk, you mastered the skill for life. What I grasped that night was also learned by awkward little steps. But unlike walking, it was a lesson I would have to learn over and over. I would continue to wobble, to fall down, and to try again. I was learning to recognize, to tell, and to live with my truth.

THE NEXT NIGHT WE WENT TO A MOVIE. For years I had loved holding hands with Burton in a dark theater, a romantic indulgence left over from teenage dating days. In the past two years, Burton had stopped taking my hand at the movies. I had tried to convince myself it didn't matter, tried to talk myself out of making an issue over who initiated what. If his hand remained on his side of the armrest, I would reach over and slip mine into it.

In the global scope of things, as compared, say, to peace in the Middle East, handholding might seem trivial. But on the second night of our visit to Florida, the geography of our respective hands mattered to me. A lot. I had told Burton about my need to feel adored. The next move was up to him. I resolved not to initiate the contact. If you must, hold your own darn hand, I told myself.

After we finished eating our popcorn, Burton reached straight across the armrest and took my hand in his. My heart fluttered as if it had wings. Burton's hand felt warm and strong, and it lingered on mine throughout the film.

One night in Florida I succumbed to a morbid fascination: viewing Monica Lewinsky in her first television interview since the Bill Clinton blue dress debacle. Identifying with spurned wife Hillary as I did, I was revolted by how the young ex–White House intern batted her big blue eyes and flipped her dark hair around and affected airs of innocence. Even unflappable Barbara Walters seemed charmed. But I got my revenge on the little home-wrecker. I threw pillows at the screen.

My disgust with Monica and her paramour did not, however, diminish my enjoyment of our vacation. Burton's ribs had healed enough that we played several rounds of golf. We walked barefoot along the sand and spotted stingrays flapping their fins in clear blue gulf waters. We consumed mounds of stone crabs. I wore my new pale peach trousers and shirt to an Italian trattoria, though there was no violinist present to complete the scene I'd imagined when I bought the outfit, and though I knew it would not have met Brenda's standards for sex appeal. We viewed several more movies, and Burton took my hand in all of them.

It was nice to know my husband and I could have fun again. It was lovely to feel appreciated. If I hadn't yet graduated to feeling adored, appreciated would do for now.

When Burton canceled twice with Onsite, I had privately wondered whether he would make it to any program of his own. But a few days after we returned from Florida, he departed for The Meadows in Arizona.

Almost five months had passed since my husband promised to remain faithful until completing his own program and I had scribbled his commitment on the back on an old sales receipt. Hoping Burton would attend such a program had kept me from giving up. It had saved me from crippling despair and bought me some relief from doubts about my husband's ability to be true. The right program might help Burton understand his deceptions, in which case maybe, just maybe, he could stop them. The right program could mean we'd have a future.

On the other hand, five days did not seem time enough to inspire changes in behaviors that had taken place, on and off, for years. No psychotherapist could vaccinate my husband against cheating. No program could guarantee he would open up to his feelings and let himself be vulnerable. He might refuse to submit to the process, as he had most of the time at Onsite. For that matter, what the hell did I even know about this particular process? What if The Meadows failed to make a difference? I was afraid to think about it.

Dropping Burton off at the airport, I watched him wheel his black bag through the sliding glass doors into the terminal, and I burst into tears.

THE UNIVERSE WORKS IN UNEXPECTED WAYS. On his first night in Arizona, Burton phoned from the Wickenburg Inn. I expected him to sound glum. Instead, he sounded gleeful.

"You won't believe what happened," he said. "After I checked into the hotel, I walked over to the stables. I told the stable manager I planned to drive out to Eureka, Nevada, in the spring. He pointed to the corral and said, 'The dude over there comes from Eureka.' 'What's his name?' I asked. 'Mike Laughlin,' he said."

"You've got to be kidding," I responded. A few weeks before, Burton had read in *Western Horseman* magazine about wild mustangs running free in a mountain range near Eureka, Nevada. Having long wished to see such animals, he had phoned the cowboy who was mentioned in the article. Mike Laughlin had been busy at the time but said he would call back. Burton had not heard from him.

"I walked over to the corral and said, 'Laughlin, you owe me a phone call.' 'Who the hell are you?' he asked. 'Burt Farbman, from Detroit,' I told him. 'No shit,' he said. 'I lost your number.' We made plans to ride together this week. I think meeting him was a sign. I'm meant to be here."

While I was glad Burton had found something positive in an experience he had dreaded, I was wary, too. I hoped horseback riding would not be the only benefit of his trip. Knowing how impulsive Burton could be, I also hoped he wouldn't skip the program altogether to spend the week riding with his new friend Mike.

To my relief, Burton attended the program every day and called home every night. We later learned The Meadows advised against outside distractions, including telephones. Such restrictions would not have discouraged my defiant husband even if he had paid attention when the rules were given, which he hadn't.

When he called, Burton told me how pleased he was to have his own room and to ride with Mike in the late afternoons. He said he enjoyed his four fellow group members, all of whom were staying on campus for more intensive therapy. He also told me his group leader, a middle-aged woman named Gail, wanted him to admit he was angry. "I don't think I am," he said. "Gail insists I must be angry at someone from my childhood. I can't figure out who."

For three days, Burton said, "I'm not getting much out of these sessions."

For three days, I replied, "Give it time."

As much as I longed to, and as hard as the Old Me would have tried, I had learned I could not control his reactions. This was his experience, not mine.

"I'll stick it out," he said. "It's my dime."

BURTON HAD BEEN GONE FOR FOUR DAYS. I lay in bed thinking about how much more energy I had been putting into my marriage than I had before our troubles began. And about how I wished Burton would experience some sort of breakthrough at The Meadows. But as hard as I might wish, the prospect grew dimmer by the hour. He had one day to go.

The phone rang. "I had a very interesting day," Burton said.

My heart jumped. "What happened?"

"I realized I was angry at someone. Who do you think it was?"

"Your father for dying and deserting you when you were a child?"

"Not my father."

"Your mother for putting so much pressure on you and not recognizing your A.D.D.?"

"Not my mother."

"Then who?"

He told me that Gail, his therapist, had called him to the center of the room. He sat in a chair with two empty chairs facing him. Everyone else sat on the floor, their eyes closed. The lights were off. Gail asked him to imagine the innocent and trusting boy he once was.

"I pictured a cute little kid with big, sad eyes. I invited him to stand behind me and told him I had some adult business to take care of, but he would be safe with me."

Gail asked whom he wanted to invite into the room. His parents, he said. He imagined his mother and father sitting across from him.

"I told them how surprised they'd be at my business success and how proud they'd be of their grandsons. I thanked them for all they'd done for me."

I sat and listened, as still as the blank TV screen. But my heart pounded.

Gail asked him if he had a higher power. He said he believed in God. Did he pray through an intermediary? "No," he said, "I go straight to the Big Guy." Gail asked if he could visualize God standing behind his parents. He doubted he could, but he tried. Soon he began to see what he called a dark reddish-purple robe with light glowing inside the hood and from where the hands and feet should be. Gail wondered if he could turn his need to control over to the higher power he saw. He didn't think so, but he concentrated on the weight on his shoulders. All of a sudden, he pushed it across the room. When his parents left, Gail asked if he'd like to bring in anyone else. He requested his stepfather, Jack, who had died more than twenty years ago.

"I hadn't thought much about Jack since he died. But I heard myself say I wanted him there, and I wanted my mother back with him. When he came in, I went nuts. I yelled and cried. Gail handed me Kleenex. I'd blow my nose and throw it on the floor and keep yelling. I screamed, 'You schmuck! You putz! You taught me to hate. I was a sweet little boy before you came into our lives.' I told my mother I didn't blame her for bringing that jerk into our home. After Dad died, she did the best she could. But I needed to tell my stepfather how I hated him, and I needed her to know it."

Goose bumps popped up on my skin. "That was a breakthrough," I said. "I'm surprised you could let go like that."

"So was I. I remember as a kid what happened when the family would go to a restaurant. My stepfather would bully waitresses so bad that I'd leave an extra tip on the table, and I didn't have extra money to leave. I knew I detested Jack when I was a kid. I had no idea I still hated him so much."

Hanging up, I felt all my nerve endings tingle. The colorful squares of the patchwork quilt at my feet seemed to brighten and dance before my eyes. I didn't know what Burton's experience meant, but I believed it could mean something important. Some new beginning. One that could possibly change the way he saw his life. Saw himself. Saw our marriage.

*Chapter Fourteen*

# FINDING MY HEART

<del>————————</del>

THE GREATEST CATALYST FOR CHANGE IN A RELATIONSHIP IS
COMPLETE ACCEPTANCE OF YOUR PARTNER AS HE OR SHE IS,
WITHOUT NEEDING TO JUDGE OR CHANGE THEM IN ANY WAY.
*The Power of Now,* Eckhart Tolle

Now THAT BURTON HAD UNLOCKED a hidden part of himself, I
wanted to do the same. Despite all the studying and praying and
counseling and learning to speak my truth, part of me still held back.
Part of me resisted giving and receiving love. I wanted to overcome
this tough little core deep inside. Experts said I needed to get in
touch with the pure and carefree girl I once was. Since attending
my Living Centered program, I had tried and failed to do that
many times. I had not been able to find the elusive essence that psychologists called my inner child. Nor could I recall a time when I
felt carefree.

Scrutinizing my past made me feel like a traitor. Both my parents were nice people who cared about me, who did not drink to
excess or beat or abandon me and were no more flawed than most of

us. But our childhoods influence the adults we become, and the adult I became had crafted a little wall around her heart. Going back helped me understand why.

One moment was chiseled in my mind. I was about twelve years old, standing outside the closed door of my parents' bedroom. As I lifted my hand to knock, I heard a muffled sound from within—the sound of my mother's crying. I heard Mom tell Dad about some old friend who had snubbed her, heard him respond that she shouldn't waste her energy thinking about it. Standing there with my hand suspended in the air, I remember resolving never to let myself be hurt the way my mother was. I stacked and mortared a few stones around my heart that day.

My eavesdropping episode sparked in me a desire to boost Mom's confidence. Soon after, having spent a day at the country club swimming pool, I rushed up the driveway, eager to report what my mother's friend had said about her. Mom stood at the blue Formica counter in our kitchen, wearing a shapeless flower-patterned housedress, smoothing butter and patting flour all over a standing rib roast.

Breathless, I said, "Mom, I ran into Aunt Beverly at the snack bar." Beverly was a social aunt, not a blood aunt, an old friend of my mother who didn't phone much anymore. "Aunt Beverly said she loves your sense of humor. She said you're the life of any party."

"Funny she didn't invite me to her last one. I was good enough for her when she wanted to get into the club. I'm not good enough anymore."

I remember feeling crushed by my mother's response. But I kept on trying to bolster her morale for many years to come.

Mom's mother, Deborah Wilkus, seemed to get invited everywhere. My elegant grandmother wore suits by Norman Norell and Pauline Trigere and carried Chanel and Gucci handbags. Her strawberry blonde hair swept back like a queen's with a pouf of extra hair pinned to the crown. She and my grandfather, David, had cruised to Europe and brought back lacquered French cabinets and wondrous little English Battersea enameled boxes. They had traveled for weeks at a time, leaving their offspring with a governess and chauffeur.

Having made up her mind to give her daughters more love and attention than she had received, Mom doted on my sister and me. She drove us to piano and ice-skating lessons. She led Brownie troop meetings, attended school plays, planned mystery trips and birthday parties, told us how talented, pretty, and smart we were.

Dad came from a family of achievers, too. His uncle Albert Kahn's architectural design for an entire plant under one roof with no dividing walls allowed Henry Ford to develop the assembly line in the first decade of the twentieth century. One of Great Uncle Albert's brothers started a company that eventually became part of U.S. Steel; another designed important public works including the Hoover Dam. Such illustrious roots proved daunting for my father, who, I sensed, felt he didn't measure up to the high family standards.

Dad's mother, Mollie, the source of my middle name, was a go-getter, too. Mollie, who was Albert Kahn's sister, started a business reproducing architectural drawings early in the twentieth century. She ran Multi Color until she bore children and turned the company over to her husband, Walter Fuchs, a German immigrant. Mollie died in the 1940s; Walter remarried.

I was born while my father, a first lieutenant, navigated bomber airplanes over Germany. When Dad returned from serving in World War II, he went into the blueprint business with his father. Several years later, when Walter and his second wife, Stella, died in the plane crash, Dad took over the company. He never seemed to enjoy his work. He escaped to the golf course in summer, to the TV in winter. He complained about bills. Income from properties Mom had inherited funded summer camp and private school for my sister and me and the occasional extra Fair Isle sweater or pair of Weejun penny loafers. My parents' marriage consisted of strained conversations, random blowups, and awkward silences. Dinner table conversation revolved around Anne's and my field trips or geography tests.

Jim Rowe told me that children from dysfunctional families

typically react one of two ways: they become rebels or perfection-ists. To make things better at home, I pursued perfection. Miss LaForge, my fourth grade teacher, called me her "little chickadee." I won spelling bees and captained the safety girls and hoped if I were talented enough or popular enough, I might somehow turn our home into a place where parents hugged and called each other Sweetheart.

Lacking warmth from her mother, father, and husband, my mother sought it in vain from me. While part of me was determined to play Mom's Little Miss Fix It, another part of me fought against the role, resenting Mom's neediness. That resistant part showed up at my bedtime. When Mom tried to kiss me goodnight, I couldn't help jerking my face away. Mom joked that she risked whiplash just putting me to bed. She settled for a compromise in which she lowered her cheek within inches of my face while I smacked my lips. She called it an air kiss.

As a girl, I worked part-time for Dad's company. Riding in my father's car to and from the office, I'd listen to him talk about accounts he was pitching and tell him about invoices I had filed. Those rare moments of connection with my father made me feel disloyal to my mother.

My childhood desire to be perfect stuck with me, taught me as an adult to stuff down feelings that might have led to less-than-perfect behavior. Like talking myself out of an attraction to another man. Or not snapping at my children for interrupting me on the phone. Over the years, I trained myself to disregard doubts and fears, to value thinking more than feeling, as if my head were a superior senior and my heart a lowly freshman.

Jim had said that recalling myself as a little girl could help me recapture some of my early joyfulness. But my antennae weren't tuned to that station. Even when I looked at photographs of myself as a youngster, I didn't pick up on a sense of joy.

ABOUT FIVE MONTHS AFTER OUR COUPLES PROGRAM, in spring of 1999, I visited my ailing mother at her apartment. After two failed foot surgeries and a broken leg, she could no longer walk. Marks from the tires of her electric wheelchair marred her white walls. My mother had always been such a neat housekeeper that I winced to look at those black scars, knowing how she must hate them.

That night I walked into my mother's bedroom. Photos of her children and grandchildren crowded her dresser top. Among them I spotted a small sculpture, glazed matte green, that I had made as a teenager in ceramics class. It depicted a young girl sitting on a rock, naked and slender, with one arm thrown across her eyes.

Later that night, I lay in bed trying again to visualize an inner child that I had begun to doubt existed. The image of my sculpture popped into my mind. I had created the likeness of a girl about eleven years old, vulnerable and exposed. She covered her eyes as if to protect herself from what she was seeing, as I should have done instead of appointing myself my mother's confidante. Having given that little sculpture to my mother many years ago, I now realized it was also a gift to myself.

In the process of seeking an inner child, I had sought a younger, happier self. If that child was submerged deeper within me, I hoped to meet her one day. For now, my childhood seemed better captured by my sculpted little girl. I wondered where she would lead me.

CHARLEVOIX IS A SMALL RESORT TOWN near the tip of your ring finger, if you use the back of your left hand as a map, which everyone from Michigan does. I never knew a Michigander who wasn't proud to live in a state conveniently situated at the end of your arm. Charlevoix is a Cindy Crawford type of town. Not just a pretty face, but smart, too. Smart enough and lucky enough to be blessed with three lakes. She snuggles up to Lake Michigan, which rewards her with breathtaking sunsets. She overlooks Round Lake, a small harbor crowded with boats in the summer. And she backs up to Lake Charlevoix, a clean version of Lake Como with new cedar shake or clapboard-sided cottages instead of old Italian stone villas.

On a cold, gray morning in early spring of 1999, soon after

rediscovering my sculpture, I zipped on a lightweight ski parka, inhaled the brisk air, and loped down the thirty-plus cement steps in our front yard. I turned west on Belvedere, passing John Cross Fishery, where I bought sublime smoked whitefish to create the mousse I had served countless guests with drinks on our porch. I passed the lower gate of what had become the most famous house in town, the ex-residence of Patsy and John Ramsey. In fall of 1996, I had taken scouting slides of the Ramseys' beautifully restored Victorian home. A magazine had accepted my proposal for a feature. I was scheduled to produce the story the following summer. The tragic murder of their young daughter, JonBenet, later that year put an end to that assignment.

I crossed Bridge Street and headed down Antrim, past the Charlevoix Cinema, which sold popcorn with just the right amount of salt. I traveled through a neighborhood of mostly modest and older two-story houses. Hordes of tourists whom local residents called Fudgies (for the fudge they bought) would descend on the town in July. For now no one worked outside pruning bushes or pulling weeds; no children played catch in the streets.

As I walked, I asked God to help me connect with my childhood self. Over the past couple of years, I had developed a habit of talking to God wherever I was. I had decided God wasn't a location snob who preferred a synagogue, say, to a shopping center. I didn't think He cared if I were down on my knees. Whether I drove in my car or walked along a sidewalk, God was still glad to hear from me. At least that's what I deduced from the fact that whenever or wherever I prayed, I felt a greater sense of peace.

I turned left on Park Street and followed it downhill to Boulder Park on the shoreline of Lake Michigan. Several quirky homes here were made of boulders capped with cedar shake roofs, built in the 1940s and '50s by Earl Young, a local builder. Some were owned by friends of ours. I was glad they were unoccupied. Whatever it was I felt drawn here to do, I didn't want an audience.

I scrambled through a border of weeds down to a sandy stretch of beach. The steel-gray color of the lake reflected the sky. Waves splashed against boulders that in previous years had been covered by water. As I scanned the shoreline, I looked for a rock that resembled the one I had made out of clay many years before. Amid dozens of granite boulders extending out into the lake, I spotted one about four feet wide and three feet tall with a gently rounded top. Climbing up on it, I imitated the pose from my sculpture—right leg curled back around the rock, right arm shielding my eyes.

I sat still for a few minutes when, to my surprise, I heard the small voice of a young girl in my head. She called herself Little Suzy. She had been lonely and unappreciated for many years, she said. She had felt left out when I put my mother's needs before hers and ever since when I ignored her fears. Wind chilled the tears that ran down my cheeks. Out loud, I promised not to ignore her again. Sliding off the boulder, I began to pick up stones and fling them into the water. With every throw, I cried out protests, until I ran out of breath and complaints.

Elated to have gotten in touch with my heart, I headed north toward the public beach and came across a slender piece of gray driftwood. I picked it up and used the point to carve a large heart in the sand. Inside, I wrote: "Welcome Home, Little Suzy." Hoping to find a heart-shaped stone as a token of the occasion, I scanned the shoreline as I walked on. Thousands of round and oval stones lay strewn across the sand. Receding waves revealed thousands more layered on top of each other. Not a single stone had the shape I sought.

Reaching the playground, I wanted to reward the child I had found in me. I headed for a large, steel-framed set of swings, sat on a rubber strap, and began to pump. I swung higher and higher until my scuffed Reeboks flew over the water and scraped the sky.

Below me, a plump young girl walked past holding a leash with a small dog straining at the end. She picked up her furry little brown and white pet and placed it on a nearby rotating wood platform. Giggling, she pushed the animal around in circles.

I dragged my feet in the sand and slowed to a stop. This girl seemed so innocent and playful. I wanted to know her age.

"Hi," I called out

"Hullo."

"What kind of dog is that?"

"Part terrier and part who knows what. My mom calls him 'Best of the Neighborhood.'"

"What's his name?"

"Sylvester. He's my best friend."

"He's a lucky dog. What's your name?"

"Emily."

"How old are you, Emily?"

"Eleven."

Somehow, I already knew.

I HAD TWICE ENGAGED in what psychotherapists called anger release work. The first time was with my small group at Onsite, the second with the large group at Debbie Ford's program. Both times I had experienced some relief, but I was never sure whether that relief came from venting energy or from managing to do what was expected of me. Both times I felt self-conscious, as though I had to perform for an audience. I decided to try it on my own.

A steep hill rose up from the beach and flattened into a woods where a path was trampled down. Leaving Emily and Sylvester behind, I climbed the hill and followed the path, searching for a sturdy branch. The ground was strewn with stray pinecones, broken twigs, and the remains of brown leaves. A fragrance of cedar blew through dark evergreens. Near the end of the path, a branch lay off to one side. It measured about two feet long and was covered with smooth gray bark. I picked it up, smacked it against a tree to knock off the tip, and carried it home.

Our house was quiet. Burton had driven to the farm to spend the afternoon with his horses, including Gypsy, who was back up north where she belonged. I passed the blue glass medicine bottles clustered on curved shelves flanking our kitchen sink window. Burton and I had collected them years before, stopping at antiques shops on the drive north. These bottles had originally contained alcohol-based medicines that were popular in America during Prohibition. I liked their symbolism—our house in Charlevoix was a healing place. On the porch outside the kitchen, I kept a wicker hamper in which I stored my gardening tools. I opened the lid and pulled out my leather gloves.

Upstairs, the windows in Andy's room overlooked the Sitners' house next door, a house I had featured in *Better Homes and Gardens*. I had been thrilled when it made the cover of the magazine. The house appeared unoccupied now. To be safe, I lowered the matchstick blinds.

Placing an old throw pillow on the floor, I sat down beside it and pulled on my gardening gloves. Alone in the darkened room, I lifted my branch and pounded that pillow as hard as I could. With every stroke, I shouted out hurt and anger I had dragged around inside me for too long. I don't know whether it was the solitude or the practice I'd had before, but this time I was ready. This time I let go. This time was for me.

JIM HAD SUGGESTED that if I ever could visualize my inner child, I should write her a letter with my right (dominant) hand and let her respond with my left. This technique could help bring unconscious thoughts to a more conscious level, he explained.

Putting away my gardening gloves, I still felt charged with energy. I pulled a legal pad out of my briefcase, picked up a pen, and sat down on a sofa in the library. "Dear Little Suzy," I began, and wrote two pages about the problems I'd had trying to reach her. "I'm sad that I was out of touch with you for so long," I concluded. "But I'm glad we can spend the rest of our life together."

I switched the pen to my left hand and waited to see if anything would happen. Within a couple of minutes, my hand began to move.

Dear Suzy,

Boy it feels weird writing you like this.

You are so much smarter than I am I don't know why you want to hang out with me, but I am glad you do. I will try to make you happier by reminding you of your feelings. I know you're not comfortable with them, but maybe not trying to control everything will calm you down. I hope you won't reject me again. I will try not to feel like I'm not good enough for you.

Love, Little Suzy

I came a long way that day. I had moved forward in a journey I began six months before, on the day I realized I needed help. It was a journey I would travel for the rest of my life. A journey to know myself, a self I had abandoned a long time ago. There were, I had learned, many forms of betrayal.

ON A SUNNY SUNDAY MORNING several days later, I walked another beach. Burton and I had come to Palm Beach, Florida, to visit our friends John and Terry. Burton had already flown back to Michigan; our hosts had left for church. Alone, I drove to the ocean, parked the car, and kicked off my shoes. Walking fast along the sand, I came upon a family playing in the surf. A little girl of five or six ran after her father, splashing him with water, throwing herself at his legs and laughing. I slowed down to follow them, reveling in the joy of this exuberant child. I could not recall ever having felt so comfortable with my father.

I savored the sensations—the sun warming my arms, the cold water chilling my toes, the smell of brine. I listened to seagulls cry and thought about how hard I had worked to get in touch with my heart. Gazing ahead at the sand, I caught my breath. I hadn't even been looking for it, and there it was. All by itself. Waiting for me to take notice, to pick it up and treasure it. Flat and pale, cool and smooth, about the size of a quarter: a perfect little heart-shaped stone.

EMOTIONAL RECOVERIES, LIKE PHYSICAL ONES, come with plenty of setbacks. Home again in Franklin, I found myself caught in yet another tug of war. Burton kept insisting he wanted me to take off more time with him. To do so would mean cutting back on my job. I didn't know how much of my will to continue my magazine work was motivated by creative satisfaction, and how much was spurred by a stubborn fight for independence I had launched as a child.

Having worked on writing our story for several months, I had found the process more rewarding than any magazine assignment. I had once reveled in seeking out beautiful homes, composing proposals, styling photo shoots, and completing manuscripts. Lately these tasks seemed to interfere with work I felt called to do. Arranging strawberries on a plate or draping a towel just so over the edge of a bathtub contributed to pretty pictures. But they did not feel like my highest creative good.

Seeking a way to respect Burton's needs as well as my own, I had come up with a compromise. I would cut back on my magazine projects and continue to write our story while traveling more with my husband. Although I preferred working in a quiet office close to home, home wasn't home without Burton. And my laptop made it possible to work anywhere.

The problem was my ego. People would ask: What do you do? I liked claiming that I was a regional editor for national magazines. Any occasion might arise where I would need a handy credential to prove what I considered my worthiness. A class reunion. Our holiday letter. An encounter with an old neighbor. I enjoyed having a title to flaunt as other women did their killer tennis serve or their new Prada bag. I didn't want to reveal that I was trying to write a book. I had heard too many others make that claim. (That's great, I'd respond. Yeah, sure, I'd think.) Clearly, my ego was running the show.

I wanted to confront my dilemma. At the foot of our Jacuzzi bathtub, a small wooden tray held chunky white candles. In recent months, I had lit those candles and plunged into hot baths to pull myself through anxiety attacks. One night I decided to turn the foot of the tub into an altar.

I cut out two tiny slips of paper. On one, I printed the word Ego. On the other, Fear. I inserted the slips into a small silver heart-shaped box and placed the box on the wooden tray. Striking a match to the candles, I turned off the room lights and knelt down in front of my glowing altar. I asked God to help me let go of my fear of being a nobody, to help me see I was important, just by being me.

I opened the box, took out the slips of paper, and touched them to a candle flame. When the fire drew close to my fingers, I stood up and dropped the burning scraps into the sink. Turning on the lights, I picked up one charred sliver to throw it out. The piece marked Fear had turned black and flaky, and I tossed it into the wastebasket. When I picked up the other scrap, I noticed it had only partially burned. A different word remained, the word *go*.

Once I'd have called it coincidence, but I've come to believe the universe works in unpredictable ways. We just need to be open to them. I think the universe spoke to me that night. It told me to keep going. Go with my husband. Go with my story. Go with my heart.

*Chapter Fifteen*

# TOUGH TALKING

I ALWAYS IMAGINED WHEN I WAS A KID THAT ADULTS HAD SOME KIND OF INNER
TOOLBOX, FULL OF SHINY TOOLS: THE SAW OF DISCERNMENT, THE HAMMER OF
WISDOM, THE SANDPAPER OF PATIENCE. BUT THEN WHEN I GREW UP I FOUND
THAT LIFE HANDED YOU THESE RUSTY BENT OLD TOOLS—FRIENDSHIPS, PRAYER,
CONSCIENCE, HONESTY—AND SAID, DO THE BEST YOU CAN WITH THESE, THEY
WILL HAVE TO DO. AND MOSTLY, AGAINST ALL ODDS, THEY'RE ENOUGH.

*Traveling Mercies: Some Thoughts on Faith*, Anne Lamott

As far as I knew, Burton still owed the twenty thousand
dollars he had promised to cover some of his ex-mistress's mortgage payments. Since raising the subject in Jim's office, I hadn't
dared to bring it up again. My brain had declared the topic off
limits. Not to mention verboten, and unsafe at any speed.

In spring, six months after Burton first told me about the
expense, I found the courage to initiate a conversation. Interroga-
tion would be more precise. We sat at the pine lunch table of
our farmhouse, eating a pizza—cheese and pepperoni on Burton's
half, mushrooms and green peppers added to mine.

"Did we pay off Jody yet?" I asked.

"No. I meant to do it last week, but I forgot. And it's me, not we."

"I stand corrected."

"It's a stupid waste of money," he said.

"That, we agree on."

I wiped a bit of grease from my lips with a paper napkin. Using his fork, Burton removed a shred of green pepper from the slice of pizza on his plate and deposited it on mine.

"What will you do when Jody calls to thank you?"

"Don't worry about it. For twenty grand, I deserve a thank-you."

"Maybe when you send her the check, you should include a note. You could tell her you already know she's grateful and not to bother to call."

"Stop trying to control me."

"I'm not trying to control you. I'm just trying to stand up for my feelings."

Thinking about it later, I realized he had a point: I was trying to control him. But I was also standing up for my feelings. I felt proud of myself for that.

The Old Me would have been unable to resist taking a shot or two. Not one of your better investments, eh? You gotta pay to play. Or something equally snide. Instead, I pretended I was a grownup. I dropped the subject.

The matter of the mortgage payments did not, however, disappear from my mental radar screen. Two or three weeks later we were back home in Franklin, reading the paper one morning. Sufficient time had passed.

"Did you send Jody the check?" I asked, monitoring my subject pronoun.

"Yes."

"Did she call to thank you?"

"No."

"Did she write you a note?"

"No."

Burton is a master of the monosyllable when he feels so inclined.

"Did it make you wish you could see her again?"

"No. It's over between us. Don't worry about it."

And so I didn't worry about it. At least not most of the time.

To this day, I cannot decide if Jody's failure to call or write with thanks was the height of good manners or bad.

*Chapter Sixteen*

# UPS AND DOWNS

—⣿—

IT'S NO GOOD TRYING TO FOOL YOURSELF ABOUT LOVE.
YOU CAN'T FALL INTO IT LIKE A SOFT JOB, WITHOUT
DIRTYING UP YOUR HANDS. IT TAKES MUSCLE AND GUTS.
*Look Back in Anger*, John Osborne

BURTON AND I PULLED OUR GOLF CARTS over spongy ground toward the eleventh tee. It was one of those magical spring days when the sun shone with the promise of T-shirt months to come. But the most magical part of the day was that my husband and I were actually enjoying each other's company. It was a relief to no longer pretend things were okay when they weren't, as I had once tried to do.

I thought back to one of those days I'd spent pretending, a less happy day on the same Franklin Hills golf course, almost two years before. I had been stuck in that bleak period when I sensed something was wrong with my marriage but didn't know for sure, and for sure didn't want to know. During the week, Burton kept disappearing. I sat in my office following up with editors or phoning designers, trying not to worry about my husband's comings and goings. On weekends, I thought up activities Burton and I might enjoy together. On the weekend I remembered, I had talked him into a round of golf.

Although Burton had once encouraged me to play golf with him, for several months he had avoided playing with me. It's easier with the guys, he'd said. You start from the same tees, move along at the same pace. Nevertheless, I had continued to work at my game. On the afternoon I remembered, my swing happened to be cooperating. I'd been scoring bogies and double-bogies, though Burton had not played to his usual seven or eight handicap.

As we drove in our golf cart, I had chattered away, spouting encouragement. You'll do better on the back nine. It's only a game. Burton had remained morose, continuing to mishit his shots. He'd kept his eyes focused on the ball, the fairway, the rough, the scorecard. On anywhere but me.

The seventh hole was long and straight, edged with woods on either side. Burton faded his drive into a thick cluster of trees.

"This doesn't look like your hole," I'd chirped.

"The problem with women is they feel compelled to talk on the golf course," he'd snapped.

I would show him. I wouldn't speak for the rest of the damn round. And so I'd hit my woods, irons, and putts in silence, neither cheering nor complaining. On one hole, I topped a four iron, and my ball had skittered into the rough.

"You're not following through," Burton muttered.

I could not help myself. I shot back, "The problem with men is they feel compelled to correct women's swings on the golf course."

Since that unhappy round two years before, Burton and I had worked hard to bring our relationship back to health. Almost six months after our couples program, our marital condition had progressed from near terminal to near stable. Although I wasn't yet ordering the champagne for the party to renew our wedding vows, there was cause for hope.

Now we were back on the same golf course. "I was thinking

about how far we've come," I said. I reminded him of the remark he'd made about women golfers a couple of years before.

"Did I really say that?" he asked.

"Yup."

"I owe you an apology for a lot of reasons," he said.

THE TEMPTATION TO LAPSE BACK into old habits, attitudes, and reactions lurked around every psychic corner. No sooner would I think we were making progress than a setback occurred. A change of heart did not come easily, for either of us.

In those volatile months, I needed frequent reassurance. When Burton didn't show me affection for several days, my first instinct was to tell myself to buck up and cut the self-pity. But Little Suzy did not let me ignore my heart for long. Sooner or later (read: later) she forced me to pay attention to my feelings.

For a few days, Burton had been acting distant. I had tried not to notice. One morning, as he gathered his keys and his mobile phone to leave the house, I spoke up.

"I've been feeling unappreciated. I need you to tell me you love me more often."

He shoved some papers into his briefcase. "I've been saying it a lot," he grumbled.

"No you haven't. I keep track. I'm still feeling very vulnerable."

"You're exaggerating, Suzy. I say it all the time."

"I need to hear it more often. I owe it to Little Suzy to tell you how I feel."

He snapped his briefcase shut, grabbed the handle, yanked open the door to the garage, snarled, "I love you," and slammed the door behind him.

Jim had warned me not to shortchange myself in what I needed from Burton. My strained relationship with my father had conditioned me to accept behaviors I shouldn't, Jim advised. He told me to ask myself: Is this satisfying and enriching or does it just feel familiar? Burton's response that morning had felt neither satisfying nor enriching. As I dressed for work, pressure built in my chest.

When I arrived at the office, the message button flashed on my phone. I punched in my voice mail. In a very tender, very appreciative tone of voice, my husband said, "This message is for Little Suzy and Big Suzy from Little Burt and Big Burt. We want you to know we love you very much."

Soon after, I received an invitation to join a group visiting top private art collections in Manhattan. I was eager to attend, yet apprehensive again about leaving Burton on his own. Nonetheless, I told him I longed to go, and asked him to join me.

"I'd rather be up north," he said. "Go without me."

The Old Me might have tried to convince him to come. The New Me realized if we couldn't make it through one weekend apart, we wouldn't make it through the rest of our lives together. The New Me was in charge of this conversation.

"If it's okay with you, I'll go by myself," I said.

"No problem."

On Saturday our group visited high-rise apartments filled with artworks by Kelly, Rauschenberg, Bartlett, and Gober, of a quality I normally viewed only in museums or leading galleries. That night at about eleven, I returned to my hotel room, thrilled by all I'd seen. I called Burton to share my excitement with him. There was no answer at our home. Or on his cell phone. The light did not blink on my hotel phone. I called the operator anyway. No messages, Mrs. Farbman. Yes, she was sure. I pulled my cell phone out of my purse. Nothing on the message display panel.

There's probably a good explanation, I told myself.

At about eleven-thirty, I tried to phone Burton again. Still no response. My belly slam-dunked. Had he run back to her?

In my head, I replayed what Jim had told me earlier that week. "Burt's recent behavior shows he seems very committed to your marriage," he had said. I vowed to Little Suzy to honor my promise not to repeat what I'd done before—shame, blame, suppressing my instincts. The whole yucky routine. I reminded myself I could not control Burton's activities and that whatever happened, I could handle it. I lay down in bed, closed my eyes, and prayed. Miracle of miracles, I fell asleep.

At twelve fifteen, a ring awakened me. Burton called from his car, sounding concerned. "I'm sorry I couldn't reach you sooner," he said. "I was driving through a no-service zone. I hope you didn't worry. I love you. Go back to sleep."

I did just that. I drifted back to sleep, happy Burton had stayed out of trouble, and grateful I had handled the situation with grace.

A SIGNIFICANT BIRTHDAY GETS OUR ATTENTION. It encourages us to look at where we've been and where we're going. On May 6, 1999, six months after our couples program, I turned fifty-five. In my early fifties, with my marriage foundering, I had dreaded this approaching milestone. It flashed like a neon sign on the horizon of my future, advertising my advancing years and my receding prospects for true love. Now that I had started to feel better about myself, now that there seemed to be a chance I might someday attend Andy's wedding on his father's arm after all, the milestone didn't seem quite so terrifying. But something about Burton's behavior troubled me.

My girlfriend Mary Lou threw a cocktail party in my honor. Mary Lou's small but chic apartment on Chicago's near north side combined old pine cabinets with white overstuffed sofas, antique checkerboards, and baskets of white begonias. Drinks there and dinner out with a few close friends and family members were just what I wanted, all I could handle in my still fragile state of mind.

My girlfriend Sandy composed an alphabet of compliments, starting with Amazing and ending with Zillions of hugs. Brenda read a thoughtful note on a card featuring a bear she had photographed at the South Pole. David, Andy, and Amy all spoke loving words. Burton said something sweet, but I had a sense he was holding back.

After the toasts, I lifted my champagne flute. "You all know this hasn't been an easy year for Burton and me," I said, wiping my eyes with a cocktail napkin. "Your support has helped us through some very tough times. Some of the most important people in my world are here in this room tonight. Having you in my life makes the second half of my fifties feel like a safer place."

The next morning Burton and I piled our bags into the back seat of the truck, next to his leather saddle. I had agreed to accompany my husband to Nevada in his dark green, four-door Ford 350 dualie, with a dual rear wheel section that bulged like a boxer's biceps.

Heading west from Illinois, we turned north on Highway 218 in northern Iowa. Rain pelted the windshield. Burton sat behind the wheel, staring at the road, hardly speaking. "Crappy weather." "Where do I turn?" I sat beside him, trying to concentrate on the maps and guidebooks surrounding me. We had driven for a few hours when the pressure in my chest boiled over.

I realized I had fallen back into my old habit of trying to talk myself out of my feelings. For a few days leading up to my birthday, I had felt neglected again. Rather than speak about it to Burton, I had told myself: Give it time. Time had not done the trick. Burton hadn't warmed up in spite of the fact that we were now doing exactly what he wanted to do, gallivanting across country on his fantasy outing.

Barely holding back tears, I said, "Lately, I haven't felt as though you appreciate me."

"Lately I haven't appreciated you," he snarled. "Reading that damn book every night pisses me off."

For the past three weeks, I had insisted we spend fifteen minutes each night reading out loud. We had been studying Gay and Kathlyn Hendricks' *Conscious Loving: The Journey to Co-Commitment.* The Hendrickses recommended a relationship based on honesty, individual development, having fun together, and recognizing that our attitude determines our reality. According to the book, "If either person is being less than 100 percent, the ground is ripe for power struggles."

Our relationship had not been 100 percent on either side. Obviously, not on Burton's. Screwing other women was as low as you could get on the commitment scale. But I couldn't claim 100 percent either. There were plenty of times I didn't pay attention when Burton spoke, times I'd interrupt him or criticize him to my girlfriends or make plans and wait to the last second to tell him someone he disliked was involved.

I hoped the Hendrickses might provide us with a new model for our relationship. So far, my hopes had not been met. Burton had declined to take his turn reading. While I read to him, he stared at the ceiling, sighed with impatience, or dozed off.

Burton took his eyes off the road and glared at me. "I resent you for being so programmed and forcing me to be so programmed," he fumed. "If I haven't seemed affectionate, it's because I haven't felt affectionate. The fact is, I haven't felt intimate toward you for a while."

I felt as though he had stomped on my heart. I had put my life on hold to share his fantasy with him and to bring us closer together. Yet he didn't feel intimate toward me? Tears sprang to my eyes; I squeezed them shut. Silently, I asked God to let me know if it was time to move on. When I opened my eyes, the windshield wipers flipped back and forth, still chasing the rain.

"If that's how you feel," I whispered, "what am I doing here?"

"The whole point of what we've been through is to be able to talk honestly," Burton said. "Don't jump to conclusions."

At our couples program, we had viewed a videotape on sexuality. A psychologist had suggested we could become more aroused by thinking about our genitals. The advice had given me something to focus on other than where my lover's organ had been. When Burton first confessed to his betrayals, I didn't know how I could ever make love with him again. Like wasps at a picnic, troubling thoughts swarmed through my head at bedtime. Did Jody practice exotic techniques? Did Burton feel different inside her? Did she have any sexually transmittable disease? With time such thoughts had subsided. I knew that physical intimacy contributed to our emotional healing.

Now, as we drove without speaking, past the town of Waterloo, past stubbly cornfields and old barns, I felt crushed. I had gone through so much to make love with him again.

I sighed. "I've always been attracted to you. I still am."

Burton took his eyes off the road and looked at me. "It's strange," he said. "After telling you what was bothering me, I've started to feel better."

The crazy thing is that the minute he started to feel better, so did I. The rain had subsided. A streak of blue sliced through the clouds overhead. We had reached the small town of Nashua. An old wood suspension bridge spanned the mud-colored Cedar River. Houses hugged the bank on both sides. Burton slowed down and pointed to the bridge. "How about a walk?"

We parked near a dark brick, Prairie-style home with projecting flat roofs. "That looks like a Frank Lloyd Wright," Burton said. I agreed. We both admired the work of the legendary architect, who had also designed the small, striking house in Bloomfield Hills, Michigan, where my sister's husband grew up. A neighbor working in his yard confirmed our guess. Discovering an unexpected architectural gem seemed a good sign. I'm a sucker for good signs.

The rickety bridge swayed as we crossed it, stepping carefully on each shaky board. On the far bank, Burton stopped, gave me a shy smile, and took me in his arms.

"I take back what I said about not feeling intimate," he murmured. And he kissed me. Ever so gently. I'd go so far as to say: intimately.

ON OUR TRIP WEST, WE WERE TYPICAL TOURISTS. We visited the Jolly Green Giant in Blue Earth, Minnesota. Burton, at six feet tall, reached the top of the Giant's boots. We admired the Corn Palace in Mitchell, South Dakota, a building dolled-up with domes, towers, and turrets and paved with murals made from corn, grains, and grasses. We played poker with locals in Deadwood, South Dakota, at the saloon where Wild Bill Hickok was shot, and gazed at the heroic faces of Mt. Rushmore. We even co-wrote a trip song and sang it for Andy, who joined us in Eureka, Nevada.

In Eureka, we also met up with Mike, Burton's cowboy friend from Arizona. He drove us out to a mountain range where, as Burton snapped photos, forty wild horses thundered across the road within a hundred yards of our truck. Later that night, I did something I'd never done before. I presented my husband with an invitation. On the back of a postcard picturing a horse, I penned in a message: *Hot to trot? You could get lucky tonight.*

The trip I first viewed as a concession to my husband reminded us of how much we enjoyed each other's company. Once again that serene state wouldn't last for long.

*Chapter Seventeen*

# Opening Up

———— ∞∞∞ ————

IF I SEEK STABILITY IN SAMENESS, I RUN THE RISK OF FORCING
MYSELF AND THOSE AROUND ME TO CONFORM TO SOMETHING
WE NO LONGER ARE—TO BE WHAT WE WERE YESTERDAY.

*Forgiving and Moving On*, Tian Dayton, Ph.D.

Self-help books present anonymous case studies of couples who make it back from marital disaster. They don't enumerate the twists and turns along the way. Living through the real thing means struggling day by day, with anguish or relief, highs or lows, at every point. Progress comes in small steps, and many go backward before they go forward. Every day I fought for patience. Every day I undertook the challenge of trying to be honest with my spouse while not forcing his reaction.

It should have been enough already. Enough fighting. Enough making up. Enough learning to express our own needs and feelings and to honor each other's. But our hearts heal at their own rate. That rate has nothing to do with the Gregorian calendar.

Back in Michigan, a chill settled over our relationship again. I remained downstate to work on some magazine assignments, while Burton flew up north. One afternoon we spoke long distance.

"I don't want to be the richest corpse in the cemetery," Burton said. His father had died at forty-seven, so Burton had been surprised to make it to fifty. He wanted to enjoy whatever time he had left. "I don't care if my friends are still working their butts off. I didn't get this far by following the crowd."

I saw his point. If he continued to work and suffered a heart attack from stress, I'd regret having urged him to keep going. But the prospect of retiring at fifty-five made me feel like a mare put out to pasture too soon. I had come up with a compromise. I'd begun training a freelance writer to take over my job downstate. I intended to continue as a regional editor in northern Michigan, a place Burton and I both loved. On the phone, I reminded Burton of my plan, explained I needed time to finish some assignments in Detroit.

"My plan is to be up north all summer," Burton snapped. "You do whatever you want."

The Old Me would have struck back: I just schlepped across the country with you, Burton. I'm doing my best to work things out. You could try to be nice about it. But the New Me took charge. "Okay," I said, in the most pleasant tone I could manage. "I'll talk to you later." And I gently placed the receiver back on the cradle.

It had taken me more than thirty years to learn that when my husband acted like a jerk, I needed to let him act like a jerk. What you resist persists—a line from one of my self-help books. I had been amazed to discover that what I did not resist often tended to correct itself. Developing the patience to wait for such a correction, however, was as challenging as developing a reliable three-wood shot.

A few uncomfortable minutes later, Burton called back. "I'm sorry I sounded so mean," he said. "If you need to be home, don't worry about it. Come and go whenever you have to."

Honest to goodness.

"IS YOUR MARRIAGE MEETING your needs?" Jim asked.

I paused, feeling foolish that my needs weren't clear to me. "I guess my needs would include having fun and receiving affection," I ventured. "My marriage is meeting my need for fun at about seventy percent. For affection, about fifty percent."

Jim lifted an eyebrow. "What about your need for fidelity?"

I was embarrassed by my oversight. I shrugged. "I figured that goes without saying."

"Don't assume Burt realizes your need for fidelity," Jim cautioned. "If that's an important need, make it clear. Make it a conscious part of the relationship."

That night in bed I shared the conversation with Burton. I hesitated to ask, but forced myself. "What about your needs?"

"My needs aren't being met," he growled. "I need to be away from the office. When I'm there, I feel the stress building up. When I stay in town and don't go to the office, I feel guilty. I want to travel. I want to play. I want someone to play with."

We had come so far, yet these disagreements still disturbed me. I drew a breath. "I hear you say you want more time off, and you want me with you," I said. Mirroring back his words gave me something to say when I was too unnerved to come up with anything better. "I hope we can find some middle ground."

"Hmmph," Burton said. He turned his back to me and went to sleep.

*Not feeling very loved or nurtured,* I wrote in my journal. *Am I avoiding facing the death of my marriage? Is B's remoteness something he can't help or something he uses to control me? Would being alone ultimately be kinder to my self-esteem? How can I continue to love someone who hurts me so?*

ONE SUMMER AFTERNOON UP NORTH, Burton came in for lunch after a horseback ride. We munched on tuna sandwiches at our farmhouse.

"I heard somewhere that most divorced couples end up as good friends," Burton said. "Once they get over their anger, they realize they still have a lot in common."

I shook my head. "Most divorced people I know can barely stand to be in the same room. But things might be different for us. We'll know we did everything we could to make this marriage work. If we end up divorcing, it will be because our needs were so different, and I couldn't take care of my needs and make you happy, too."

Burton squinted at me, chewing the last bite of his sandwich. "It's not your job to make me happy. It's my job to make me happy." He shoved back his chair, stood up, and strode out of the house.

About fifteen minutes later, he returned. "I went for a walk," he said. "I didn't like the way our conversation was going. I realized I don't want to get divorced. Maybe instead of worrying about not being together, we should concentrate on having a really good time when we are together."

Having prayed intently as I went to sleep that night, I awoke the next morning dreaming of being hugged by an affectionate little girl, about five years old. I sensed she was my younger inner child. Not the sadder but wiser eleven-year-old with whom I connected in my writings. Rather, the spunky little me who performed at my grand-parents' dinner parties. The gutsy little me who entertained guests with fingers climbing to "The Inky Dinky Spider." She was the me who delighted in the applause of her dignified, grown-up audience. Me, the childhood star.

I turned over in bed and kissed the soft pink part of Burton's cheek, above the stubble. I snuggled against his chest the way I used to before his morning disappearing acts began.

"Why don't we pick one day and try to be as romantic as we can?" I said. "We'll see if we still know how."

"Good idea."

Burton gazed at the ceiling fan whirling overhead.

"What are you thinking?" I asked.

"About not being so passive."

Minutes later, Burton left the farmhouse, heading to the

Belvedere Golf Course for an early tee time. Still upstairs, I smelled the aroma of hazelnut coffee. When I walked downstairs, a surprise waited on the kitchen table. Burton had picked a bunch of yellow flowers and put them in a vase. Although he normally set a table only under duress and generally forgot that the spoon goes on the right, he had set the table for me. There was a place mat, a napkin, a coffee cup, a bowl of Raisin Bran, and a spoon on the left. Against the vase of flowers, Burton had propped an old snapshot of his parents. Below the photo lay a handwritten note: "From my mother and father and—most of all—me, thanks for being you."

PEOPLE WITH A.D.D. OFTEN EXHIBIT unpredictable, erratic behavior. Knowing this did not make Burton's mood swings any easier to deal with. Soon Burton turned cold and unresponsive again, and I found myself fighting off discouragement for the umpteenth time. When I realized I was stuffing down my feelings once more, I forced myself to pay attention. Tired as I was of bringing up the subject, on this summer morning I brought up the subject.

"I'm feeling sad," I said to Burton. "I need you to show me you appreciate me."

He scowled. "I can't think about you every damn minute of the day."

"I don't need every minute. Just a few times."

"What's a few times?"

"Maybe once every four hours."

His eyebrows drew together the way they do when he computes numbers. "Once every four hours. That's six times a day. I guess I could handle that." He gave me a hug and left for the golf course.

When I trotted downstairs, another note waited on the kitchen table. "Good morning again, my little sweet. You are special to me everyday. There are just some days I don't show it. Today is a good day to show it." On the bottom of the page, he had drawn two smiley faces.

I THINK MANY WOMEN RESIST INTIMACY just as we long for it. We fear it will cost us our independence. We worry it will smother us. Minutes later, driving to the golf course, I sensed a strange conflict inside. I was touched by Burton's sweetness, yet I felt myself back away. I had yearned to be treated lovingly, worked hard for it. Still, I hesitated. I had learned to distance myself from men as a child, siding with my mother against my father, trying in my ineffective way to protect her. But I wasn't a child any longer. I was a grown woman, working to be the person I wanted to be—loving and accepting, not critical and judgmental. Or ambivalent.

I didn't understand my response. Was I afraid to trust Burton's behavior? Afraid he might withdraw his affections and hurt me again? Did I worry that by becoming too close to my husband, I might lose myself? I pulled into the Belvedere parking lot, turned off the ignition, and sat quietly, asking God to help me open my heart to love.

Soon after, my girlfriend Lynne and I approached our drives on the fairway of the first hole. We waved to Burton's foursome, including Lynne's husband, Michael, a near-scratch golfer, on the adjoining fairway. My ball sat up on the turf. I took out my five wood—a safer bet than my three wood—and hit my second shot straight down the fairway almost one hundred and thirty yards. As I put the club back in my bag, a caddy with short blond hair and ruddy cheeks drove up in a golf cart. He handed me a scorecard with my name scrawled on the front.

Inside the scorecard, Burton had written a note with the blue marking pen he used to place identifying dots on his golf balls: "In case it is four hours since the last time I said the L word, this is for you." His caddy handed me a golf ball and drove away. On the back of the ball, with the same marking pen, Burton had drawn in XO. That ball remains in my locker, unused to this day. I wouldn't risk losing it in a woods or pond. Not with my three wood. Or any other club.

Spotting Burton again on the eleventh green, I pulled up my golf cart, disturbing Michael, who missed his putt and glared at me.

Nonetheless, I approached Burton's caddy, whose face broke into a grin. I took his hand and poured several peanuts onto his open palm. "Give these to my husband," I said. "Tell him this is how I feel about him."

*Chapter Eighteen*

# THE LAST TO KNOW

——⦵⦵⦵——

AFTER A WHILE YOU LEARN . . .
THAT KISSES AREN'T CONTRACTS
AND PRESENTS AREN'T PROMISES
AND YOU BEGIN TO ACCEPT YOUR DEFEATS
WITH YOUR HEAD UP AND YOUR EYES OPEN
WITH THE GRACE OF A WOMAN
NOT THE GRIEF OF A CHILD.
*After a While*, Veronica A. Shoffstall

U NLESS WE'RE A CELEBRITY HOUNDED by paparazzi, we don't always know when we become the topic du jour. No checkout-counter racks confirmed that my husband had been running around. His behavior did not interest *Entertainment Tonight*. I didn't begin to hear rumors about Burton's cheating until months after it had stopped. For this I am grateful.

That night at Onsite after Burton broke up with Jody on his cell phone, he repeated what he'd told her: we had agreed to try to reconcile.

"What did she say?" I'd asked.

"She said she was happy for me."

"Happy?"

"Happy that I had made a decision."

I had fought off the urge to roll my eyes. There is a lovely Yiddish word, *rachmones*, which translates as compassion, a highly valued trait in the Jewish tradition. Although rachmones was a trait to which I aspired, I did not think it applied in the case of someone who stole someone else's husband. Especially my own.

"Jody asked if I had told you her name," Burton had said. "I said yes. If I was going to make our marriage work, I needed to be honest. She asked you to do her a favor—not mention her name to anyone. She said she liked to keep her business private."

Tell her I'd like to keep my husband private, I thought.

"She doesn't have to worry," I said. "I don't want to advertise for her."

And so, although I confided to close girlfriends that Burton had had an affair, I did not say with whom. For many weeks, I never uttered Jody's name outside of Jim's office. My best friends did not ask who she was. They politely called her "Burt's ex-mistress." Over time, I came to understand their tact. They didn't need to ask Jody's name. They knew it.

ONE MORNING ABOUT FIVE MONTHS AFTER Burton broke off the affair, I talked to a dear friend on the phone. As I put on my makeup, I said, "I don't think Burton has cheated on me since he promised he wouldn't. But I keep worrying about the future."

"She does have a reputation for hanging on," my friend said.

I dropped my mascara brush into the sink.

"She?" I asked. "Who are you talking about?"

In a voice as confidential as a Swiss bank account: "Jody."

I blinked a black smudge onto my lower lid.

"I have never mentioned her name," I said. "Do you think many people know who she is?"

"Your good friends do."

I PLAYED GOLF WITH JULIE a couple of months later. As I drove our cart toward the eleventh tee, she turned to me and asked, "Is South Lyon finished?"

I swerved over the edge of a bed of petunias. "I hope so," I said, parking the cart by the forward tee. "I think so," I said, pulling my driver out of my bag. I walked to the red markers, teed up my ball, and took a practice swing. I turned to look at Julie. "Let me put it this way: if she's still in, I'm out."

I flexed my knees, dropped my hands slightly, swept the club back, hit the ball straight down the middle, and caught the slope for an extra ten yards. I loved my Big Bertha Hawkeye.

"Nice drive," Julie said.

I admired the shot myself. I admired my brave words even more. I hoped I meant them.


HAVING PROMISED NOT TO MENTION JODY'S NAME, I remained reluctant to do so. I discussed her only with my closest friends, like Barbara, who phoned a few weeks later.

"My mother left a message on my answering machine demanding that I call her right away," Barbara said. "When I got back to her, she was frantic. She said: 'Everyone in the building is gossiping about Burt Farbman and Jody Sommers. Say it isn't true!' I told her, 'Take it easy, Mother. It's old news. Suzy and Burt have worked things out.'"

I shook my head. "Very interesting," I said. "If word has gotten around the senior circuit, our little scandal must be common knowledge."

There was a time when any of these conversations would have chopped a divot from my heart. Keeping the fairway of our lives green and free of weeds had once seemed so important. As time passed, I realized that our being the subject of gossip hardly mattered anymore. What mattered was that Burton and I were making progress—uneven, but still progress. Our marriage was growing stronger. And so was I.

AFTER FIRST COMING TO GRIPS with my husband's betrayals, I wanted nothing more than to blot his treachery from my mind. If there had been a pill to provide instant amnesia, I'd have gulped it down, with or without water.

Nobody came up with such a remedy. The experts recommended facing, not running from, the pain. And so I forced myself to feel my feelings and share them with Burton. I found that honest conversation helped us to better understand why our marriage fell apart. I hoped it made history less likely to repeat itself.

At one point, I remember making some uncharitable reference to Burton's ex-mistress. "If you knew Jody under different circumstances, you'd like her," he'd said. "I'll bet you'd even be friends."

"I'm evolving spiritually, but I'm not that evolved," I replied.

"You should be mad at me. Not at her."

"I know that," I said. "You were the one who promised to love, honor, and be faithful. She was only looking out for herself. I should feel sorry for her for getting into dead-end relationships. I know I should be more compassionate. But I still hate her."

"If it hadn't been Jody, it would have been someone else. I was completely out of touch with my feelings."

FOR SEVERAL MONTHS, I WROTE about our experience mostly to help myself understand it. I did not show Burton what I was writing. I wanted to be as honest as I could, and free of his influence. Nor did Burton urge me to share my prose with him. Slowly, I started to believe our story might give hope to some other despairing wife. I began to want to reach her.

Ten months after our couples program, eight since I'd begun writing, I sat across from astrologist Susie Cox. My chart lay on the desk of her office at the Canyon Ranch Spa in Tucson, Arizona. She looked at the paper, frowned, and shook her head. "You've been through a difficult time," she said.

She pointed to wedges within a circle. "Your professional life and your health look fine," she said. I knocked on my head. "The rest of your houses look fine, too. Except for this one." She tapped a pie-shaped section marked with squiggly lines. "This house describes your relationships with men. You have trouble trusting them, and not just in romance. You probably had problems with your father, too."

"My relationship with my father was strained," I said. "My husband broke off an affair a few months ago. I've been working to get over how he hurt me. I may write a book about it."

She nodded. "A lot of people need to hear what you have to say."

Susie Cox's advice added to my dilemma. While I believed our story might help others, healing my marriage mattered deeply to me. Considering how Burton guarded his privacy, I could not imagine his consenting to a public revelation of our problems.

I was sharing a casita with my toned and athletic girlfriend Sandy. Her typical Canyon Ranch schedule included a twenty-mile bike ride up a mountain followed by one hundred laps in the swimming pool. My activities consisted mostly of beginner hikes and stretch classes. This probably accounted for the fact that Sandy's tummy and thighs were firmer than mine. I tried not to notice.

Burton had flown to Denmark on a shooting expedition with friends. After my spa activities, I hurried back to our room to check the message light on our telephone. Mostly, it blinked for Sandy. Her boyfriend, Charley, had left several tender messages. He missed her; he hoped she was having fun; she deserved to get away. Burton had left me few messages, and those he did leave were brusque. Catch you later. Call me back.

Once when we spoke, Burton suggested he might change the colonoscopy appointment he had scheduled for the week ahead. Since I had intended to drive him, I asked him to let me know so I could make other plans.

"If you're so busy, forget it," he snapped. "I'll find someone else to take me."

I had hung up feeling as though he'd run my heart through a paper shredder.

Soon after talking to Susie Cox, I reached Burton on the phone. "I met with an astrologer," I said. "She predicted a lot of people will want to read our story."

"Great," he said. His voice said otherwise. "Do what you have to do. I'll react accordingly."

Through thousands of miles of slender fiber optic cable, I could feel the chill. He was shutting me out again.

To SHAKE OFF THE TENSION, the next day I took a class in African dancing. A striking black woman with wild hair wrapped in kente cloth led several of us to the pulsing beat of live drummers. We kicked our legs and swung our arms with abandon. After, we thanked our musicians by kneeling down and pounding our hands on the floor.

Despite the energy I had released, I kept thinking about how curt Burton had been. I wanted to cry, but tears wouldn't come. Back in our room, I picked up a book of essays by Iyanla Vanzant. "When you surrender, give up the fear thoughts, and give up the control of a situation, you open the way for a miracle." I read the sentence again and again.

Soon after, I sat waiting in the lounge. Sandy had suggested that a cranio-sacral massage might help realign my energy. As I waited for some much-needed realignment, I closed my eyes. I prayed for help in surrendering my fears—fears of further upsetting Burton if I persisted in wanting to share our story, fears of letting myself down if I didn't.

"Suzy Farbman." A gentle voice brought me back. A woman in a pink uniform introduced herself as Sarah and led me into a small room. I hung up my robe and lay down under a bed sheet. Sarah ran her hands lightly over the sheet, stopping at my pelvis. "I sense a lot of blocked energy in your reproductive organs," she said. "You don't feel very nurtured or loved."

She knew. I hadn't mentioned a word about my problems, but she knew. My body had given me away. Suddenly, tears I could not cry earlier spilled from my eyes. Tears of grief for how my husband had hurt me. Tears of gratitude for the help I had received in putting my heart back together. And tears of understanding. I understood that however hard I tried, I could not control Burton's feelings. I had to let go.

"Cry if you need to," Sarah said in a tone as soft as her touch. "Tears help eliminate toxins."

Sarah stroked and I sobbed through the entire treatment. After, Sarah led me to a small, private room with two beds. "Rest here as long as you want," she said.

I didn't need to stay for long. I felt better than I had in days.

I FELL ASLEEP THAT NIGHT MARVELING at the changes I'd made. A message from Frida Kahlo, a dead person, had inspired me to throw out a rewarding and lucrative career for the bizarre notion of writing a book exposing my husband's and my flaws. I'd gone from *Vogue* magazine to affirmations. And now astrology. African dancing. Energy realignment. I was living beyond the safe, trimmed hedges that ringed the comfort zone of my former life. I felt a little strange. But vibrant. Even brave.

About midnight, a loud burst of noise awoke us. The sky boomed and flashed in a violent thunderstorm. Sandy and I sat up in our beds, admiring the spectacle. When the drama subsided, the heavens grew as still as a baby dozing off after a tantrum.

I peered toward Sandy through the darkened room. "I had the strangest feeling that thunderstorm was meant for me," I said. "The universe sent me a message. I shouldn't run and hide. I should make my own thunder and lightning and proclaim my truth. Does that sound crazy?"

"Not at all," she said.

Some of our best ideas are the craziest. When we get them, there will be plenty of people to tell us we're crazy. I was glad Sandy wasn't one of them.

"I need to thank the universe," I said.

I climbed out of bed, dropped to my knees, and pounded my hands on the floor.

*Chapter Nineteen*

# STARTING OVER

———∞∞∞———

I DON'T WANT TO START ALL OVER AGAIN
WITH SOME OTHER JERK. I LIKE THE JERK I'VE GOT.
Kathie Lee Gifford, *20/20*

B<small>URTON AND</small> I <small>SAT BY THE LAKE</small> where we'd held our twenty-fifth anniversary sing-along, seven and one-half years before. From a CD player in the nearby log cabin, Willie Nelson wailed "Mama Don't Let Your Babies Grow Up to Be Cowboys." Across the lake, maple trees had started to blush, thinking about the future. I was thinking about the future, too. Burton and I had talked a lot about what had happened between us, and I had begun to believe we had a future again.

Burton closed his eyes, stretched out his legs, and leaned back against the log swing. "I am so relaxed," he said. "It feels great to settle down after years of stressing out about business."

"And about a secret life."

He laughed. "You had to get that in."

I touched my index finger to my tongue and pressed it to the air with a hiss.

"A point for you," he conceded.

We swung back and forth, enjoying the sun on our faces, a luxury I allowed myself only in late afternoons. It felt good to be able to talk honestly to my husband. I had monitored my words for so long.

"Did I tell you about Shirley Kramer?" I asked.

"What about her?"

"She called Barb the other day, demanding to know if you were having an affair with Jody. The rumor had spread all over her building. Barb told her we had worked things out. At least we gave our senior citizens something other than their blood pressure to talk about."

Burton's eyebrows pinched together. He took my hands in his. "I am so sorry for what I've put you through."

He stood up and ambled along the shoreline. Picking up a smooth round stone, he threw it, side-hand, into the water. It jumped a dozen times before settling below the surface. Burton had taught himself to skip stones as a little boy at his family cottage on Lake Erie in Canada. He lived there during summers, with his mother and sisters. His father, a practicing doctor, showed up on weekends. Burton could make a stone leap and dance and defy gravity for a few magical seconds.

I walked up to him and he handed me a stone. I tried to imitate his flick of the wrist. My stone sank. He tossed another. I counted seven skips.

We strolled into a sandy area overgrown with dark green reeds and carved with hundreds of deer hoofprints. Burton pointed out how marks left in the sand by the buck bore an extra depression in back.

"Rutting season lasts about two weeks," he said. "Dozens of does hide in the woods. The buck rubs his antlers on tree trunks to mark his territory and claim the females in it. If another buck comes after one of his does, he'll fight him to the death. The male will risk his life for sex."

Burton flashed me a smile. "That's one for me," he said.

I WAS HAPPY TO BE ABLE TO LAUGH about our problems with my husband. But something still grated, like a grain of sand in my shoe. When we sat back down on the swing, I asked, "Do you know what bothers me?"

"What?"

"You won. You got to go as far as you wanted. When the kids were grown and it was my turn, you wouldn't support me. You found someone else. I wasn't willing to lose you. I gave up a job I loved to spend more time with you."

"You gave up your magazine job not only to spend time with me," he said. "You gave it up because writing about us became more important to you than writing about houses."

I had intended to continue my magazine work in northern Michigan. Yet when I should have been out scouting for prospects, I had found myself at home, bent over my laptop, trying to understand what had happened with us. It was true that writing about our experience had come to interest me more than writing about houses. I believed I had found a story I was meant to tell. At the moment, however, I did not give Burton the satisfaction of saying so.

"My career was never just my career," he continued. "It was always *our* career. Years ago you chose to put my work ahead of yours. You backed me up one hundred percent. Whether it was organizing an event or entertaining clients or figuring out which lawyer to hire, I could always count on you. We built the company and our reputation together. It's not that *I* won. *We* won."

I ran my finger back and forth over a groove in the arm of the log swing. "Okay," I said. "We won. But I wasn't ready to stop. You burned out; I didn't. I helped you to reach your goals. I had goals, too."

"I know I let you down. After so many years of hard work, I

needed to take care of me. When you weren't around for me anymore, I found someone who was. What I did wasn't fair. It was cold and dishonest and selfish. It took a crisis to shake us up. I'm just thankful we were strong enough to get through it."

If Burton weren't a salesman, he wouldn't have sold me on marrying him in the first place—a man with a poor education and seemingly dim prospects, a man who lost his job the day before my bridal shower. He's a convincing salesman because he believes in what he says. And because he can be maddeningly logical.

A fact of life: raising children takes time. Unless they have Mary Poppins for a mother-in-law, one or both parents must sacrifice some of their own professional ambitions to carve out that time. When I got pregnant, Burton and I agreed his earning potential in real estate surpassed mine in journalism. We opted for the money. His became the primary career in our family. Most women of my generation made similar sacrifices, although the best-adjusted among us may not have considered them sacrifices.

Some mothers were smart enough to realize up front what it took me years of parenting to understand: those times I resented the intrusion of my children, I got it wrong. Now I look back on the meetings or parties I missed because one of our boys was home sick or had a role in a school play, and I realize those events weren't as important as they seemed. By attending the baseball games and science fairs, even if I'd rather have been working on an article or making cocktail conversation with grown-ups, I was investing in the future. I was putting time and attention into an account that would reap joyful dividends as our children grew into loving, independent young men.

And yet Burton betrayed me. There are days when I still smolder over the injustice. When I drive through Detroit and witness boarded-up houses and barred doors, when I travel to Chicago or New York—cities where I gave up chances to live—and catch my breath over the skylines and busy streets, when someone my age wins a Pulitzer or gives a commencement speech, I wonder what else might have been. We make our choices and we live with them. We can't change what has happened; we can only change how we look at it. We can dwell on blame and regret. Or choose to forgive, learn, and move on.

Talking about what bothers us aids the process of forgiving. That night, voicing what had troubled me and hearing Burton's take on the subject didn't change the past. But it opened up my heart again.

A red canoe waited at the edge of the lake. Burton put in his tackle box, sat in the stern and paddled. I relaxed in the bottom of the bow, facing him, trailing my fingers in the warm water. Sun slipping below the trees turned the sky into a luminous painting of shifting pinks and golds.

Burton hooked a lure to the end of his monofilament line. After several casts, his rod dipped. "I've got one," he said. "It's a big one." He began turning the reel, drawing the line in and letting it play out with the patience and skill of a seasoned fisherman. As his catch neared the boat, he lifted it into the air. Two silvery bass clung to the same lure.

"Look at that!" Burton exclaimed. "I have never seen two fish on one lure."

"Two-on-one. Your ultimate fantasy," I said.

We both laughed.

Burton removed the fish from the hook as gently as I'd seen him extract splinters from our boys' fingers when they were little. With a flip of their tails, his catch darted off. A hawk swooped and soared above us, sky-pink showing through the tips of its wings. Birds chattered. Water glistened. Sun warmed our shoulders.

"Heaven can't be any better than this," Burton said as he cast his line out again.

I nodded. "The angels are up there right now, looking down and taking notes."

LARGE URNS SPILLED OVER with pale purple delphiniums, hydrangeas, and roses. Politicians, celebrities, and some Fortune 500 mainstays sprinkled the bejeweled crowd. Back downstate, we were attending the wedding of a daughter of our old friends Bob and Susu at the Ritz-Carlton Hotel in Dearborn. I sat next to Burton in my gold aisle seat, waiting for the ceremony to begin. Violins played. In front, gathered beneath the chupah—the canopy under which the bride and groom would exchange their vows—were four rabbis and a cantor. "A rafter of rabbis," Burton murmured. "A quintet of clergy," I said.

I gazed at the chupah, admiring the simplicity of ivy vines spiraling around white birch branches. "I can't help thinking about something," I said.

"That all these people are whispering about us?"

"No. I was thinking how I used to adore weddings. They were a chance to renew our love."

Burton gave me a sad smile. He took my hand in his.

Blonde and petite, Cathy glided down the aisle in a white strapless gown with pale lavender stripes. She and Charles beamed at each other as they repeated their vows.

At the end of the ceremony, the rabbi placed a glass, wrapped in a napkin, on the floor. "Cathy and Charles," he said, "as you begin your lives together tonight, your marriage is whole and intact. You stand here before God with pure love in your eyes.

"Life will deal you trouble and heartache. The glass that represents your perfect marriage today may shatter into a thousand pieces tomorrow. With enough love and caring, you will survive the sorrows. You will never put the glass back together the way it was. But you may create something new from all those pieces. What you create may be more beautiful than anything you would have known if the glass hadn't broken in the first place."

Charles stomped. Guests shouted "mazel tov!" I blinked back tears.

During dinner, the band struck up "I Will Survive." "My theme song," I said. "Let's dance."

We squeezed onto the crowded parquet wood floor and performed the Social, a simple but showy routine we had mastered years before. We slowed down for the following number, a romantic ballad.

"There's your friend," Burton muttered.

I opened my eyes to see divorce lawyer Alan Felstein dancing with his wife, Sheila. Although I had never officially met with Alan, knowing he was around had made me feel a little less helpless.

"Do you know why I'm glad we're getting along so well?" Burton asked.

"Why?"

"So I don't have to be nice to Alan Felstein."

Later, the photographer came up to our table. As guests lined up behind us, I whispered to Burton, "It would be good for my image if you'd pose for the picture French-kissing my ear."

He laughed. "It wouldn't be good for *my* image," he said. But he did put his arm around me.

The next morning, Burton arose early to fly up north for the day. He woke me before he left.

"You were a great date last night," I said. "I think I like weddings again."

He leaned down to kiss my eyelids, my nose, and my lips, and he said, "I think I like you again."

*Chapter Twenty*

# A NEW MARRIAGE

———— ✦✦✦ ————

THERE IS SOMETHING ABOUT TWO PEOPLE HAVING MOVED
THROUGH THE STAGES OF LIFE TOGETHER THAT SPIRITUALLY
FERTILIZES THE GARDEN THEY SHARE. THERE IS AN INEFFABLE DEPTH
TO HAVING WALKED THE WALK WITH SOMEONE FROM THAT LAND
CALLED "WHO WE USED TO BE" TO WHO WE ARE TODAY.

*Enchanted Love*, Marianne Williamson

IN ONE OF THE TOUGHEST YEARS OF MY LIFE, I often wondered if I would ever laugh again, or feel carefree. I kept on going, step by step, though I didn't know where. There were times I lost my footing and times I lost my breath. But I never lost hope.

Burton and I have forged a new marriage, complete with the history of our old one. We remember the thrill of that first kiss by firelight. We remember how we trembled when those early bills dropped through the mail slot onto our worn beige carpet. We remember savoring the sweet taste of lobster when Burton closed a deal. We remember starting our own company.

*233*

We also remember Squeaky the Squirrel, our sons' graduations, and hundreds of moments in between. Anyone who didn't drive the carpools or rejoice at the bar mitzvahs, cheer the home runs or groan at the strikeouts, anyone who didn't edit the term papers or sweat the missed curfews or worry about the drinking—anyone who wasn't part of those exasperating, scary, rewarding moments would never care about our kids the way we do. And if someday grandchildren wail their way into our lives, they'll be all the more welcome because they'll be both of ours. Because they'll be our legacy. Because we'll know how close we came to losing the chance to enjoy them together.

WHILE BURTON'S EARLY RETIREMENT contributed to our problems, it also gave us the time to learn from them. We worked hard to understand where we went wrong and why we split so far apart. I believe the lessons we learned apply to all couples. Whether or not they have the luxury of spare time or money. Whether they travel across country to attend a couples program or drive a few blocks to consult with their minister. Whether they see a private therapist or join a local support group, buy a stock of self-help books or borrow them from the library.

We learned to fight the urge to blame and hold grudges.

We learned to put our marriage first, to play together, to cherish each other, to focus on our blessings.

We learned that refusing to talk about difficult subjects did not make them go away.

We learned to speak our truth and to let go of the outcome.

We work on these lessons every day. The first year was the toughest. Since then, we've struggled less and enjoyed each other more. Over the year that followed, certain moments brought so much joy that they helped to make up for all the heartache.

ON A SUMMER DAY less than two years after our visit to Onsite, Burton and I walked through Burt's Pass at our farm. I had named the old logging trail several years before when my husband spent a summer clearing out overgrown branches with a chain saw. Ridges rose up on either side of the trail. These ridges—geologists call them eskers—were formed of gravel and sand dragged by the last glaciers to rumble through northern Michigan, about 10,000 years ago. In recent months, I had found solace roaming these hillsides. Knowing their age helped me to see how temporary our problems were.

Maples, beech, and saw-toothed aspens crowded the hills on both sides of Burt's Pass. On a day such as this, the sun transformed green leaves into glowing stained glass. The forest turned into a chapel.

Burton said, "As a boy, I opened myself up to loving my father. When he died, a door slammed in my face. Then my mother went back to work, and I felt like she'd abandoned me. Until lately, I've been afraid to get close to anyone again."

"I locked myself off, too, for different reasons," I said. "From my mother to protect against her neediness, from my father out of loyalty to my mother. For a while, those locked doors protected us."

Twigs crackled beneath our feet. The late afternoon sun cast tiny spotlights on mossy mounds and fungi poking from decayed wood. A warm breeze blew, and thousands of trees whispered back.

"Let's find someplace and meditate," Burton said.

"Nice idea," I said, thinking the suggestion was more than nice; it was unprecedented. "You pick the spot."

Burton pointed up a hill. We climbed over matted brown leaves and clumps of grass and sedge and sat down beside each other on the thick trunk of a fallen tree. Burton took my hand and closed his eyes. I had never prayed with anyone before, I mean really prayed, except maybe reciting the Sh'ma in temple as a young girl before my father turned Catholic, but I didn't count that. The moment I closed my eyes, the atmosphere changed. Buzzing bees, chirping birds, and quivering leaves all seemed to hum along with the beating of my heart. I tuned into another frequency, a higher energy plane.

When Burton opened his eyes, I asked, "Did you feel it?"

He pressed my hand to his chest.

A MONTH LATER, BURTON AND I STOPPED for lunch in Greektown, a Detroit neighborhood filled with bars and restaurants, flashes of flaming saganaki, cries of "Opa!" and background music straight out of *Zorba*. At that point, Greektown was one of the few lively and safe areas left downtown.

We munched on crisp romaine lettuce and soft feta cheese at the New Hellas Cafe. "I wonder if Andy would have come home if you and I hadn't worked things out," I said. Our younger son had recently returned from New York to join his brother in running our company.

"Maybe not. He took our problems really hard. Having both our sons in the business is a dream come true. But the biggest bonus is the two of us." Burton broke off a chunk of bread, rubbed it in the salad dressing on his plate, and chewed. "I believe I had only one chance at true love. After I was successful, I'd never have known whether a woman wanted me for myself or for my bankroll."

"What bankroll?"

"Exactly. When we came back from our honeymoon . . . "

" . . . you had thirteen cents in your pocket."

After lunch, we drove to Stroh River Place, a complex of renovated office and apartment buildings east of downtown. Our son David had purchased the old Parke-Davis pharmaceutical research plant here. Built around 1900 and designed by David's great-great uncle Albert, it had stood vacant for many years. David was converting it into loft condominiums. This was my first visit since the reconstruction began.

The four-story red brick exterior had been sandblasted. Large open windows wore a layer of plastic film within. Outside, you could admire their tall rectangular and arched shapes. Because it was a Sunday, there were no trucks or workmen present, and we parked in front. Using a set of metal implements, Burton jimmied the padlock that fastened the temporary plywood front door. The door squeaked open.

"No respectable landlord goes anywhere without his tools," Burton said.

"I love being with a professional," I said.

We entered a concrete cavern, empty except for a few scaffolds and some piles of wood boards. This level would contain indoor parking, Burton explained. We climbed up an old stairwell. Metal walls bore the crackled traces of old paint. Dust flickered in the light from a window. Textured brick walls enclosed the fourth floor. Tall galvanized metal studs defined the shapes of future apartments.

Burton led me to a window covered with opaque plastic sheets and pulled a piece aside.

"Look at this view," he said.

We peered through the opening. The gray-blue Detroit River sparkled in the sunlight. Factories, smokestacks, and houses studded the opposite shore of Windsor, Ontario. The view took my breath away. So did the challenge of the renovation and the risk it represented.

"Will this project succeed?" I asked.

"I think so, though it will take some time. I hope so. We have a lot at stake."

We watched a freighter glide past on the river.

"I always told David it didn't mean much to develop another building in the suburbs," Burton said. I heard a strain in his voice. "I told him if he wanted to do something more than just try to make money, he should focus on the city. These apartments could help improve the future for Detroit."

"You and I worked hard trying to make things better here," I said. My throat tightened, too. "What a thrill to watch our sons help turn this town into someplace people would want to be again."

"And to live to see it together."

WE HAD REACHED THE STAGE when many of our friends' children were getting married. Wedding dates filled our calendar. Two years after David and Amy's wedding, Burton and I were invited to that of another David—David and Anessa. The groom's father, Michael, had introduced Burton and me thirty-four years earlier.

I asked Burton if he would wear a wedding ring for the evening. "Sure," he said. I scurried off to our safe to retrieve his platinum band, one of the pair he had bought from Tiffany's almost two years before but had never worn.

I loved watching that little flash of metal all night. The simplest gesture—when Burton scratched his head or popped a shrimp into his mouth—seemed as graceful and glorious to me as watching Nureyev leap across a stage.

When we returned home from the wedding, I took the ring to put it back in the safe. I slipped the circle around my thumb. It flopped over my knuckle.

"It was fun to dance with an officially married man tonight," I said. "That was the first date I ever had with someone wearing a wedding band. And he was wearing it for me."

"I enjoyed it," he said. "I'll wear it whenever you want me to."

These days he wears his wedding band all the time.


THE FOLLOWING WINTER, A STORM ROLLED across the Gulf of Mexico. Rainwater leaked from the light fixture over the kitchen sink of our rented beachfront cottage. We cracked open the sliding glass door to listen to the ocean churn. Slats of vertical blinds rattled in the breeze. Handing me a glass of strawberry/orange juice spiked with vodka, Burton sat down beside me on the sofa with the wobbly leg. More than two years had passed since our couples program.

"You once tried to get Jim to agree that cheating was normal," I said. "Do you still think so?"

Burton stirred the ice in his glass with his finger and licked off the juice. He spoke slowly. "'Normal' is a word people can use to justify dangerous behavior. For a while, I did think of running around as normal. Now I see how wrong I was. I've had a chance to stand back and look at what I did. I made a terrible mistake. I've come to understand how important it is to have a loving, caring relationship with one person.

"At the time, Jim told me that 'common' might be a more accurate word than 'normal,' but that we had a chance to build a relationship that was more than common. He could have given me a better answer."

Whether from the drink or the stormy night or the conversation, I felt light-headed. I waited.

Burton narrowed his eyes the way he does when he concentrates. "Jim could have told me: You're hurting Suzy, but she can always leave you. So can your kids and your employees and your friends. Poof. Good-bye. At the end of the day, the only person you have is yourself, and you can't leave you.

"Jim could have told me: You're the one you're cheating. You're cheating yourself out of a pure relationship, out of being able to sleep without stress and wake without conflict. You're giving up the chance to feel good about yourself. You're pushing away a friend you could play with all the time. You could be a little boy one day and pretend you're a racecar driver the next. You're missing the opportunity to walk down the beach, hand in hand, feeling love with all your senses."

Later we took off our clothes and stepped into the hot tub on the screened-in porch. Steamy water swirled around us.

"There's something else Jim could have told me," Burton said. "You're giving up the chance to be romantic with someone you adore and to share your deepest thoughts and know she cares. You're giving up the ability to cherish the woman who sleeps next to you and to open your eyes in the morning and look at her and think: Am I the luckiest guy in the world, or what? You're missing the possibility that your favorite evening of your whole life could be that night with the one you love.

"If I were Jim, that's what I'd have said to me. But Jim couldn't have known I'd come to feel this way. You can't know it unless you've lived it."

# EPILOGUE

THE PAST EXISTS ONLY IN MEMORY, CONSEQUENCES,
EFFECTS. IT HAS POWER OVER ME ONLY AS I CONTINUE
TO GIVE IT MY POWER. I CAN LET GO, RELEASE IT,
MOVE FREELY. I AM NOT MY PAST.

*Caring Enough to Forgive*, David Augsburger

FIVE YEARS HAVE PASSED since Burton and I began bailing out
our sinking vessel. We still hit bumps and turbulence, but we keep
paddling. We're committed to making our marriage work. And it is
working. Better than ever. For both of us. Has this marriage been
saved for the long run? I am betting on it, and I only wager on what
I consider a pretty sure thing.

Small hurts can still tug at my heart. When I'm unable to reach
Burton on the phone or he arrives home late, I might feel a shudder
pass through me. But it does pass, and I shudder less these days.
Burton tries hard to return my calls promptly and to let me know
where he is. If he plans to leave the house early in the morning, I ask
him to wake me to say goodbye. The ache of arising to an empty bed
lingers. My heart remembers.

Trust is a delicate web. It takes years to weave and seconds to rip apart. Learning to trust again is learning to live with the fact that at this very instant, on this very day, things are okay. Learning to live in the moment is one tough assignment. I'm still working on it. Like my golf swing. That's improving, too.

A couple of years ago, I asked my girlfriend Lori how she learned to trust her husband again. She said, "I trust myself not to let anyone mistreat me any more."

At the time, I thought she was dodging the question. I've come to see the wisdom in her words. I hope I can count on my spouse to give me 100 percent for the rest of my life. At this point, I think I can. I have the peace of mind that comes from knowing I'm giving him the best I've got. From believing he's giving me the same. And from knowing if I ever can't count on him again, I've developed the tools and inner strength to survive.

The truth is: it's not Burton I need to trust. It's my favorite threesome—me, myself, and I.

I will fight the tendency to lose myself to someone else for the rest of my life. Habits lodge deep within us, like some dormant germ, waiting for the right conditions to erupt again. I still back off more than I should to Burton's opinions and feel anxious when he snaps at me. I still need to improve at speaking up for myself. Lots of women do. One told me how, after thirty-five years of marriage, she confronted her husband's tendency to take over a conversation. "Excuse me," she told him. "My lips are moving, but I'm hearing your voice."

I no longer feel the need to operate the controls for anyone else. I've grown better at relaxing and enjoying the moment, at believing I am where I'm meant to be. I feel more able to handle what comes my way. Not that I am asking to be tested. I hope, for instance, never to be seated near Jody Sommers at a dinner party. It is a long distance to the level of enlightened master. I have many frequent flyer miles to go.

When I experience twinges of doubt, I pause to wonder what lessons my doubts are trying to teach me. I realize I'm still wounded and give myself credit for how far I've come. I speak to Burton about what's bothering me. And I pray. I'm grateful that God's infinite virtues include infinite patience, or by now He'd have blown me off as a pest. A better title for my saga might be: Dear God, It's Me Again.

BURTON JOINED ME IN STUDYING *A Course in Miracles*—a miracle in itself. The course combines spiritual and mental training. It helps me to understand that forgiveness is a choice and love is the path to forgiveness. It teaches me how to travel that path. On most nights, Burton reads a passage from the course out loud, and we discuss its meaning. These moments of spiritual connection provide us with a regular and safe context for talking over the kind of problems we used to avoid.

While I practice forgiveness, I do not forget. I no longer want to. Remembering the pain helps us to remember the lessons that came with it. It makes us less likely to lapse back into old patterns, like criticizing each other or deceiving ourselves that greater happiness lies elsewhere. Real gifts emerged from that pain—deepened self-esteem and awareness and a more caring, conscious relationship. Carl Jung observed, "Seldom or never does a marriage develop into an individual relationship smoothly and without crisis. There is no birth of consciousness without pain."

I've come to believe that men are little boys who grew taller but who still need a lot of positive attention. When Burton strayed, I used to think if I could only look pretty enough, he'd be mine again. Now I realize looks weren't the issue. Neither was sexy lingerie. The issue was companionship.

We renovated a farmhouse on the farm and moved there. Burton loves living for months among his horses and corn and oat fields. He fills bird feeders outside the house and watches the bluebirds, finches, and hummingbirds that visit our yard. One morning not long ago I woke up and walked into the kitchen. Burton stood looking through the window at a dozen gray doves pecking at birdseed scattered on the frosted ground. I padded over in my slippers, my hair matted down, black mascara forming half moons under my eyes. As we gazed out the window together, Burton put his arm around me and said, "I love sharing the same space with you." I don't think he even noticed the mascara.

We talk a lot about what happened between us. We laugh about it, too. On my last birthday, Burton said, "Fifty-nine years ago, your mother and father gave me a great gift." Later, I mentioned I had written his compliment in my journal. "That's good," he said. "Someday when our kids come across it, maybe they won't think I was a complete shmuck after all."

As HE DID WHEN HE QUIT SMOKING, Burton walked away from his career without looking back. When clients call with real estate needs, he refers them to our sons. He helps David and Andy to analyze deals but insists they make the final decisions.

Burton remains busy and productive. He became the chief volunteer officer of the YMCA for southeast Michigan. He spearheaded a program for Wayne County to help eliminate drug houses in Detroit. (His favorite part of the job: his official gold badge.) He amassed an array of Nikon lenses and became a good enough photographer to have sold his pictures in an exhibit to benefit the new downtown Detroit Y.

I still struggle to accept Burton's having retired in his fifties. Work has always held greater value than play for me. During the day, when I hear the plunk of aces and jacks on a computer screen or find Burton slouched in front of the television watching *My Cousin Vinnie* for the fifth time, I can catch myself thinking: he's wasting his talents. But because I don't have the right to judge the way Burton spends his free time, I pray to become more accepting and less judgmental. Some days I even manage it. One night I asked Burton to switch roles with me. We talked about his retirement from each other's point of view. I was surprised to see how well he understood my ambivalence.

I'd like to say I've escaped the ambivalence that has haunted me. I haven't. But I have recognized the gift that comes with it. The good part of ambivalence is the capacity to see both sides of an issue. That open-mindedness gave me the ability to distance myself from the demands of fear and pride. Early on, it allowed me to get past Burton's lack of credentials—those pertaining to money and education, the ones that mattered in my socioeconomic circle. Later, it helped me to acknowledge my part in our problems, to appreciate the benefit of what we went through, to forgive my husband. It enabled me to work with Burton to bring our marriage to a happier, more gratifying level.

I remind myself how fortunate we are that Burton could afford to retire and that our sons took over. I appreciate how relaxed Burton has become, and know that reduced stress could help him live longer. I consciously enjoy the added time we spend together— taking long walks, golfing, traveling. I remain creatively challenged through my writing, and Burton supports my need to work.

In *Gift from the Sea*, Anne Morrow Lindbergh writes about the bittersweet realities of middle age. "Perhaps middle age is, or should be, a period of shedding shells. . . . Perhaps one can shed . . . one's pride, one's false ambitions, one's mask, one's armor. Was that armor not put on to protect one from the competitive world? If one ceases to compete, does one need it? Perhaps one can at last in middle age, if not earlier, be completely oneself."

Burton has proven a better shedder of shells than I. In my old shell, I clung to the rocks of responsibility and ambition. I focused on what I could or should have been doing other than enjoying my husband's company—deadlines to meet, mail to open, calls to return. I was distracted by thoughts of the magazines I longed to read, the time I should be spending with my mother, the parties I was missing. The old me was enslaved by the day-to-day obligations we all have, obligations that prevent our enjoying the moment at hand. The mantra of the old me: What if?

In my tender new shell, I have begun to realize that the sun will rise and set whether or not I miss a party or rewrite a passage. I am learning to sit and do nothing, to let my thoughts tumble and play, to relax and trust the unknown. I have begun to appreciate what Deepak Chopra calls "the wisdom of uncertainty." The mantra of the new me: Whatever.

Perfection is an illusion, forever beyond reach. Until lately, nothing was good enough for me—not my hair, my body, my marriage, my achievements. I've begun to believe that good enough is good enough. While I no longer write out a daily list of things for which I'm grateful, I think about them several times a day. My gratitude lists are between God and me now. Giving thanks for all that is right in my life, I see how blessed I was all along. How blessed I am.

Though I still wouldn't mind thicker hair.

BETRAYAL COST ME MY INNOCENCE, my illusions, my pride. But every loss came with a gain. Working my way through heartache—one step, one sigh, one prayer at a time—taught me patience. It led me to understand the importance of listening to my inner voice. It helped me to realize how out of touch I was with my own needs and how limited my expectations were. It showed me that I held back from giving my marriage all I had to give. I've come to see how much deeper a relationship was possible if both Burton and I did the work to get there.

What if a genie appeared and promised to change everything? What if this genie could snap his fingers and take it all back, blotting out that terrible day when Burton's cell phone rang and my stomach dropped through the floorboard of the car? What if the genie could eliminate the two years I suffered in silence, spare me from confronting Burton's and my inadequacies, wipe away the agony and regrets?

I'd say: Thanks. But no thanks.

Surviving the fires of hell tempered me. It turned me into the freer, more emotionally tuned-in, more open and, yes, content woman I've become. Without the torture of the past few years, I would never have mustered the energy and will to change my ego-based way of thinking. I would still be the more anxious person I was for the first fifty-some.

If our story can bring hope to one couple who are hurting, we're willing to share it. That is the Twelfth Step described by AA. It's more than a step. It's a leap of faith.


NOW AND THEN ANOTHER WIFE, hearing what Burton and I have been through, will take me aside. I'll know what she wants to ask. I'll know from the look on her face, that same barely-holding-back-tears expression that once captured my face. I'll know from her voice, which will be strained by the tightening in her throat. My throat tightened that way, too.

She'll ask: What did you do to get Burton to change?

As controlling as I once tried to be, I understand the question.

"I didn't do anything to change him," I say. "I started to take care of myself. As I changed, he changed."

Burton changed because he wanted to change, not because I wanted him to. He changed because for many years there was more right than wrong about our marriage. He changed because he still loved me. And because, in spite of appearances, he was a man of character.

When Burton was in the grips of his career, he often awoke at night, his face moist, his heart pounding. I stayed up with him, sometimes for hours, to give him a chance to talk through the problems. More recently, in the middle of the night, Burton will take me in his arms. He'll press his lips to my forehead and hold them there for a long, long time, and he'll murmur how much he loves me. I will silently thank God for the deeper bond my husband and I have forged.

Then I'll turn over on my side, gather my cool pillow beneath my ear, and drift off to sleep with a smile that reaches all the way down to my heart.

THE WEEK OF OUR THIRTY-FIFTH WEDDING ANNIVERSARY, Burton and I drove back from Florida, where we'd spent part of the winter. We played some of the courses on the Robert Trent Jones golf trail in Alabama. The Old Me would have pushed to get home sooner, worrying about whether our housekeeper had left on an outside floodlight and burned out the bulb. Or fretting that our septic system had malfunctioned and caused a smell in the house. The New Me admired the trees, the birds, and the ponds on the golf courses we played and didn't even look at her watch—except to make sure we made it to our tee times.

Continuing our drive home, we stopped in Atlanta to visit our future in-laws. Our son Andy had become engaged to their daughter Amy a couple of months before. Carol and Bob invited almost forty friends for dinner at their home to meet us. Radiating southern hospitality, everyone hugged us and raved about our son.

Carol and Bob surprised us with a big anniversary cake. As guests stood and sang to us, I thought about how these people would become Andy's new extended family, and ours. I thought about how fast time had passed since Burton and I married, and what we had gone through since then, and how lucky we were to share this moment. As Burton and I blew out the candles together, I realized what this moment meant. The evening was more than a celebration. It was a victory. When I tried to voice my thanks, I had a hard time getting out the words.

# In Burton's Words: Giving Up Deception

EVEN THOSE WHO GAIN RENOWN . . . ARE NO MORE EXEMPT
THAN THE REST OF US FROM ENCOUNTER WITH LIMIT,
WITH DEFLATION AND WITH MORTALITY.

*The Middle Passage, from Misery to Meaning
in Midlife*, James Hollis

I LIVED WITH DECEPTION since I was five or six years old. I was a cute little kid, a decent athlete with a funny sense of humor. I came from a nice family. I thought I was okay. All of a sudden, I walked into a schoolroom and discovered I couldn't read. Blam! I felt like the moron of the class.

I tried and tried to read, but I couldn't learn how. Fifty years later, I learned my early trouble with reading was a result of my A.D.D. At the time, I just thought I wasn't as smart as other kids. I figured out ways to disguise my problem. I'd skip school or manage not to be available in class. I'd find something I could do or change the conversation to hide what I couldn't do. I mastered the control of my environment. I was too stubborn to cheat on tests, but I became an artist at bullshit. I deceived my parents and my friends. I faked out my teachers. All but one. Mrs. Bockoff flunked me in fourth grade. She said, "Burton doesn't know how to read."

One day when I first started Sunday School, the rabbi asked my class about a passage from the Torah. I told him what I thought it meant. He said "*No.*" I remember the disgust in his voice. Then he turned to a student everyone knew was bright, and got the answer he wanted. That was the last time I volunteered to talk out loud in class.

Over time I learned to read, but I wasn't good at it. I had to take special courses because I couldn't keep up with the other kids. I'd hide my textbooks so no one would know what classes I was taking. I became argumentative. I'd distract the teacher. She'd say, "It's a beautiful day." I'd ask, "How did you come up with that?"

I kept this bullshit routine going for years. When my friends went to college, I talked my way into taking some courses. I rarely went to class. Rather than sit through lectures I didn't understand, I'd go to the student lounge. I'd play bridge with other kids or challenge someone to Ping-Pong. No one could beat me at Ping-Pong.

School gave me the chance to understand what deception was. I became a pro at it. My deceptions spread to other areas of my life. I'd figure out ways to do things I wasn't supposed to do, like driving before I had my license. When I was thirteen, I'd get up at five in the morning, hot-wire my mom's 1956 Oldsmobile, and drive through Rondeau Park near our cottage in Ontario. I'd come home before my mother woke up, park the car, and water it down with the hose. She never found out.

I developed a second social life. As a teenager, I'd take out a Jewish girl. I'd pretend she was my girlfriend, but I'd have a Gentile girl on the side. I remember when I was about sixteen, I picked up a beautiful blonde at the Totem Pole Drive-In. We drove to some other state—Kentucky, I think—to stay with her sister, who lived in a converted barracks. I had never met anyone so poor. There was one bare light bulb in the ceiling. It was winter and cold outside. The house was heated by the kitchen stove. The only extra place to sleep was a crib in the living room, so that's where I slept. My legs hung over the side.

When I took this girl home with me, my mother said, "She's not our kind, Burton." I asked, "What's our kind?" She said, "You know." So I figured it out. For my parents' sake, I'd have a Jewish girlfriend. She'd think I was crazy about her. But I'd be out screwing someone else. Over time, it became a habit to have two lives.

As a married adult, I had reinforcement for deception. I knew lots of guys who were running around. Some would rationalize it by saying, "I work my ass off. My wife spends the money; my kids spend the money. What's in it for me? So I go out and find a broad and have some fun." For much of my life, I considered deception my friend. It gave me something to do. I could make a private phone call or buy a secret gift. I could visit someone Suzy didn't know about.

Some guys were blatant about their cheating. I never was. My secrets were my secrets. Nobody knew about my private relationships. Suzy was a loving wife who wanted to believe what I told her. While it was easy to deceive her, it was never fun. My secret life had intrigue, but it was scary and dangerous.

Whatever I did, I never intended to leave Suzy or let her leave me. I believed we'd be together forever. Then that day in Florence she pulled the plug. She talked about coming back on her own, taking care of herself. I thought: My wife is thinking about going away and having a good time without me. I could lose her. I don't know why it hadn't dawned on me before that what I was doing could destroy our marriage.

By the time we got to Italy, I was really sick. I was so caught up in deception that I didn't know who I was anymore. Suzy had always been my support. She was my anchor, and I had cut myself off from her.

I always felt my screwing around was my problem, not Suzy's. I planned to take it to the grave. I didn't look at my behavior as cheating. I saw it as just doing what guys do. If Suzy never found out what I was up to, what was the harm? Who was I hurting? It took me most of my life to figure out the answer. I was hurting myself.

A few years after we got married, there was a trend to so-called open marriages. Both members of a couple agreed to carry on outside relationships. Neither Suzy nor I bought into the idea. We didn't think an open marriage could work. Someone was going to be jealous. That was human nature.

Now I see leading a double life didn't work either. It may have been considered acceptable by much of the adult male population, at least much of the adult male population I knew. But it was stressful. It wasn't healthy. In my case, it prevented me from having a full and honest relationship with my wife. Somewhere deep inside, I knew what I was doing wasn't okay.

IT WASN'T MY STYLE to do anything halfway. I did what I did 150 percent. In school, I was as bad a student as I could be. When it came to building a career, I gave it everything I had. When I got involved with another woman, I got seriously involved. A casual, one-night stand would have had no meaning for me. I never randomly screwed around. I was too well known for that. I had to consider my family and my reputation. My deceptions were planned out, discreet.

Before my relationship with Jody started, I was already in bad shape. I felt burned out from the stress of business. I had worked hard since age nine, when I took a paper route for the *Detroit News* and added one for the *Free Press* and expanded both routes. Then I whitewashed basements and delivered bagels and drove a cab and researched mortgage titles—all before going to work full-time. I put in more than thirty years of working seven days a week whenever I could. I built a company, negotiated the contracts, shouldered the risks, and monitored the uncertainties of each deal. I attended a million meetings and juggled the politics. As hard as reading was for me, I forced myself to read every word of every document. Growing the business took total concentration.

I used to go through the numbers twenty times to make sure I was right. Then I'd work backwards. I'd figure out how much margin we had in case I'd made an error. I'd worry about every little thing that could go wrong—a paragraph in a lease, the cost of construction, getting zoning and site plan approval, wondering whether we'd find tenants, trying to secure nonrecourse financing. Were we building the right product in the right place at the right time? Were we charging the right fee? A serious mistake could take us down.

Eventually I had a team of professionals to handle different aspects of a development, but they reported back to me. I was the leader. My lieutenants knew their own segments, but I was the captain who understood how the whole deal worked.

I faced the trials every businessman faces. Our comptroller would come into my office and tell me about our problems. He'd say we couldn't pay our bills. When he'd leave, I'd close the door and shake for about three minutes. Then I'd walk out and throw my arms around my guys' shoulders and rally the team. I'd say, "These problems are temporary." I'd say, "Don't worry; we'll make it happen." Inside, I'd wonder how. By the time a deal ran into trouble, it was too late to turn back; we owed too much money. We had to push forward.

I finally brought the company to the next level. We paid off our bills and had money in the bank. The effort burned me out. I couldn't work anymore. I knew what had to be done next. The company needed to get financing and bring in new blood to allow us to expand. I didn't have the energy for it. I was finished. Luckily, our sons were talented and ready to take over.

I DIDN'T CARE ABOUT MAKING THE FORTUNE 500 LIST. I wouldn't want to be one of the world's wealthiest men even if I could. I've seen what that kind of success can do to a guy. If he's rich enough, he tends to lose all sense of reality. Significant wealth has the power to destroy whole families, to mess up children and grandchildren and even great-grandchildren.

I always respected Rocky Marciano. He retired at the top of his game, a world heavyweight champion. Some people accused him of wasting his talent. I saw him as a winner. I saw myself the same way. I was a champion, too. I played for the love of the game. That meant giving my career the best I had every day. It meant taking the risks and the punches, playing it straight, and once in a while getting a deal just right. When I was too tired and beaten up to keep playing at my peak, it was time to go. I retired at the top of my game. My career wasn't my whole life; it was a part of my life.

When I tried to tell Suzy how I felt, she didn't hear me. Or she didn't want to hear me. That's when I started to lose my feelings. I took time off from work, and Suzy was against it. I was alone a lot. I had lots of toys, but no one to share them with. Suzy was busy with her career. We'd have dinner together and go to a show or go out socially, but that was about it. I was bored, and I was lonely.

The relationship with Jody started around the point when Suzy's mother got sick, and Suzy was spending so much time with her. At first Jody was just a friend—someone to talk to or ride horses with during the day. It was fun hanging out with her. At the beginning, I thought, "I love my wife; this is just a fling." By the time Jody became more than a friend, I was numb to my feelings.

Now I ask myself why I got into the affair. I could say it was my wife's fault because she wasn't spending enough time with me. But that's bullshit. It was my fault. I did it because I was weak and felt rejected. I was looking to build up my ego. Suzy wanted our lives to continue the way they were. I wanted change.

Jody was attractive and available and willing. I knew Suzy wouldn't appreciate my friendship with her, but I had no guilt or remorse because I lost touch with who I was. I had no reality check. All I cared about was getting through the next hour.

At some point I realized carrying on an affair was destructive. I couldn't be in two places at once, physically or emotionally. By the time I realized that, I was in too deep to get out of the other relationship. I didn't care if I lived or died. I thought to myself, "If Suzy leaves me, she leaves me."

I went to a few sessions with the psychologist who diagnosed my A.D.D. He told me that some guys who screw around want to get caught. Maybe I did. Maybe I wanted Suzy's attention.

IN THE PAST WHEN I FACED A PROBLEM, I would take action to stabilize the situation. When the boys were young, some kids toilet-papered the trees and bushes in our yard. My instinct was to remove the stuff right away, to get back to normal. I rushed outside at seven in the morning and yanked tissue out of the branches.

In the case of our marriage, I had gone too far. No one action would bring us back to normal. In telling Suzy the truth, I started to get rid of my own sense of guilt. But I created a new problem: I hurt her more than I ever thought I could. I wondered how I could have done such a thing when I'd always considered myself a nice guy. Emotionally, I had hit my wife with a left upper cut as hard as I could hit her. I had no idea how tough the hurt would be for both of us to overcome. If we hadn't been able to work through it, Suzy would probably have been angry for the rest of her life. I would have felt I made a terrible mistake in being honest.

If I hadn't gotten the facts out in the open, we'd have faced a different set of problems. Our marriage would have kept deteriorating, even if we had stayed together. By admitting everything to Suzy, I defused the chance for Jody to threaten me or make trouble, though I didn't think about that at the time. I confessed when I did because I sensed our couples program was the last hope for our marriage. If I didn't tell Suzy then and there, while we could still get some help, I knew we were finished.

Our couples program showed me the trouble we were in. When I understood how I had hurt Suzy, my emotions came rushing back. I felt terrible. Just holding her, I could feel her stomach tighten. I remember lying in bed and starting to make love. She said, "I can't do this."

When I told the guys in my forum about my confession, some of them called me crazy. They wondered why I didn't hold out for a few more hours. I said I felt like a businessman hounded by his creditors, a guy who owes five bucks for every dollar he earns. When his creditors put so much pressure on him that they force him into bankruptcy, in some ways he's relieved.

At first, I was relieved. Before long, I felt deprived. I missed my deceptions. I didn't know what to do with my time. My sense of loss turned into anger and resentment. I sulked or I blew up. I felt sorry for myself. I'd been a bullshitter for years. All of a sudden, I'd given up my deceptions. I had no place to hide. I thought to myself: You moved too fast, you idiot.

Suzy and I saw Jim for a while, but I felt like I was on trial. I missed Jody. I felt guilty for what I'd done to both women. I hated seeing Suzy so tortured. Living with the stress of deception seemed easier than the agony I was feeling.

A couple months after our program, a friend asked how things were going. I told him, "If you're going to screw around, be smart about it. Don't get caught." I'm sure he thought, "Burt's back to normal; he'll be out there again." Even I figured I'd get back to my deceptions; I'd just be more clever the next time. Until then, I'd behave and let things cool off.

I was too involved in justifying what I'd been doing to figure out why I'd been doing it. I needed someone objective to help me understand my behavior. I couldn't have made the changes I've made without first getting help.

I didn't really start to heal until I went to my own program. At The Meadows, I finally began to turn around. Instead of challenging authority the way I always had, I did what they asked. I wrote when they wanted me to write, talked when they told me to talk. I told the truth. Nobody judged me.

The Meadows helped me begin to open up and look at my

history, to find words for my feelings. It gave me a r
After I got so mad at my stepfather, I wondered what
dealt with. I realized I had never worked through the se
donment I had felt when my father died.

One afternoon a few months after my program, I loc ...yself
inside the farmhouse and thought back to my childhood. Remembering how I felt as a little boy, I started to cry. I visualized my parents. I yelled at my father for fighting so much with my mother and for getting sick and dying and leaving me behind. Then I yelled at my mother for going off to teach every day and coming home at night in a bad mood, and for expecting me to be the man in the family, and for bringing that jerk of a stepfather into our house.

After I vented all that anger, I came to see that my father didn't choose to die and that my parents did the best they could. I recognized how my early experiences determined the adult I became. I had developed a desperate need to control situations, to force people to do things my way. Once I understood where that need to control came from, I could start to let it go. I began to appreciate other peoples' feelings and to encourage them to make their own decisions.

A couple months later, I asked myself a key question: Who suffers when I pull this stuff? The answer was: I do. Everybody around me might suffer, but I suffered the most. When I realized I was hurting myself, I became able to stop the deception. That's when I knew I could be trustworthy.

Suzy's not as sure she can trust me as I am. I can't blame her. If I stood behind a horse that had kicked me once, I'd be cautious. If he started shifting in the wrong direction, I wouldn't stand around wondering which way he was going to move. I'd race out of there. I tell Suzy she's earned the right to doubt me. What matters is I trust me.

After about six months of living without deception, I realized something that surprised me. I actually didn't want to screw around any more. I'd rather take a nap. I'd get some rest, and I'd feel better

...an if I had run around like a maniac and come back to face Suzy. I hated having her ask what I was doing in South Lyon. It ate me up to lie to her. She'd ask, "What did you do all day?" I'd have said something stupid like, "Oh, I groomed my horse for three hours. He had a lot of burrs in his tail." And I'd have wondered how she could believe me.

I'm thankful Suzy and I both got help. I'm thankful she was strong enough to rise above how much I'd hurt her. I'm thankful for our initial bond and our history. We had something worth saving, something to build on. We moved forward together. One of us couldn't have done it alone.

IT TOOK TIME TO GET TO KNOW MYSELF and find out why I was so unhappy. By then I was in the process of retiring. I don't know if I could have been so introspective while I was running the company. Business took a toughness and a concentration that might have prevented me from being vulnerable.

When I first got home from my program, I created an exercise. Every morning, I'd look in the mirror and say: I love you, Burt. At first, I saw all the things I didn't love. There was a coldness in my eyes. I was uptight and calculating. I'd do whatever it took to get my way, like pressure Suzy to go up north when I wanted or make the boys feel guilty if they didn't have time to join me for lunch. But seeing that unlikable guy in the mirror, I'd ask him: What can I do today to help me love you more tomorrow? I'd try to be nicer, more thoughtful, more honest.

At some point, I crossed the line. I couldn't return to my secret life. Maybe it was when the mirror said: I love you back. My deceptions cleared up like a case of acne. It was as though one day I looked in the mirror and my face wasn't broken out. I didn't see that coldness in my eyes anymore.

I don't say everything I do today is right, but my intentions are right, in all aspects of my life. Not just about refusing to cheat on Suzy any longer, but about how I handle decisions or talk to my friends. I only do what makes me feel good about myself. I used to get angry or upset if someone pissed me off or disappointed me. Now I stop to ask: How can I see this differently? I want to look at life through eyes of love, not of ego.

I DISMANTLED THE LAYERS of my deceptive life, the arrangements I had made so Suzy wouldn't find out what was going on. I had gotten a special cell phone I'd turn off when she was around. I had signed up for a separate credit card. I rarely used it, but I had it just in case. I had taken a post office box so there was someplace my secret bills could come. It feels good to be rid of that stuff.

I've found plenty of outlets for my energy. I've become passionate about photography. I ride horses and play golf and even read books. I've taken on new positions in the community. I no longer wake up and wonder, "What am I going to do today?" I have so many interests I don't feel a desire for extra distractions.

I consciously try to be someone Suzy would want to be married to. I draw pictures for her and write funny notes on them. I make her submarine sandwiches for lunch. I check in a lot. Suzy has changed, too. She's easier to be with and less critical. She's more responsive and relaxed. We spend a lot of time together. Today, I'm proud of our relationship.

After you've been married for a long time, you know what reactions to expect from your spouse. I know how Suzy will respond if I want to go to a shoot-em-up movie. Or if I come up with a crazy idea like putting in a swimming pool at the farm. I've always known what would worry Suzy or make her jealous or angry. But while I could predict her reactions, I didn't know what she was thinking. Now I encourage her to tell me. I don't jump on her anymore when she says something I'd rather not hear.

Talking about our problems helped us get through them. I hated thinking about what I did to Suzy, but she needed to talk about it, and I respected that. Nothing was off limits. When you restrict what your spouse can say, you cut her off, which makes your problems worse. You can only explore each other's thinking when you're not ashamed to express your true thoughts. To expose parts of yourself that aren't so perfect, you need to know your partner will stand by you no matter what. You need to feel safe.

We've both changed a lot. Earlier in our marriage, if Suzy and I disagreed about whether to go out for Italian or Chinese food or spend an afternoon at a racetrack or a lecture, we each wanted our way. We've learned that if we're true partners, we can give and take. We can subordinate our egos. Today Suzy and I have equal power in our marriage. In the past, I wouldn't let Suzy make plans with a couple if I didn't like the husband. These days, I'll go along. I might even have a good time. We base our choices on love for each other. We win or lose together. I have what I've always wanted and didn't know how to find: a best friend.

SOME GUYS FIGURE THEY HAVE A RIGHT to cheat on their wives. They do it for the sex or the sport. They do it to boost their egos or because of peer pressure. Some feel justified because their fathers cheated, as though an unwritten law was handed down: If it was okay for their dads, it's okay for them. I came across a journal my father had written while he was married to my mother. It suggested he had had an affair. Suspecting that my father had run around made it a little more acceptable for me. I'm sorry I passed that legacy on to my sons. I don't think it influenced Andy, but it affected David. After I got help, he sought counseling, too. I'm proud of the strength that took.

Since I've gotten over my need to be deceptive, I speak to other guys who act the way I did. Some are good friends. I suggest they may want to reconsider their behavior. Usually they say they admire me, but they couldn't do what I've done. Some probably do admire me. Others probably think I'm a jerk. But even if my friends don't hear me, or don't want to hear me, I hear myself. It helps me to talk about what I've learned.

Most of the guys I know don't want to change their ways. A

husband may stop cheating if he's taking some heat at home, but chances are he'll be back at it before long. He'll say, "It feels good to get laid in the afternoon." I'll say, "There are better ways to feel good."

Some guys think having an affair is a kind of reward. I say it's more of a booby prize. You show me a man with a mistress, and I'll show you a man who's asking for misery. After two or three dates, his mistress will start making demands, and the fun will stop. He'll end up taking grief from his mistress and his wife. He'll find himself deceiving both of them. Both women will feel neglected or scorned. He'll stand in the middle wondering whose fault it is. It's no mystery. It's his fault.

Not long ago I invited a couple of buddies to spend a weekend up north. One of them said, "Cool. We can chase puss." I told him, "You can chase all the puss you want, but not with this hound. My puss-chasing days are over."

He looked at me like I was nuts. "What's gotten into you?" he asked. I said, "When I told Suzy what was going on, I suddenly saw the pain I had caused her. I don't know why, but I hadn't thought about it before. I'll never forget what she said to me."

My buddy didn't ask, but I remember Suzy's exact words. I remember how her mouth quivered. She said, "All I ever did was love you and try to make you happy." I told my buddy, "I could never hurt Suzy like that again. I'm into a new phase now. It's called peace of mind."

IF A HUSBAND AND WIFE AGREE to go separate ways, that's their business. From what I see, most husbands run around in secret and try to rationalize it. They complain their wives don't understand them. They insist their mistresses love them more. They tell me how much they care for these other women.

I don't judge guys who run around. I was there. But I don't humor them either. I tell them what I finally figured out: You're not in an arranged marriage. Your wife is the person you chose. She's the mother of your children. She shares your history. She loves you and cares about you, yet she's the one you hurt most. Even if she doesn't divorce you, at some point she'll become numb or depressed or she'll flip out. If she tolerates your cheating, she devalues herself.

And whether or not they want to hear it, I tell them something else I learned: You're not just cheating your wife. You're cheating your kids and yourself. You may think you're getting away with something. But you're a loser, too.

Sometimes a man ditches his wife of many years for a younger woman. At first, he gets a kick out of the hunt. A guy of sixty can win someone guys of thirty compete for. He's thrilled. He thinks his conquest is the most beautiful, adorable girl in the world. She loves the package that comes with him—the things she can buy, the places she can go. About six months later, the infatuation wears off. He finds himself stuck with a mate who isn't as beautiful or adorable as he thought, who doesn't know what Watergate was and can't stand John Denver. She discovers he's not as rich or connected as she hoped, he has stomach problems and likes to go home early. And when he wants to talk to someone on his level, someone who understands him and shares his past, that someone is gone.

NOW THAT MY HEAD IS CLEAR, I really enjoy my interests. I get a kick out of shooting trap and knocking off eighteen or twenty clay pigeons. Or breaking eighty in a round of golf. Or taking a good photograph—it blows my mind when I capture the effect I wanted.

That kind of satisfaction beats sitting in some other woman's kitchen listening to her complain because you won't leave your wife or your kids or because she's broke. The real world has a way of grabbing you by the balls. When you're involved in an affair, sooner or later you'll stand back and wonder what you're doing. The bottom line is: most mistresses do what they do to have a good time and get what they can—the jewelry, the cars, the cash.

Cheating on your wife will cost you. A guy can romanticize an affair all he wants, but at some point his mistress will say, "I'm leaving. Just give me money." And he'll ask himself: What am I doing here? I could be home reading the paper, smoking a cigar, hanging out with my kids.

Plenty of the guys I know believe their girlfriends stay with them out of love. Give me a break. Some of these men have mugs like Frankenstein. But they have wallets like Wilt Chamberlain. They have women falling over them because they've got bucks. Period.

Once you're involved in deception, you find yourself lying to everybody—your family, your mistress, your secretary. You drive yourself nuts trying to keep it going. You've got to remember what you said to whom. You've got to cover your tracks. Deception takes a toll on your health. It forces your body to keep releasing stress hormones. Herbert Benson, a Harvard doctor, says most health care visits are stress-related.

With the stress I was under, I'm grateful I'm still alive. Onsite saved my life. I wasn't ready to be saved, but it was a start. Jim Rowe saved my life. The Meadows saved my life. The guys in my forum saved my life, just by listening. Suzy saved my life. When she agreed to hang in there with me and try to work things out, it was like God told me: Get it right this time. This is your last chance, buddy.

Today I've found my moral compass. My mind is clear as to what's right and wrong. I speak my truth and hope I can reach some of the guys I care about. They relate to me. I'm an athlete. I was good at business. We ran around together. If I can help any of them begin to wake up in the morning with a clear head, I'm willing to try.

I saw a brave young man from Cambodia on TV. He received a Nobel Prize for his work in helping to do away with land mines. His legs had been blown off. He was muscular and well built on top, but below the waist there were stumps. He said, "I don't like showing my body to people. I do it because I hope it can help others."

I don't like exposing myself either, but maybe I can help someone else who is ready to be helped. Each time I tell our story, it hurts a little less. At first I worried about damaging my reputation. Then I realized our problem is a common one. If Suzy and I had divorced and word of my cheating had gotten out, I think our reputations would have survived. I hope the positive things Suzy and I have done will outweigh any negative perceptions.

In any case, I don't care what people know any longer. I'm at peace with myself. If our story can be helpful to others, it is worth telling. I hope our children will benefit from our experience. Our sons will have adult problems, too. The way we've faced ours gives them permission to work through obstacles they'll have to deal with.

TODAY THE FIRST QUESTION I ASK MYSELF about any choice is "Can I be honest?" I no longer think about how to pull off a deception. I think about doing what is right. I don't worry about what I can and can't say. I say whatever I want because it's the truth. Suzy has the same right.

Suzy never laid a guilt trip on me. I feel bad enough about the affairs. If Suzy had thrown them up to me every day, I don't know how bad I'd feel. Suzy's strength amazes me. For a while I was such a shmuck to her, but she was able to get past it and turn the experience into something positive. If the roles had been reversed, I doubt I could have gone through what she went through for me.

On the day the World Trade Center fell, all I wanted to do was hold my wife and cry with her. I thought about the precious relationships that had been lost that day and how lucky we were to still have ours. Overnight, life became more unstable. That tragedy helped me remember how important Suzy is to my sense of stability.

There are two types of forgiveness. One is external; someone else gives it to you. The other you give to yourself. Internal forgiveness is harder to achieve. Suzy has come a long way toward forgiving me. I'm tougher on myself. I made the mistakes, and I'll have to live with them forever. Not one of them was worth it.

What hurts me most is to know I wasn't a man of honor. When I'm lying on my deathbed, I won't be able to look back and know I was faithful to my wife. I can't change that. All I can do is learn from yesterday and try to be a better person today. A better father. A better friend. A better husband.

*Appendix*

# A READER'S GUIDE

———— ∞∞∞ ————

## Infidelity Today

How prevalent is infidelity? In her insightful book *After the Affair*, Dr. Janis Spring, Ph.D., reports, "... by the *most conservative* [italics mine] estimate ... in the United States, 1 in every 2.7 couples— some 20 million—is touched by infidelity." That number equals almost 4 out of 10 husbands and 2 out of 10 wives. In *Infidelity*, a program that aired frequently on CNN in 2003 and 2004, couples therapist Dr. Shirley Glass reported that 45 percent of married men and 25 percent of married women admitted to infidelity. The CNN program also contended that middle-aged couples today admit to adultery at twice the rate of the preceding generation.

I asked psychologist Ted Klontz, co-director of Onsite, how likely any marriage is to make it through the kind of rupture Burton's and mine survived. He said, "For most people, understanding how they got into a situation that violates everything they believed in and changing their behavior is just too much work." He estimates that only 1 in 4 seriously troubled couples will see adultery as a turning point rather than a death knell. Klontz added that research shows that learning a new behavior, like listening better or criticizing less often, takes seven years to become automatic. "Most people think it's easier to get out of a relationship than to change. They figure the next one will be better," he says. "Generally, it's not."

Couples therapist Harville Hendrix, Ph.D., is even less optimistic. In *Getting the Love You Want*, Hendrix writes about struggles that can cripple a relationship after romance fades. "The last stage of the power struggle is despair. When couples reach this final juncture ... the pain has gone on too long ... Perhaps as few as 5 percent of all couples find a way to resolve the power struggle and go on to create a deeply satisfying relationship."

Many variables determine a married couple's ability to weather infidelity. Terri Orbuch, Ph.D., project director of a long-term study on marriage and a senior research scientist at the University of Michigan, says these include:

- how close, committed, and happy the relationship was before the infidelity,
- the ability of the betrayed partner to forgive, to have compassion for the betrayer, and to imagine why he or she behaved they way they did,
- whether the betrayer admits to doing wrong and sincerely apologizes.

Many articles and books have been written on the subject of infidelity. The following sections list resources, organizations, Web sites, and books that offer help, insight, and hope.

## Couples Programs

ONSITE, Cumberland Furnace, Tennessee
Private intensive therapy. Coupleship I programs: Experiential
therapy involving group work, sharing, and action techniques
focuses on healing and building relationships. Lodging and
meals included. Coupleship II enrichment program and couples
equine therapy program also available. Visit Web site at
www.onsiteworkshops.com or call 615-789-6609 or 800-341-7432.

THE MEADOWS, Wickenburg, Arizona
A multidisorder facility treating trauma and addiction. Couples
workshops help couples explore difficulties and join together in
recovery. Also available: workshops on men's sexual compulsivity
recovery, women's sexual concerns, love addiction/avoidance, and
setting/using boundaries. Meals included. Visit Web site at
www.themeadows.org or call 800-632-3697.

THE GOTTMAN INSTITUTE, Seattle, Washington
Research-based couples workshops, with no group work or public
disclosure, teach tools for making marriage work. Gottman-
trained therapists are located in various states. Visit Web site at
www.gottman.com or call 206-523-9042 or 888-523-9042.

## Other Organizations and Web Sites

ASSOCIATION FOR COUPLES IN MARRIAGE ENRICHMENT (ACME)
International, nonprofit, nonsectarian organization of trained
married lay couples. Events and group discussions that strengthen
relationships and increase intimacy in various communities.
Visit Web site at www.bettermarriages.org or call 800-634-8325
or 336-724-1526.

AMERICAN ASSOCIATION OF MARRIAGE AND FAMILY THERAPY
(AAMFT)
Mental health professionals who diagnose and treat family disor-
ders in U.S., Canada, and abroad. Facilitates research, develops
standards, publishes journals and tapes. Directory of therapists by
area. Visit Web site at www.aamft.org or call 703-838-9808.

BEYOND AFFAIRS NETWORK (BAN)
Comprehensive listing of support groups nationwide, helpful Web
sites, books, and articles. Peggy Vaughan, psychologist, and James
Vaughan, Ph.D., share their own story of surviving infidelity in
their book *Beyond Affairs.* Peggy offers telephone consultations.
Visit Web site at www.dearpeggy.com.

COALITION FOR MARRIAGE, FAMILY AND COUPLES EDUCATION
(CMFCE)
A nonpartisan, nonsectarian clearinghouse for information, books,
and articles on strengthening marriage and reducing
family breakdown. Annual conference teaches latest relationship-
building conflict management skills. Visit Web site at
www.smartmarriages.com or call 202-362-3332.

CO-DEPENDENTS ANONYMOUS (CoDA)
A 12-step program for understanding and recovering from
codependence and developing healthy relationships. Nationwide
listing of contact persons for self-help support groups. Visit Web
site at www.codependents.org.

IMAGO RELATIONSHIPS INTERNATIONAL

International organization of therapists providing individual counseling, workshops, and seminars for couples. Based on Imago Relationship Therapy methods developed by Harville Hendrix, Ph.D., and Helen LaKelly Hunt, Ph.D. Visit Web site at www.imagorelationships.org or call 800-729-1121 or 407-644-4937.

MARRIAGE BUILDERS

In-depth Web site of psychologist, author, and radio host Dr. Willard F. Harley Jr. includes a discussion forum and helpful articles on infidelity. Telephone counseling available. Visit Web site at www.marriagebuilders.com.

MARRIAGE SAVERS, INC.

Trains clergy and mentor couples nationwide in supporting troubled marriages. Helps develop community marriage policies. Visit Web site at www.marriagesavers.com or call 301-469-5873.

PREP, PREVENTION AND RELATIONSHIP PROGRAMS

Developed by psychologists and co-directors of the Center for Marital and Family Studies at the University of Denver, Howard Markman, Ph.D., and Scott Stanley, Ph.D. PREP instructors around the world help strengthen and enrich relationships. Visit Web site at www.PREPinc.com or call 800-355-0166.

RETROUVAILLE

An international organization sponsoring live-in weekend and post-weekend programs for married couples featuring presentations by other married couples and priests. Catholic-based, though couples of all faiths are welcome. Visit Web site at www.retrouvaille.org.

## Selected Bibliography

*After the Affair:*
*Healing the Pain and Rebuilding Trust When a Partner Has Been*
*Unfaithful*
by Janis Abrahms Spring with Michael Spring
Clinical psychologists offer sensitive suggestions for emotional
support and strategies to overcome the crisis for both hurt and
unfaithful partners.

*Conscious Loving:*
*The Journey to Co-Commitment*
by Gay Hendricks, Ph.D., and Kathlyn Hendricks, Ph.D.
A program for clearing away unconscious reactions that under-
mine your relationship.

*Daily Affirmations for Forgiving and Moving On*
by Tian Dayton, Ph.D.
One of many inspiring books of daily affirmations that help in
letting go of resentment and grief.

*The Dance of Anger:*
*A Woman's Guide to Changing the Patterns of Intimate Relationships*
by Harriet Lerner, Ph.D.
Advice on understanding and reducing anger and using it to effect
change in relationships.

*The Dark Side of the Light Chasers:*
*Reclaiming Your Power, Creativity, Brilliance, and Dreams*
by Debbie Ford
Guidance and practical exercises on learning to live authentically.

*Enchanted Love:*
*The Mystical Power of Intimate Relationships*
by Marianne Williamson
Essays and prayers illuminate and enhance the spiritual dimension
of partnerships.

*Everything You Know About Love and Sex Is Wrong*
by Pepper Schwartz, Ph.D.
A guidebook of fresh, practical solutions for intimate satisfaction.

*Getting The Love You Want: A Guide for Couples*
by Harville Hendrix, Ph.D.
An insightful guide for understanding how childhood issues affect adult relationships.

*Infidelity:*
*A Survival Guide*
by Don-David Lusterman
A therapist shows how marriage can overcome infidelity and become stronger.

*Not "Just Friends":*
*Protect Your Relationship from Infidelity and Heal the Trauma of Betrayal*
by Shirley P. Glass, Ph.D., with Jean Staeheli
Statistical and case studies as well as advice about preventing and coping with emotional and physical infidelity, especially occurring in the workplace.

*Passionate Marriage:*
*Love, Sex, and Intimacy in Emotionally Committed Relationships*
by David Schnarch, Ph.D.
A sex therapist shares couples' stories to show how emotionally committed relationships are "crucibles" of personal development.

*The Power of Now:*
*A Guide to Spiritual Enlightenment*
by Eckhart Tolle
A look at how relationships can be a portal to spiritual growth.

*Relationship Rescue:*
*A Seven-Step Strategy for Reconnecting with Your Partner*
by "Dr. Phil" McGraw
A popular psychologist pinpoints problems and recommends steps
for taking personal responsibility.

*The Seven Principles for Making a Marriage Work*
by John Gottman, Ph.D. and Nan Silver
Practical advice and exercises backed by scientific research on
building and enhancing a relationship.

*The Sex-Starved Marriage:*
*Boosting Your Marriage Libido: A Couple's Guide*
by Michele Weiner Davis
Lessons in bridging the desire gap and restoring intimacy.

*The Surrendered Wife:*
*A Practical Guide to Finding Intimacy, Passion,*
*and Peace with Your Man*
by Laura Doyle
Down-to-earth, entertaining advice on how to give up attempts to
control and manipulate your spouse.